PAUL SELIGSON
CAROL LETHABY
TOM ABRAHAM
CRIS GONTOW

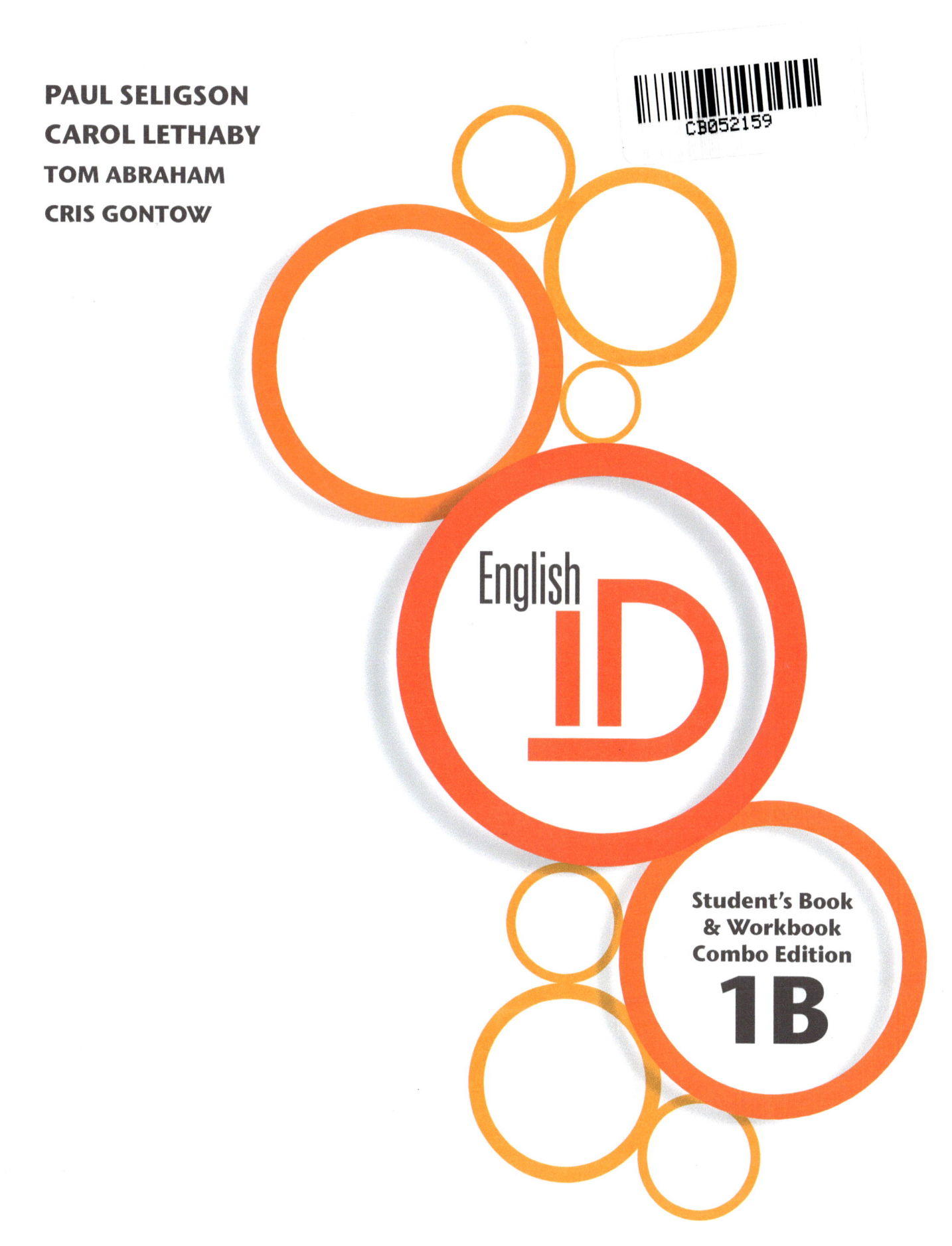

English
ID

Student's Book
& Workbook
Combo Edition
1B

Richmond

ID SB Language map

		Question syllabus	Vocabulary	Grammar	Speaking & Skills
6	6.1	What's in your refrigerator?	Food & drink	Countable vs. uncountable nouns	Talk about food & drink Describe what's in your refrigerator
	6.2	What do you eat for lunch and dinner?	Food portions & containers	Quantifiers: *some* and *any*	Talk about morning food & healthy eating
	6.3	How often do you eat chocolate?	Food and nutrition	Quantifiers: *a little, a few, a lot of*	Use quantifiers to talk about activities you like / don't like
	6.4	How many meals do you cook a week?	Food Cognates	*How much* vs. *how many*	Talk about food and nutrition Take a class survey
	6.5	Are you hungry?	Menu food		Scan a menu Order food from a menu
		What would you like for lunch?	Restaurant phrases		Order food in a restaurant
	Writing 6: A food diary		**ID Café 6: Role-play a restaurant situation**		**Review 3** *p.84*
7	7.1	Do you live in a house?	Rooms & furniture	Past of *be: there was / there were*	Describe your home Compare a home then and now
	7.2	Where were you last night?	Party items Past time expressions	Past of *be*: ➕ ➖ ❓ / short answers	Talk about a party Ask & answer about last week
	7.3	Where were you last New Year's Eve?	New Year's Eve celebrations	Prepositions of place	Describe New Year's Eve celebrations Describe positions of objects
	7.4	Was your hometown different 10 years ago?	Dates Places in a city	*there is / there are* & *there was / there were*	Talk about changes to cities Compare your hometown in the past and now
	7.5	Do you enjoy weddings?			Predict from context Describe a special event
		How about a barbecue on Sunday?			Make invitations
	Writing 7: An online review		**ID Café 7: Describe a party**		
8	8.1	When did you start school?	Life events Past time expressions	Simple past regular verbs ➕ ➖	Talk about past events Write a biography Pronunciation of past tense verbs
	8.2	Did you go out last weekend?	Ordinal numbers & dates Simple past irregular verbs	Simple past irregular verbs ➕ ➖	Talk about what you did yesterday / last birthday Pronunciation of past irregular verbs
	8.3	Where did you go on your last vacation?	Vacations	Simple past ❓ / short answers	Ask and answer about your last vacation / Pronunciation of *Did you*
	8.4	When do you listen to music?	Everyday activity verbs	Subject questions vs. object questions	Do a pop quiz Write questions for a class quiz
	8.5	Can I use your phone?	Phone phrases		Understand a story Tell a story
		Could you help me, please?	Phrases to make requests		Ask for favors and respond
	Writing 8: A vacation message		**ID Café 8: Call a friend for help**		**Review 4** *p.110*
9	9.1	How did you get here today?	Transportation	*How do / did you get to …?*	Ask & answer about personal transportation Describe transportation problems
	9.2	What do you do?	Jobs	Articles + jobs	Talk about occupations & dream jobs Talk about commuting & keeping in shape
	9.3	Where are you going to be in 2025?	Future plans	*going to* for future	Talk about future plans Make predictions Pronunciation of *going to* / *gonna*
	9.4	What are you going to do next year?	Life changes	Present continuous for future *going to* vs. present continuous	Talk about intentions and plans Write New Year's resolutions
	9.5	Would you like to be a nurse?	Jobs		Make connections Discuss occupations in the future
		Could I borrow your pen?			Ask for permission
	Writing 9: A reply to a blog post		**ID Café 9: Speculate about life in the future**		
10	10.1	Do you look like your mom?	The body & face Adjectives (appearance)		Talk about parts of the body Describe physical appearance
	10.2	Are you like your dad?	Adjectives (character)	Comparatives with *-er* & *more* *Like* as verb & preposition	Talk about a timeline Make comparisons
	10.3	Who's the most generous person in your family?	Personality types Adjectives (character)	Superlatives with *-est* & *most*	Describe personality and places
	10.4	What's the best place in the world?	Geographical features	Comparatives & superlatives	Sentence stress Talk about surprising facts
	10.5	What's your blood type?	Parts of the body		Understand facts
		Is your English better than a year ago?			Make choices
	Writing 10: A family profile		**ID Café 10: Talk about making changes to physical appearance**		**Review 5** *p.136*

Grammar p. 148   Sounds and usual spelling p. 158   Audioscript p. 164

ID WB Language map

		Question syllabus	Vocabulary	Grammar	Speaking & Skills
6	**6.1**	What's in your refrigerator?	Food & drink	Countable vs. uncountable nouns	Talk about food likes & dislikes
	6.2	What do you eat for lunch and dinner?	Food portions	Quantifiers: *some* and *any*	Talk about a daily diet
	6.3	How often do you eat chocolate?	Food & nutrition	Quantifiers: *a little, a few, a lot of*	
	6.4	How many meals do you cook a week?	Recycle food portions	*How much* vs. *how many*	
	6.5	What would you like for lunch?	Courses & ways to cook	*I like* vs. *I'd like*	Ordering food
7	**7.1**	Do you live in a house?	Rooms & furniture	Past of *be*: *there was / there were*	
	7.2	Where were you last night?	Party items	Past of *be*	Talk about parties
	7.3	Where were you last New Year's Eve?	Celebrations	Prepositions of place	Talk about your town
	7.4	Was your hometown different 10 years ago?	Places in a city	Past of *be* ⊕ ⊖ ❓	Describe a town in the past
	7.5	How about a barbecue on Sunday?			Make invitations
8	**8.1**	When did you start school?	Biographies		
	8.2	Did you go out last weekend?	Ordinal numbers & dates	Simple past ⊕ ⊖ Prepositions	
	8.3	Where did you go on your last vacation?		Simple past ❓	Pronunciation *did you* /dɪdʒə/
	8.4	When do you listen to music?	Everyday activity verbs	Subject questions	Talk about past routine
	8.5	Could you help me, please?		*Could*	
9	**9.1**	How did you get here today?	Transportation	Recycle simple past	Talk about how you get to places
	9.2	What do you do?	Jobs		Talk about jobs
	9.3	Where are you going to be in 2025?	Future plans	*going to*	Talk about future plans / predictions
	9.4	What are you going to do next year?	Life changes	*going to* vs. present continuous	
	9.5	Would you like to be a nurse?	*borrow / lend*		Ask for permission
10	**10.1**	Do you look like your mom?	The body & face Descriptions of people		Describe a person
	10.2	Are you like your dad?	Adjectives (appearance & character)	Comparatives	
	10.3	Who's the most generous person in your family?	Personality types	Superlatives	Express opinions about people & places
	10.4	What's the best place in the world?	Geographical features		
	10.5	Is your English better than a year ago?		Recycle comparatives & superlatives	

Audio script p. 56   Answer key p. 62   Phrasebank p. 67   Wordlist p. 71

Welcome to English ID!

Finally, an English course you can understand!

Famous **song lines** illustrate language from lessons.

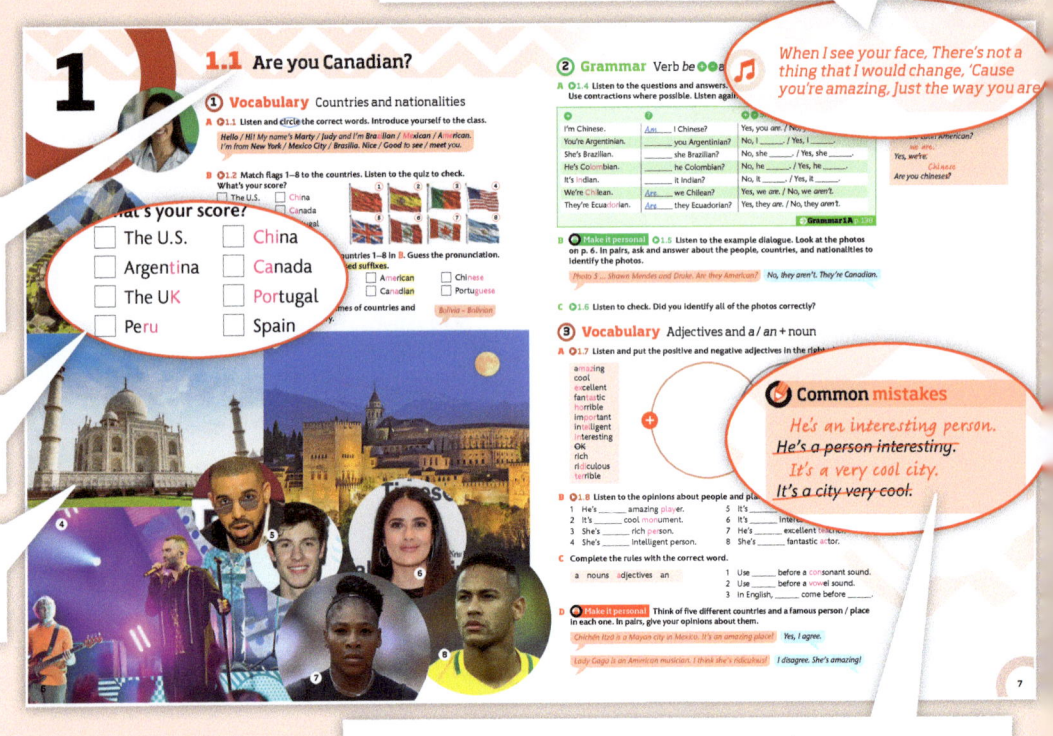

Lesson titles are questions to help you engage with the content.

Word stress in pink on new words.

Contextualized Picture Dictionary to present and review vocabulary.

Focus on **Common mistakes** accelerates accuracy.

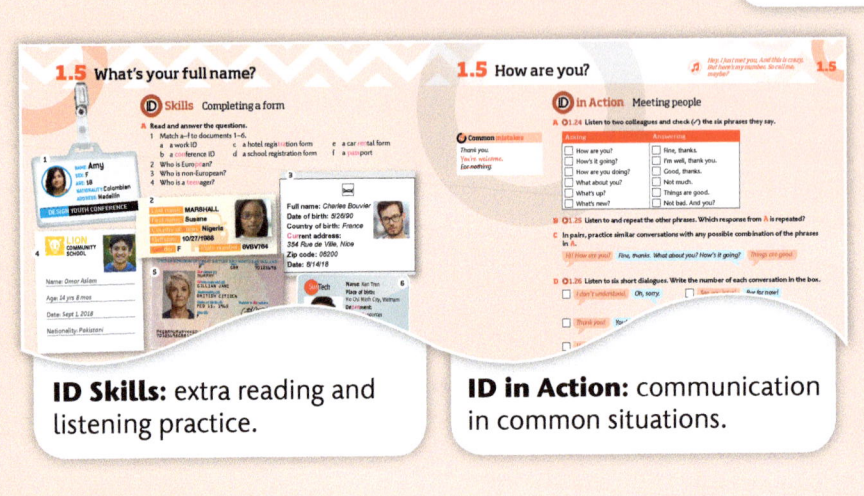

ID Skills: extra reading and listening practice.

ID in Action: communication in common situations.

Authentic videos present topics in real contexts.

ID Café: sitcom videos to consolidate language.

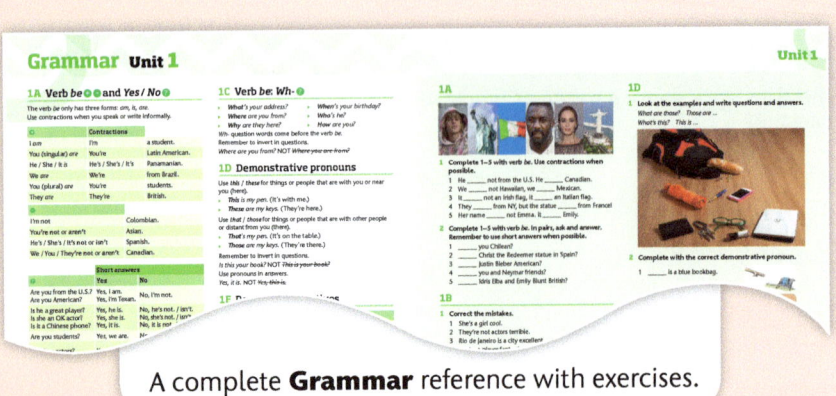

A complete **Grammar** reference with exercises.

Reviews systematically recycle language.

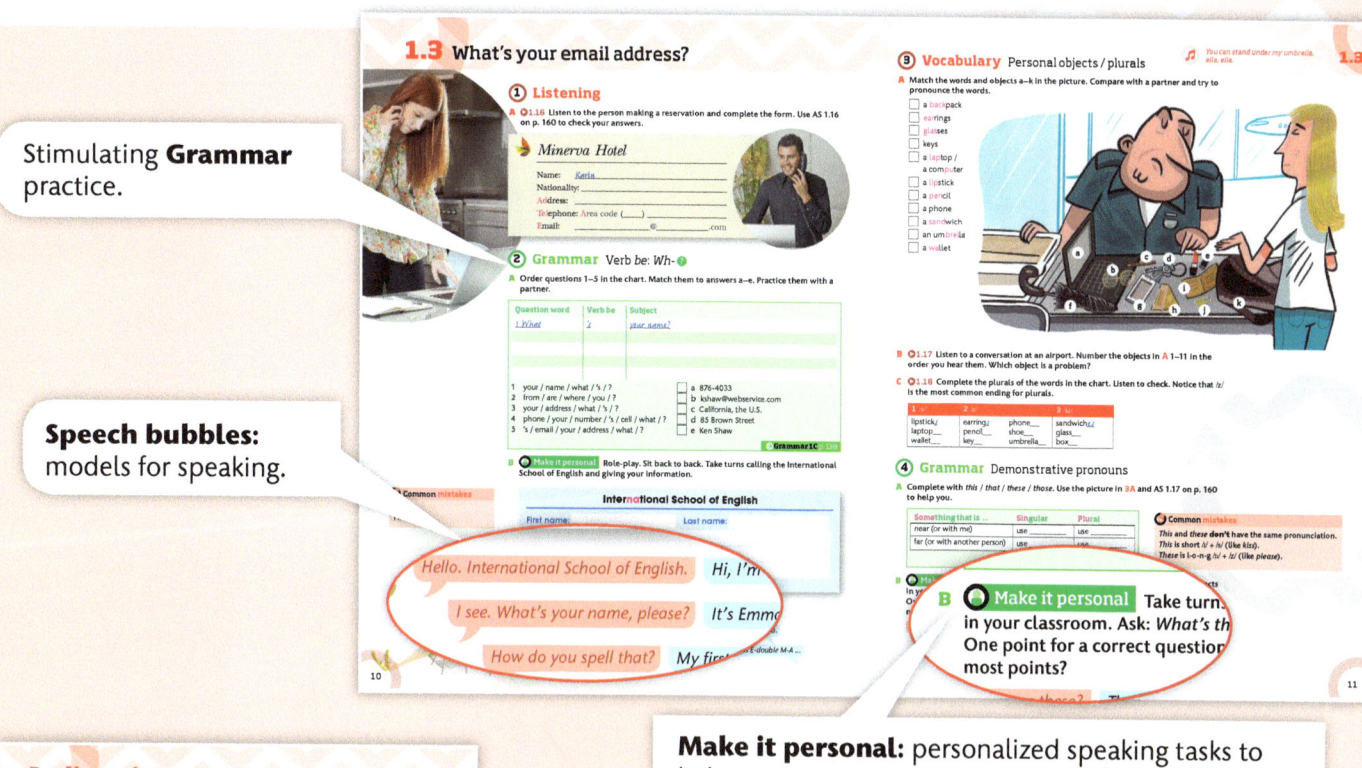

Stimulating **Grammar** practice.

Speech bubbles: models for speaking.

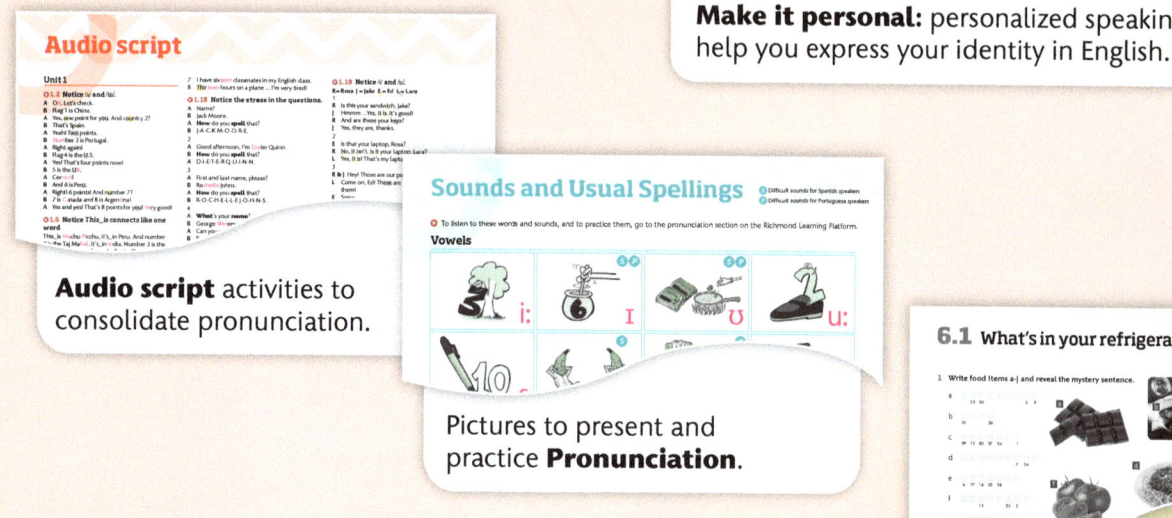

Make it personal: personalized speaking tasks to help you express your identity in English.

Audio script activities to consolidate pronunciation.

Pictures to present and practice **Pronunciation**.

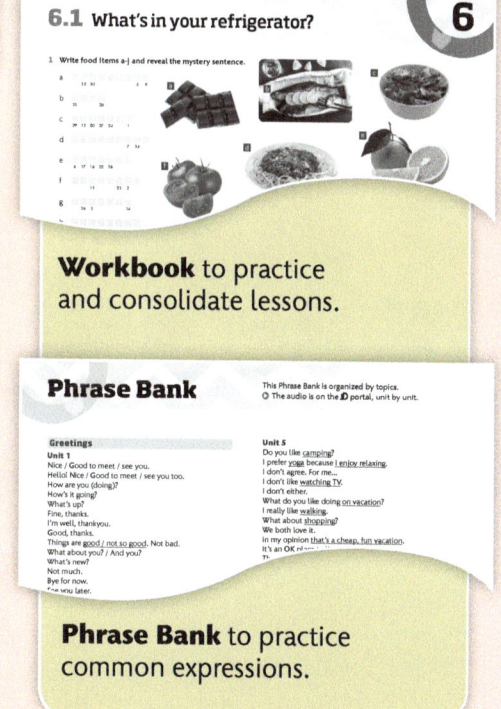

Workbook to practice and consolidate lessons.

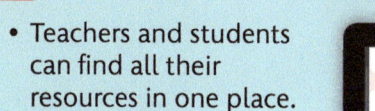

Richmond *Learning* **Platform**

- Teachers and students can find all their resources in one place.
- **Richmond Test Manager** with interactive and printable tests.
- Activity types including pronunciation, common mistakes and speaking.

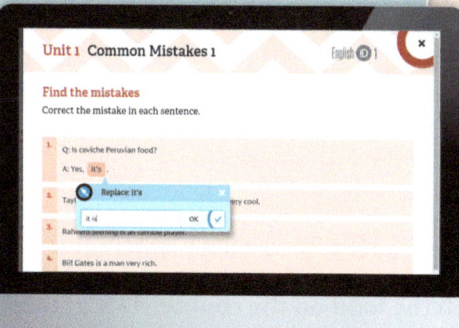

Phrase Bank to practice common expressions.

Learn to express your identity in English!

① **Vocabulary** Food and drink

A ▶6.1 Match the food on the counter 1–8 to these words. Try to pronounce them. The highlighted letters are all pronounced /ə/. Then listen to Jeff making a shopping list to check.

☐ bananas	☐ oil	☐ spaghetti	☐ tomatoes
☐ chocolate	☐ salt	☐ tea	☐ vinegar

Your sugar, Yes, please, Won't you come and put it down on me?

B 6.2 **Match the food in the refrigerator to these words. Try to pronounce them. Then listen to Jeff completing his list to check.**

☐ apples /æpəlz/	☐ chicken /tʃɪkən/	☐ onions /ʌnjənz/
☐ bread /brɛd/	☐ eggs /ɛgz/	☐ oranges /ɔrəndʒəz/
☐ butter /bʌtər/	☐ fish /fɪʃ/	☐ potatoes /pəteɪtoʊz/
☐ carrots /kærəts/	☐ lettuce /lɛtəs/	☐ sugar /ʃʊgər/
☐ cheese /tʃi:z/	☐ milk /mɪlk/	

C In pairs, cover the words in A and B, and name all the items in the photo.

Five oranges ...

D 6.3 **In pairs, listen to Sandra and Jeff. What's their problem?**

E 6.3 **Listen again and number the items in B in the order you hear them. Then ...**

1 What three items can they put in the freezer?
2 What fruit doesn't Sandra like? What food doesn't she eat?
3 What three items can they can use for dinner?

F Make it personal In pairs, ask and answer. Which items on p. 72–73 do you eat / drink

– (almost) every day?
– more or less every week?
– occasionally?
– never?

I eat bananas almost every day. I love them!

Really? I like bananas, too, but I only eat them occasionally.

2 Grammar Countable vs. uncountable nouns

A Look at the words in exercises 1A and 1B. In pairs, answer 1 and 2.

1 Circle the eight plural words. Are the other words usually singular or plural in your language?
2 Which of these foods can you have more than one of?
a coffee b egg c orange d rice e spaghetti f sugar g juice

B Read the grammar box. Then complete the sentences.

Countable nouns		Uncountable nouns
a carrot	carrots	butter
an egg	eggs	cheese
a mango	mangoes	fish
a melon	melons	ice
a potato	potatoes	juice
		milk
		water

Countable nouns have plural forms that end in ______, and the word *a* or ______ before them in the singular. We use ______ when the word begins with a vowel. Uncountable nouns have only ______ form and do ______ have *a* or *an*.

Grammar 6A p. 148

Common mistakes

We have ~~a~~ bread for breakfast.
I don't eat fish~~es~~.

C In pairs, take turns asking and answering about the items in the photo.

What's this? *It's chocolate.* *What are these?* *They're fish.*

D Make it personal Play *Refrigerator Secrets*!

1 Make a list of 10 items you usually have in your refrigerator.
2 In pairs, take turns asking and answering. Who can guess all 10 items first?

Do you usually have milk? *Yes, I do. And you?*

Do you usually have soft drinks?

Yes. I usually have two or three soft drinks in my refrigerator.

6.2 What do you eat for lunch and dinner?

① Vocabulary Food portions and containers

A ▶6.4 Match photos 1–13 to the food items. Listen to check. Which item isn't very healthy?

☐ a bottle of water
☐ a bowl of rice
☐ a cup of tea
☐ a glass of juice
☐ a piece of cake
☐ a piece of fruit
☐ a slice of bread
☐ some carrots or nuts
☐ some eggs
☐ some meat
☐ some fish
☐ some salad
☐ some vegetables

B ▶6.5 Listen to Tony recording Day One of his healthy eating plan. Write Breakfast (B), Lunch (L), Dinner (D), or Snack (S) next to the items in **A** that he eats.

C ▶6.6 Listen to Tony and his friend María. True (T) or False (F)? Correct the false sentences.

1 Tony doesn't like cake.
2 His juice is natural.
3 He thinks potato chips are healthy.
4 He eats a slice of bread only in restaurants.
5 María wants to eat healthy food, too.

D 🔘 Make it personal Each day you can eat only five of the items in the photos, and each week you can eat a particular food no more than three times. In pairs, plan your weekly menu.

How about some salad for lunch on Monday?   *OK. And let's have fish on Tuesday.*

② Grammar Quantifiers: *some* and *any*

A ▶6.7 Complete the extracts using *some* or *any*. Listen to check. In pairs, change 1–4 to make them true for you.

1 I usually have _____ brown rice.
2 I don't eat _____ red meat. I'm a vegetarian.
3 I never eat _____ sugar.
4 I have _____ bread every day with meals.
5 Do you want _____ water?
6 No, I don't want _____, thanks.

B Complete the grammar box examples and rules 1–4 with *some* or *any*.

♪ You want a piece of me,
I'm Mrs. Lifestyles of the rich and famous,
You want a piece of me.

6.2

> There's **some** coffee and _____ tea here. And there's also **some** sugar.
> Do you have **any** vinegar? Yes, but I don't have **any** salt or _____ pepper.
> Do you want **some** cold juice? It's really hot!
> Do we have **any** pasta? I want to make dinner.
>
> 1 Use _____ in affirmative sentences ➕.
> 2 Use _____ in negative sentences ➖.
> 3 Use _____ in questions when you think the answer is "yes."
> 4 Use _____ in questions when you think the answer is "no" or aren't sure.
>
> ➡ **Grammar 6B** p. 148

Common mistakes

information
Do you have any ~~informations~~?

That was ~~a~~ bad news!

NB: The word *news* is an uncountable noun, not a plural.

C ▶6.8 **Circle the correct form. Then listen to check. Are you similar to or different from Lucas?**

Judy: So, Lucas, what do you usually have when you get up?
Lucas: I only have **some / any** water.
Judy: Wow! You don't eat **some / any** food?
Lucas: Well, I have **some / any** bread and **some / any** fruit two hours later.
Judy: Two hours later? And do you have **some / any** coffee? You know, to stay awake?
Lucas: I don't need **some / any** coffee. I don't get up until noon!

D 🔘 **Make it personal** **In groups. What do you usually eat / drink in the morning? Whose morning diet is the healthiest?**

I always drink some water when I get up.

③ Listening

A ▶6.9 **Use the photos to guess what Amy is going to have for breakfast during her trip to Japan. Listen to Amy and her friend Bill to check.**

B ▶6.9 **Listen again. Choose the correct answers.**
1 Amy's trip to Japan is for **vacation / work**.
2 Tourists usually like the **Western / Japanese** breakfast.
3 Bill **often / never** goes to Japan.
4 Miso soup **has / doesn't have** a lot of salt.
5 Green tea **has / doesn't have any** caffeine.
6 In Japan, you can buy coffee in a **bottle / can**.
7 A good way to go to your hotel in Tokyo is by **taxi / train**.
8 Amy **is / isn't** nervous about her trip.

C 🔘 **Make it personal** **In pairs, compare your answers to these questions. Any surprises?**
1 Would you like to try a Japanese breakfast? Why (not)? Any other unusual meals you like or would like to try?
2 What's your ideal breakfast, lunch, and dinner? Where, when, who with, what food?

My ideal lunch is me and Justin Bieber on a beautiful beach, eating fish and drinking coconut water.

My ideal lunch is me and my family eating my mom's home-cooked food!

6.3 How often do you eat chocolate?

① Reading

A ▶6.10 **Read the title of Nelly's blog. Do you think the answer is *yes* or *no*? Then read and listen to the blog and the article and see if the writer agrees with you.**

Food & Life

HOME   ABOUT   RECIPES   MISC

Is Chocolate Really Good For You?
September 3rd by Nelly

I have a confession to make: I love sugar ♥. But I don't really eat a lot of candy. The secret to a "sweet" life 🙂 is quality, not quantity. When I really want some candy or a dessert, I always go for the most delicious and the most attractive that I can find. And they even say chocolate is good for you!

Maybe you're smiling because Nelly's blog sounds familiar. That's not surprising. Chocolate tastes good! And some claim it has health benefits, too.

- If you have a lot of pressure and stress in your life, chocolate can make you feel better mentally and physically. Chocolate gives you energy!

- Chocolate will reduce your appetite. If you eat a small quantity of dark chocolate before a big lunch, your appetite might be 15% less!

- Chocolate can improve your heart! Some even say your cholesterol may improve, too.

- Chocolate keeps your skin hydrated, and it also has anti-aging properties that help you stay young.

- Chocolate has a little caffeine, but much less than coffee. And it has some sugar. Be sure to check the ingredients before you buy. And make sure your chocolate is at least 85% chocolate.

So, is chocolate really good for you? No, not really! We usually eat it with a lot of fat and sugar, which aren't so good for you. But, the good news? A little chocolate now and again won't hurt you – and, of course, it tastes delicious!

B ▶6.10 **How much can you remember? Complete the notes about chocolate. Listen to and read both texts again to check. Repeat the pink-stressed words.**

People say:
1 It's good for pressure and _____.
2 It gives you _____.
3 Eat a little piece before a big _____, and you eat less.
4 It's good for your _____.
5 It makes you look _____.
6 But chocolate usually contains _____ and _____, so it's good to only eat a _____!

C 🎧 **Make it personal**   **Discuss the questions in groups.**
1 Are you similar to or different from Nelly?
2 Does any information in the article surprise you? Anything missing?
3 Do you keep a blog or regularly read any blogs?

> *It doesn't mention the origin of chocolate. It comes from …*

All I'm askin', (ooh) Is for a little respect when you come home (just a little bit).

6.3

② Grammar Quantifiers: *a little, a few, a lot of*

A Circle the correct words in a–d and complete rules 1–3 with *a few, a little,* or *a lot of*.

a   Nelly doesn't eat **a lot of** / **a little** candy.
b   **A little** / **a few** chocolate satisfies her.
c   If you have **a lot of** / **a few** stress, chocolate can make you feel better.
d   We all have **a few** / **a little** bad habits.

1   Use _____ with countable nouns. It means a small number.
2   Use _____ with uncountable nouns. It means a small quantity.
3   Use _____ with countable and uncountable nouns. It means a large quantity or number.

→ **Grammar 6C** p. 148

Common mistakes

I have a little of money in my purse.

③ Listening

A ▶6.11 **Listen to Sandra and Joe talk about lunch at a Mexican restaurant. What do they decide to eat?**

B ▶6.11 **Listen again and complete the chart. Which meal would you choose? Why?**

Common mistakes

six hundreds fifty grams

NUTRITION FACTS Serving Size: 1 burrito (198 g)			
Quantity Per Serving	**Chicken burrito**	**Meat burrito**	**Vegetarian burrito**
Total Fat	____ g	5 g	4 g
Cholesterol	30 mg	____ mg	____ mg
Sodium	880 mg	890 mg	730 mg
Fiber	6 g	5 g	____ g
Protein	____ g	____ g	14 g

C **Make it personal** In pairs. Use the words in 1–6 and *a lot* / *a little* / *a few* to have short conversations about you and your friends. Any surprises?

1   eat / Mexican food
2   have / English-speaking friends
3   spend / money
4   do / exercise
5   download / songs
6   take / selfies

Do you take a lot of selfies?   *No, only a few. I don't really like selfies.*

6.4 How many meals do you cook a week?

① Grammar *How much vs. how many*

A ▶6.12 **Listen to and complete the conversation with** *how much, how many, a lot, a few,* **or** *a little.*

Richie: OK, the chili's almost ready.
Grandpa: You can add some mushrooms, if you want.
Richie: _____ mushrooms?
Grandpa: I don't know! _____ if you like them or _____ if you don't.
Richie: OK – I get it. And how do I serve it?
Grandpa: With some rice.
Richie: _____ rice?
Grandpa: _____ if you're hungry, _____ if you're not.

B **Circle the correct answers and complete the examples in the grammar box.**

> 1 Use **how much / how many** with uncountable nouns: "_____ money do you have?"
> 2 There's always a plural noun after **how much / how many**: "_____ carrots are there?"
> 3 *A few* is an answer to **how much / how many**: "_____ eggs are there?" "A few."
> 4 *A little* is an answer to **how much / how many**: "_____ cheese is there?" "A little."
>
> → **Grammar 6D** p.148

C **Complete the examples with** *how much* **or** *how many.* **In pairs, research these foods and role-play choosing something to eat.**

a chicken burrito   **a hamburger**   **a salmon burger**

a veggie burger   **a tofu burger**

fat   fiber   salt   cholesterol   protein

Do you want a chicken burrito?   *I'm not sure. _____ fat does it have?*   *Five grams.*

And _____ grams of fiber does it have?   *Only six.*

D **Complete 1–10 with** *How much* **or** *How many.* **Ask and answer in pairs.**

1 restaurants do you go to every month?
2 coffee / tea / water / milk do you drink every day?
3 people do you live / work / study with?
4 hours do you work / study / exercise on the weekends?
5 time do you spend studying English / listening to music / on social media a week?
6 money do you spend on clothes / going out / traveling / food a month?
7 meat / rice / fruit do you eat a week, on average?
8 phones / computers / TVs / cars does your family have?
9 texts / emails / Tweets, on average, do you send a day?
10 times do you go out / go to the beach / play sports each month?

E ⓧ **Make it personal** **Choose a topic 1–10 in** D, **and take a class survey. Share your answers with the class.**

Most of us are on social media all the time, except Victor.

On average, we spend about X a month on clothes.

♪ *But she said where d'you wanna go?, How much you wanna risk?, I'm not looking for somebody, With some superhuman gifts.*

6.4

② Reading

A In pairs, take the quiz, but don't read the article! Try to guess the correct answers.

HOW MUCH DO YOU KNOW ABOUT WHAT YOU EAT?

by Sally Larouche

1 Which of these foods doesn't have a lot of potassium?

a potatoes b beans c bananas d apples

2 Which of these drinks is the best way to rehydrate the body?

a water b tea c sports drinks
d orange juice

3 Which of these drinks is really a food item?

a tea b coffee c milk d coconut water

4 Which of these vegetables has a lot of protein?

a beans b carrots c spinach d onions

5 Which of these foods is NOT rich in vitamin C?

a strawberries
b pears
c kiwis
d tomatoes

B ▶6.13 Skim the article and, in pairs, answer 1 and 2. Think of ten more cognates you know.

1 Words that are similar in two languages are called *cognates*. How many of the highlighted words in paragraph 1 do you recognize? Is the pronunciation similar or different in your language? Listen to check.

2 Examples can help you know the meaning of words, too. Can you guess the meaning of the highlighted words in paragraph 3?

How do we decide what to eat?

It's not easy because modern grocery stores offer many, many choices. The first step to a healthy diet is learning as much as we possibly can about the foods we eat. Let's look at the answers to the quiz.

1 Apples are good for you in many ways, but they're not rich in potassium like the other foods are. Potassium keeps our muscles strong and helps eliminate salt from the body. Apples are very nutritious, though, and have a lot of vitamin C and fiber.

2 As you've probably guessed, water is absolutely the best way to rehydrate the body. When it's hot out, drink, drink, drink, and always carry a bottle of water with you. Water also increases our energy, helps us concentrate, and prevents headaches.

3 Because it contains a lot of nutrients, including calcium, protein, and potassium, milk is a food. It's a food you can drink! But if you don't like the taste of milk, be sure to consider other dairy products, such as cheese and yogurt.

4 Do you remember Popeye? He loved spinach. Well, all of the foods in question 4 are good for you, but beans have a lot of protein, more than spinach, carrots, or onions. Maybe you eat beans often, but, if not, now is a good time to start. They taste good, too!

5 And finally, everyone knows that vitamin C is good for you, but which of these fruits is NOT rich in vitamin C? It's not the tiny strawberry. The answer is pears. The good news is that pears contain no fat and are a good source of fiber.

So ... happy, healthy eating! Please share my article with all of your friends. Thank you!

C ▶6.13 Listen to and read the article again. In pairs, take turns asking and answering the quiz in **A**. Check your answers in the article. Do you remember any interesting facts?

> *Here's one. Apples have a lot of vitamin C.*

D 🔊 Make it personal In pairs. Ask and answer 1–4. Are your answers similar?

1 Do you Google information you don't know?
2 How many times a week do you check Wikipedia?
3 Did any answers to the quiz surprise you? Which ones?
4 Does it make you want to change anything about the way you eat?

> *I use Google a lot!*
> *Me, too. I check Wikipedia every day.*

6.5 Are you hungry?

(ID) Skills Scanning a menu

A Scan the menu. In pairs, answer 1–5.
1. What do the symbols ⓥ, 🌱, 🌾 mean?
2. How many meat-free dishes are there?
3. What are the two types of starters?
4. How many main courses and desserts are there?
5. Write the price of each dish on the photos.

Fast & Fresh

Starters
Special Soup

ⓥ Totally Tomato 6.⁹⁹
Pureed tomatoes with fresh cream. Topped with croutons.

Salads

ⓥ🌾 Going Green 8.⁵⁰
Lettuce and spinach topped with the best salad dressing in L.A.

🌾 Chopped Chicken 9.⁹⁹
Lettuce and tomato topped with chopped grilled chicken.

Main Courses
All come with a choice of baked potato, fries, or steamed vegetables.

🌾 Special Steak 35.⁰⁰
1/2 lb barbecued steak topped with a light cream & pepper sauce.

🌾 Fish Fillet 25.⁰⁰
Grilled salmon in orange sauce with a baked potato.

🌱 Pasta Pomodoro 18.⁰⁰
Spaghetti with tomato and oregano sauce.

Desserts
ⓥ Chocolate Chunk 7.⁵⁰
Chocolate cake with chocolate ice cream and fresh cream.

ⓥ Annie's Apple 7.⁵⁰
Traditional apple pie with vanilla ice cream.

🌱🌾 Seasonal Fruit Salad 7.⁰⁰
Strawberry, mango, melon, pear, grapes, and kiwi.

ⓥ vegetarian | 🌱 vegan | 🌾 gluten free

CASH ONLY

i $ 6.99

B ▶6.14 Listen to the ad for Fast & Fresh and check (✓) the dishes you hear on the menu.

C Read the menu again. True (T) or False (F)?
1. Croutons are bread and are only served in salads.
2. The fish and the steak are grilled.
3. There are three different kinds of potatoes.
4. The vegetables are fried.
5. The fruit salad has strawberries.
6. You can pay by cash or credit card.

D 🔘 Make it personal In pairs. Imagine you're at Fast & Fresh. Order a three-course meal.

For my starter, I'm having … | *And I'd like …*

What would you like for lunch?

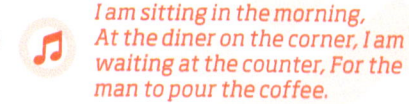

I am sitting in the morning, At the diner on the corner, I am waiting at the counter, For the man to pour the coffee.

(ID) in Action   Ordering food

A ▶ 6.15 **Listen and check (✓) the items Marie and Phil order.**

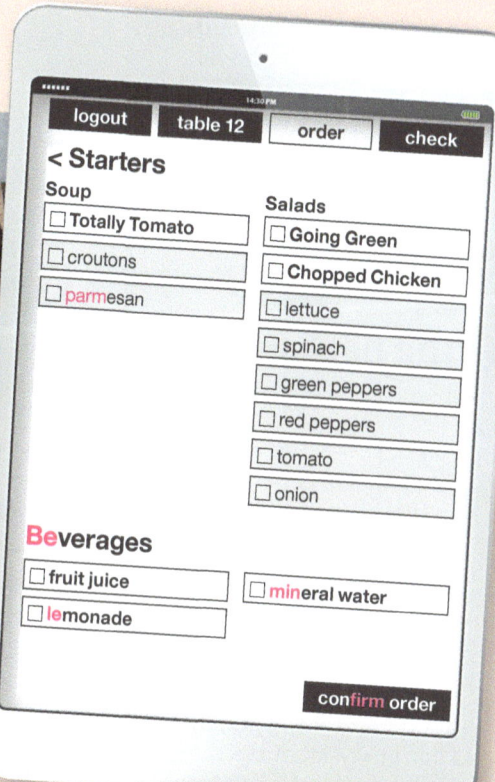

logout | table 12 | order | check

< Starters

Soup
- ☐ Totally Tomato
- ☐ croutons
- ☐ parmesan

Salads
- ☐ Going Green
- ☐ Chopped Chicken
- ☐ lettuce
- ☐ spinach
- ☐ green peppers
- ☐ red peppers
- ☐ tomato
- ☐ onion

Beverages
- ☐ fruit juice
- ☐ lemonade
- ☐ mineral water

confirm order

B ▶ 6.16 **Listen and order the second part of the dialogue 1–10. Complete the dialogue with the food Phil and Marie order.**

☐ **Server:** OK. And you, sir?
☐ **Marie:** Great, thanks.
☐ **Marie:** Yes, please. I'd like the _____, please.
☐ **Server:** OK. How are your starters?
☐ **Phil:** Can I have _____, please?
☐ **Server:** Would you like to order the main course now?
☐ **Phil:** I'll have the _____, please.
☐ **Server:** Any drinks with your meal?
☐ **Server:** Sure. I'll be right back with those.
☐ **Marie:** And I'll have _____, please.

C **Read the dialogue in B again and find three different ways to order food in a restaurant.**

Common mistakes

~~I~~ like pizza, please. *I'd*
"I like pizza" = generally.
"I'd like pizza" = now.
~~I~~ have a mint tea, please. *I'll*

D ▶ 6.17 **Listen and check (✓) the desserts and hot drinks Phil and Marie order. What's the last thing Phil asks for?**

E **Make it personal** **Restaurant role-play in groups of four. A, B, and C: you're at Fast & Fresh for a three-course lunch. D: you're the server.**

Hi! I'm Gaby, and I'm your server today. What would you like to start?

I'd like the soup, please.

Excellent choice! And for your main course?

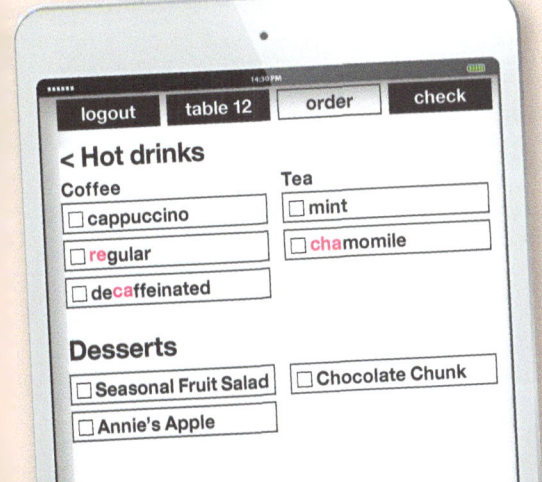

logout | table 12 | order | check

< Hot drinks

Coffee
- ☐ cappuccino
- ☐ regular
- ☐ decaffeinated

Tea
- ☐ mint
- ☐ chamomile

Desserts
- ☐ Seasonal Fruit Salad
- ☐ Chocolate Chunk
- ☐ Annie's Apple

Writing 6   A food diary

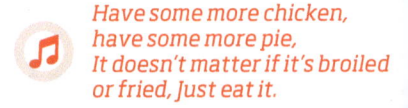

My Life in Food

The healthy eater
Monica, age 22, personal trainer

I try to eat well, as I have a very active job. I believe there's a connection between what we eat and our physical health, so I like to eat food that's fresh and nutritious.

For breakfast, I usually have fruit juice, cereal with honey, and a cup of hot water. I drink a lot of water every day, because it's important to stay hydrated. I never drink sugary drinks. However, I love coffee, and I often have an espresso after lunch.

Mid-morning, I often have a snack, like a piece of fruit. I never eat chocolate or candy. I eat a lot of fruit and vegetables. I don't eat a lot of meat, but I do eat fish because it has protein without much fat.

I always eat lunch, as I need to maintain my energy level through the day. A typical lunch for me is a big salad, with tuna, bread, and more fruit. In the evening, I'm usually tired, so I eat something easy to prepare – for example, spaghetti with vegetables.

The junk food addict
Jude, 19, college student

I eat a lot of junk food, _____ I know it's bad for me and makes me put on weight.

I never eat breakfast _____ I always get up late, but when I get to college, I usually have a donut and a cup of coffee. I drink a lot of soda, _____ it's cheap and it tastes good, and the sugar helps me to stay awake in class.

I eat a lot of snacks through the day – _____, candy bars, chocolate, and potato chips. For lunch, I usually have a burger with some fries and a bottle of soda. I hate fish, and I don't eat fruit or vegetables; _____, I like banana ice cream!

I eat dinner alone _____ my mom works in the evenings. I usually get a take-out, _____ pizza, or sometimes Chinese food. I stay up late playing video games, _____ I often eat another slice of pizza or some chocolate at night. I'm surprised how unhealthy my diet is – I know I need to change it.

A Read what two people with very different diets eat in a typical day. Check (✓) the things they eat and drink.

	Monica	Jude	You
breakfast	☐	☐	☐
water	☐	☐	☐
coffee	☐	☐	☐
fruit	☐	☐	☐
vegetables	☐	☐	☐
fish	☐	☐	☐
meat	☐	☐	☐
soda	☐	☐	☐
chocolate	☐	☐	☐

B Read **Write it right!** In Monica's diary, circle the six connectors.

✔ **Write it right!**

To improve your writing, use a variety of connectors.
- to give reasons: *because, as,* and *so*
- to give examples: *for example* (or *e.g.*), *like*
- to introduce a different idea: *however, but*

C Complete Jude's diary with *because, as, so, for example / e.g., like* and *however*.

D Complete the chart in **A** for you. Think about why you eat what you eat. Anything you need to change?

E 👤 **Make it personal** Write your own food diary in 150–180 words.

Before	Use your notes in **D** and the vocabulary in Unit 6.
While	Use connectors carefully.
After	Read a partner's diary and comment on her / his diet.

6 Party planners

① Before watching

A **Match 1–5 to their definitions.**

1 split   ☐ be certain
2 tasting   ☐ small, red, sweet fruit
3 make sure   ☐ share
4 have no idea   ☐ not know at all
5 cherries   ☐ trying

B **In pairs, guess where August and Andrea are, and what they're doing. Then watch to check.**

> *I think they're sitting in …*

② While watching

A **Listen and complete the extracts with *like, love, would like / 'd like*, or *will have*.**

August: OK. I _____ to try the beef, for sure. But I do _____ chicken.

Andrea: That's OK. You get those. And I _____ to try the fish and vegetarian dishes. I'd also _____ a bowl of rice and a salad plate. So you could get the pasta and potatoes, OK?

Server: _____ you _____ to order dessert?

Andrea: Yes, please. I _____ the white chocolate cake. And also a cup of tea, please. Thank you.

August: And I _____ a slice of Black Forest cake and a coffee. Thanks.

B **Complete 1–5 with *how much* or *how many*. In pairs, take turns asking and answering.**

1 _____ food do they order?
2 _____ main and side dishes are there?
3 _____ slices of cake do they order?
4 _____ cups are there on the table?
5 _____ dishes does Andrea order?
6 _____ cake do they eat?

> *They both order a lot of food!*

C **Match food portions 1–4 to the correct group. Then add the food items to the groups.**

bread	cereal	coffee	pie

1 A bowl of   paper, gum, _____
2 A cup of   pizza, cake, _____
3 A slice of   tea, hot chocolate, _____
4 A piece of   rice, pasta, _____

③ After watching

A **True (T), False (F), or Not Given (NG)?**

1 August and Andrea are at their favorite restaurant.
2 They're planning a surprise for their parents.
3 Andrea loves all red fruit.
4 August doesn't enjoy the Black Forest cake.
5 They thought they were trying the regular menu.
6 They don't have enough money to pay.

B **Match questions 1–6 to the responses.**

1 Are you ready to order?
2 What are you having?
3 Can I take your order?
4 What can I get you?
5 Can I get you anything else?
6 Would you like to see the menu?

☐ I'll have the chicken, please.
☐ Spaghetti and meatballs, please.
☐ Sure. Could I get the beef, please?
☐ Yes, thanks.
☐ Yes, I am. I'd like the fish.
☐ No, thanks. Just the bill, please.

C **Complete 1–5 with expressions from the video.**

1 _____ they don't know about the surprise party?
2 I think we have to try all of those things to _____ they're good.
3 Here comes the server … _____.
4 Dessert? _____ We have to try those, too.
5 _____ we just ate two main courses?

D ⊕ **Make it personal** **In groups of three, role-play the situation. Eat a lot and pay too much!**

> *Good evening sir, madam. A table for two?*

R3 Grammar and vocabulary

A **Picture dictionary.** Cover the words on these pages and use the pictures to remember:

page	
58	8 places around town
60	10 free time activities
61	4 household chores
62	14 vacation activities
64	8 house sitting jobs
67	4 traffic signs
72–73	22 food and drink words
159	16 picture words for lines 1 and 2 of consonants

B 🔴 **Make it personal** **Play *Mime it!* Think of examples for 1–8. Mime them for a partner to guess. Were any of your choices the same?**

1 Two spectacular animals.
2 Two useful *Can I ...?* questions.
3 Three boring activities.
4 Three relaxing places.
5 Three items in your fridge.
6 Two household chores.
7 Your favorite dessert.
8 One vegetable and one fruit.

No idea! Maybe a lion?

C **Circle the correct alternative to complete 1–10.**

1 _____ a good café with WiFi near here?
 a There is b Is there c Have
2 Today, _____ over 5 billion cell phones in the world.
 a there is b there are c there are some
3 Are there _____ cookies in the kitchen?
 a the b a c any
4 How _____ people are there at the party?
 a much b a lot of c many
5 _____ a great new store on the corner.
 a There is b Is c Is there
6 Can I have _____ water, please?
 a some b any c glass of
7 This vegetable soup has _____ salt.
 a much b any c a lot of
8 We _____ like watching TV.
 a same b the two c both
9 I love _____ to the gym and shopping.
 a go b going c goes
10 I hate cooking, but I don't mind _____ the dishes.
 a wash b to wash c washing

D ▶R3.1 **Complete with *some* or *any*. Listen and check. Then in pairs, role-play using different food items.**

Tina: I'm thirsty. Is there _____ juice in the fridge?
Carl: No, we didn't buy _____ juice this week. But, look, there are oranges. Do you want me to make you _____ juice?
Tina: Yes, thanks. Uh, and did we buy _____ cookies?
Carl: No, but there are still _____ cookies in the cabinet.
Tina: Great, thanks!

E **Circle the correct words.**

Dan: Do we have **a lot of / many** homework for next class?
Lee: No, just **a few / a little**. Maybe half an hour.
Dan: How **many / much** exercises?
Lee: I'm not sure, Dan. Only **a little / a few**. Why do you ask?
Dan: I have a party tonight and **much of / a lot of** my friends are going, so I don't have **many /much** time for homework! Hey, do you want to come, too?
Lee: Sure, why not? It sounds fun.

F **Match the two parts to make activities.**

cleaning	in rivers / in the ocean / in a pool
going	video games / soccer / cards
watching	museums / relatives / a friend
playing	the house / the bathroom / the car
taking	the sunrise / old movies / TV
doing	a class / a shower / a course
visiting	the dishes / the laundry / homework
swimming	online / out with friends / to the gym

G ▶R3.2 **Complete with a pronoun. Listen to check.**

1 Hi Mike, how are *you* ?
2 This is Nick and this is Steve, I work with _____.
3 Your coat is on the floor. Please put _____ on your chair.
4 That's Jessica. I go to school with _____.
5 This is David's phone. Can you give it to _____?

H **Correct the mistakes. Check your answers in units 5 and 6.**

1 A house sitter take care your house when you're away. (2 mistakes)
2 I love to walking in the beach. (2 mistakes)
3 To swim is good for you. (1 mistake)
4 I no really enjoy to do the dishes. (2 mistakes)
5 Do you know where is the soccer stadium? (1 mistake)
6 For dinner we ate a bread and a few yogurt. (2 mistakes)
7 You look hungry. Would like any biscuit? (2 mistakes)
8 It's my sister's book. Please give him to it. (2 mistakes)
9 I hate use maps, especially old maps. (1 mistake)
10 Stop! No do that! Please to sit down. (2 mistakes)

Skills practice

♪ *There's a mountain top that I'm dreaming of,*
If you need me you know where I'll be,
I'll be riding shotgun underneath the hot sun.

R3

A 🔴 **Make it personal** **Do you like doing these activities? In pairs, compare. Anything in common?**

| hate | don't mind | like | love |

clean the bathroom   cook   do the dishes
do the laundry   exercise   go online
play video games   read novels
shop in malls / online   spend money   sunbathe
take selfies   tidy my room   water plants

I don't mind doing the laundry, what about you?

Oh, no! I hate doing the laundry.

B **Try to match breakfasts a–f to the country they are typical of. Then read the blog to check your guesses.**

1 Brazil   3 Japan   5 Norway
2 China   4 Mexico   6 The UK

What's your perfect breakfast?

"On the weekend I love to eat eggs, bacon, sausage, tomatoes, mushrooms, and toast. And lots of tea! I don't have time to make such a big, cooked breakfast from Monday to Friday."
Julia, London, UK

"My favorite breakfast is eggs in hot sauce with refried beans, tortillas, and some coffee."
Juan, Guadalajara, Mexico

"I eat the same thing every day - fruit, bread, pastries, some juice, and some coffee."
Milton, Salvador, Brazil

"On weekends or special occasions, I usually eat smoked salmon and scrambled eggs with some rye bread. Other days I just have some bread and cheese – and black coffee, of course! I don't usually eat much in the mornings."
Alexander, Oslo, Norway

"I always eat rice with some fish and soup for breakfast. I don't have time to eat again until the evening so a good breakfast is important to maintain my energy level through the day."
Kimiko, Tokyo, Japan

"Rice porridge with chicken is my best breakfast. I have this about three times a week."
Lin, Beijing, China

C **Read again and name the person / people who ...**
1 eats the same thing every day? _____
2 has a different breakfast on weekends? _____
3 enjoys eggs with hot sauce? _____
4 eats meat for breakfast? _____
5 doesn't eat any meat or fish for breakfast? _____
6 eats rice for breakfast? _____

D ▶R3.3 **Listen and follow the directions. Write the letter in the correct place on the map.**
a the bookstore   c the mall
b the movie theater   d the gym

E 🔴 **Make it personal** **In pairs, are 1–5 True (T) or False (F) for your area? Any interesting differences?**
1 There's a very good restaurant near my house.
2 There is a nice park at the end of this street.
3 There's no good shopping mall near here.
4 There are no interesting museums around here.
5 There aren't any cheap hotels in this area.

There are a lot of excellent restaurants near my house.

Really?! Lucky you! There aren't any near mine.

F 🔴 **Make it personal** **Question time.**
In pairs, practice asking and answering the 12 lesson titles in units 5 and 6. Use the book map on p. 2–3. Where possible, ask follow-up questions, too. Can you comfortably ask and answer all the questions?

Is there a mall in your hometown?   *Yes, but it's only small.*

Do you go there often?   *Not really.*

① **Vocabulary** Rooms and furniture

A ▶7.1 **Match clues 1–9 to the rooms. Listen to a guessing game to check.**

☐ the basement ___   ☐ the dining room ___   ☐ the living room ___
1 the bathroom ___   ☐ the garage ___   ☐ the office ___
☐ the bedroom ___   ☐ the kitchen ___   ☐ the laundry room ___

B ▶7.2 **Listen to Tom showing his house to Anna, a potential roommate. Number the rooms in A in the order you hear them, 1–6. Which three rooms in A are not mentioned?**

C Match the words below to furniture a–s in the picture. First match the words on the left, then those on the right. How many of the words do you already use?

☐1 a bed   ☐ a sofa   ☐ an armchair   ☐ shelves
☐ a chair   ☐ a table   ☐ a bathtub   ☐ a sink
☐ a closet   ☐ a TV   ☐ a fan   ☐ storage space
☐ a refrigerator   ☐ a toilet   ☐ a fireplace   ☐ a stove
☐ a shower   ☐ a microwave   ☐ the stairs

D 🎙 Make it personal In pairs, decide which items of furniture are essential at home and which are optional. Make two lists.

In my opinion, a bed is absolutely essential.

1 Take a shower in ...
2 You can cook in ...
3 You wash and dry clothes in ...
4 Store things you don't need in ...
5 You sleep in ...
6 People usually eat in ...
7 People work in ...
8 We watch TV in ...
9 We keep our car in ...

E ▶7.2 **Listen again and list the furniture Tom mentions in each room. Do you think Anna likes the house? Why or why not?**

♫ *We're going home,*
If we make it or we don't, we won't be alone,
When I see your light shine, I know I'm home.

F 🔴 Make it personal **Give a tour of your home. Draw a floor plan and describe it to your partner. Are your homes similar?**

> *This is the living room with a big sofa. And this is my bedroom.*

② Reading

A **Look at the photo and guess what Jay says about his house. Then, read his blog post and answer the questions.**

Hi! I'm **Jay Shafer** and I live in a small house because it doesn't cause problems for the environment. Also, this way, I don't buy more things than I really need. My house is only 89 square feet (that's 8.3 m²). It has a very small living room, a tiny kitchen, a small bedroom, and bathroom. During the day, my bed is in the wall. You can have a small house, too! Dream big. Live small.

1   What rooms does Jay's house have?
2   What are some good things about a tiny house? Can you think of any others?

B ▶️ ▶7.3 **Watch the video with the sound off. In pairs, name everything you saw in one minute. Who remembered the most?**

> *two chairs*   *a toilet*

C ▶️ ▶7.3 **Watch again and circle the correct answers. Is his house comfortable?**

1   Jay's living room has two chairs and a tiny **fireplace** / **sofa**.
2   The kitchen has a sink, stove, refrigerator, and a **dishwasher** / **toaster oven**.
3   The shower is **the bathroom** / **in the bathtub**.
4   Jay sleeps in **a bedroom** / **the loft**.
5   When it's hot, he uses **air conditioning** / **a fan**.

③ Grammar Past of *be*: *there was* / *there were*

A ▶7.4 **Listen to Katie and Lenny talking about a tiny house. Complete the grammar box with *was*, *were*, *wasn't*, or *weren't*. How many syllables in *wasn't* and *weren't*?**

	➕	➖	❓	Short answers
Singular	There _____ a window.	There was no stove. There wasn't a stove.	_____ there a bathtub?	Yes, there _____. / No, there wasn't.
Plural	There were two closets.	There _____ any closets.	_____ there any bedrooms?	Yes, there _____. / No, there weren't.

When something is negative, we use *there* _____ if it's singular, and *there* _____ if it's plural.

➡️ **Grammar 7A** p. 150

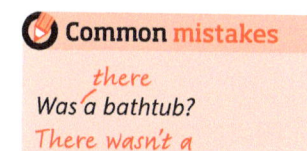

🔥 **Common mistakes**

~~Was~~ *there* a bathtub?
There wasn't a
~~No had~~ garden in my old home.

B 🟢 Make it personal **Imagine you're now living in a tiny house. In pairs, compare it to your "old home."**

> *In my old home, there was a ... but now there's no ...!*   *Were there any ... in your old home?*

① Vocabulary Party items

A In pairs, name each item and its color.

a red teapot, colored invitations, ...

- [ ] coffee
- [ ] glasses
- [ ] plates
- [ ] presents
- [ ] juice
- [ ] a cake
- [ ] tea
- [ ] water

- [ ] balloons
- [ ] birthday cards
- [ ] candles
- [ ] invitations
- [ ] napkins
- [ ] snacks
- [ ] soft drinks

B ▶7.5 Listen to Liz, a party planner, talking about how to have a good party. Number the items in **A** 1–15 in the order she mentions them.

C ▶7.5 Listen again. What does Liz consider essential for a party that is not shown in **A**?

D Make it personal In pairs, compare your last party. Which items in **A** and **C** were(n't) there?

My last party was fantastic!   *There were a lot of ...*

② Grammar Past of *be*: statements and questions

A ▶7.6 Listen to Martha and Rob, and find Martha (1), Rob (2), Jane (3), and Rick (4) in the photos.

B ▶7.6 **Order these words to make sentences. Who said them? Martha or Rob? Listen again to check.**

1 was / I / party / great / at / yesterday / a / .
2 it / was / where / ?
3 was / it / Jane Foster's / at / home / .
4 birthday / was / it / her / .
5 there / Jane's / was / boyfriend / ?
6 he / yes, / was / .
7 parents / Jane's / there / were / ?
8 they / no, / weren't / .
9 boyfriend / I / before / Jane's / Rick / was / .
10 party / great / that / the / wasn't / .

♫ *'Cause we were just kids when we fell in love, Not knowing what it was, I will not give you up this time.*

⏺ **Common mistakes**

Was your brother
Your brother was at the party last weekend?

                                    was
Were you alone? Yes, I were.

C **Read the grammar box and complete with** *was, were, wasn't,* **or** *weren't.*

	➕	➖	❓	**Short answers**
Singular	I was at home. You were … She / He / It was …	I wasn't there. You _____ … She / He / It wasn't …	Were you at home? _____ she / he / it good?	Yes, I was. / No, I _____. Yes, he / she / it was. No, he / she / it _____.
Plural	We were there. You _____ … They were …	We _____ there. You weren't … They _____ …	_____ you there? Were they …?	Yes, we _____. / No, they weren't.

Don't forget the pronoun with *Wh-*questions:

Where were you? I was at school.
When was Julia at school? She was there all day.

➡ **Grammar 7B** p. 150

D **Complete the email with the verb** *be.* **Where was Stacey yesterday?**

To: **Martin**   Today at 10:58
Subject: R U OK?   All Mail

Hi Martin!

Where _____ you yesterday evening? Sleeping again? Well, I _____ at Lina's party, and it _____ amazing! There _____ some great music from the DJ, lots of dancing and the food _____ absolutely delicious! _____ you at home? Your cell phone _____ on all night, and I couldn't talk to you. That's why I _____ emailing you now. Are you OK? You _____ at school last week, and you _____ at the party. Where _____ you now??? 🙁

I hope everything _____ OK.

Write back, text, or call me, please!

Stacey xx

E **Complete the chart of past time expressions.**

afternoon   evening   Monday   month
morning   night   summer   weekend   year

yesterday	last
evening	

⏺ **Common mistakes**

last Monday morning
I was at work the last Monday in the morning.

all evening
We weren't at home all the night.

⭕ **Make it personal** **In five minutes, find out all you can about your partner's week. Use** *Were you …?* **or** *When / Where were you …?* **+ past time expressions. Mime what you can't express in English. Change partners and report what you remember. Who had the most boring / interesting week?**

Were you at home last night?   *Yes, I was, all evening. Where were you yesterday morning?*

7.3 Where were you last New Year's Eve?

① Reading

A Which cities do the photos illustrate? What can you see in them?

The Opera House. That's in Sydney.

B ▶ 7.7 Who has good memories of New Year's Eve last year? Who doesn't? Read and write + or - next to what each person says. Listen to check.

New Year's Eve around the world

Billions of people globally welcome New Year's Eve with spectacular celebrations. How was your last New Year's Eve?

It was awesome! Our city was the first place in the world to really celebrate the New Year. And, of course, the first babies of the year were born here!
Kerry, Gisbourne, New Zealand.

Amazing! I'll never forget it. This was my first year in Sydney. There were fantastic fireworks, and there were hundreds of boats on the water!
Dave, Sydney, Australia.

It was cold! The music was good, but there were so many people along the River Thames! And there were no restrooms near us, so we didn't stay long!
Kirsty, London, England.

I was at the concert at the pyramids of Giza. It was magical! Incredible to think they're nearly 5,000 years old!
Habibah, Cairo, Egypt.

There were thousands of lights on the Eiffel Tower. It was absolutely beautiful!
Sabine, Paris, France.

It wasn't too good. I don't really like fireworks. But I was with a big group of friends. We were all asleep by 12:30!
Lindsey, Los Angeles, the U.S.

It was just like every other day. It wasn't really very special. The family was all together, and dinner was delicious, but it always is. My brother is a chef.
Larry, Santiago, Chile.

There were tons of confetti falling on Times Square. It was a fabulous sight. The snow was beautiful, too, but too many people, and all the trash on the streets wasn't very nice.
Kevin, New York, the U.S.

It was my birthday. It was New Year's Eve and then suddenly I was 12, too! Wonderful!
Jodie, Berlin, Germany.

Fantastic! I was on the beach all night. There was dancing, and then there was a terrific sunrise. Beautiful colors!
Luís, Guadalajara, Mexico.

C Answer the questions.

Who ...
1 was cold?
2 was on the beach?
3 was a child?
4 doesn't like fireworks?

Where ...
1 were the first babies born?
2 was there music along the river?
3 were there a lot of boats?
4 was there confetti?

D 🔊 Make it personal What happens in your town or city on New Year's Eve? In pairs, imagine you were together last year. Write a post to the website.

Traditionally here, people eat 12 grapes at midnight.

♫ *But here I am, Next to you, The sky's more blue, in Malibu.*

② Listening

A ▶7.8 **Where's the mouse? Listen. Match mice 1–10 to the prepositions.**

- [ ] **a**bove the TV
- [ ] **across from** the people
- [ ] **be**hind the TV
- [ ] **be**tween the sofa and the table
- [ ] **in front of** the TV
- [ ] **in** the bed
- [ ] **in** the box
- [ ] **next to** the sofa
- [ ] **on** the bed
- [ ] **un**der the table

B ▶7.9 **Listen to the couple and circle the seven mice they mention in the picture in A.**

C ▶7.9 **Listen again. Draw the mouse's new route on the picture. Describe the route to your partner using the phrases in A.**

First, the mouse was under the table. Then it was …

D 🔵 Make it personal **In pairs, follow these steps.**
1. **A:** Say where the mouse is. **B:** Point to the correct picture.
2. **A:** Point to a picture. **B:** Describe where the mouse is.
3. Close books and remember!

It's on the …

> 🔴 **Common mistakes**
>
> *mice*
> I don't like ~~the mouses~~.
> **mice = irregular plural, like *women*, *men* and *people***

③ Grammar Prepositions of place

A **Read and complete the grammar box. Which are opposites? Mime one to test a partner.**

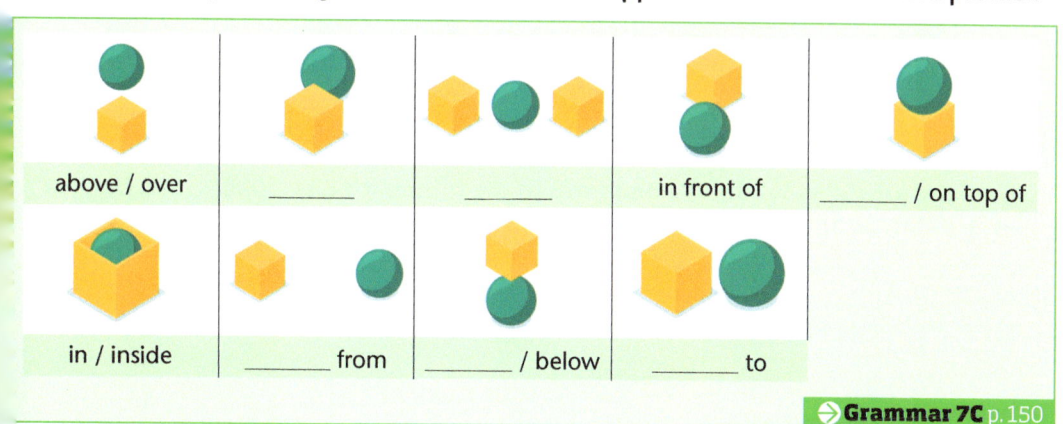

above / over	_____	_____	in front of	_____ / on top of
in / inside	_____ from	_____ / below	_____ to	

→ **Grammar 7C** p. 150

B **In pairs, say where these items are in 2A. Test each other with more items, too.**
1. the pillow / sofa
2. the plant / TV
3. the fruit / table
4. the picture / TV
5. the CDs / TV
6. the bed / chairs

The pillow is on the sofa.

C ⚪ Make it personal **Play a memory game in pairs. You each need five personal objects.**
A: Close your eyes. **B:** Move an object.
A: Look and say where the object was and where it is now.

The … was next to the … but now it's under the …

Hmm … Where was the …? Now it's between …

There was a … in front of … It wasn't behind …

① Vocabulary Dates

A ▶ 7.10 **Listen to and number the dates in the order you hear them. Then circle the correct options.**

YEAR **1980** YEAR **2000** YEAR **2013** YEAR **1985** YEAR **2005** YEAR **2017** YEAR **1997** YEAR **2010** YEAR **2023**

We say years like 1980 and 2017 as **two / three** numbers. For 2019, you can also say two **thousand / thousands** nineteen.

B ▶ 7.11 **Listen to Núria describe her hometown. Write the dates.**

I was born in Barcelona in _____. The city was very different then. In my neighborhood, there were a lot of old buildings and factories. Until _____, there were only two coffee shops (we call them "bars"), and there were no other restaurants on my street. By _____, the neighborhood was a little different, and by _____, there were many new businesses. Now it's _____, and there are families from all over the world. You can enjoy food from many countries, too!

C **Make it personal** In pairs, describe a real or imaginary city on three different dates.

> It was very different. In ..., there was ...

② Reading

A Is this photo of San Diego, California, from 1990 or 2018? In pairs, give three reasons. Which is the most convincing?

> I think it's 2018. There are a lot of tall buildings.

B Read the article about Bill Watson's trip to the future. It's now 2030! Is San Diego a little different or a lot different from his last visit? Does he like the city now?

San Diego, a changing city

by Bill Watson

As I arrive at my hotel in downtown San Diego in 2030, I am shocked. I was last here in 2018, and the city is very different. I almost think I'm in the wrong place!

Like many American cities, there has been urban renewal, and the downtown area has been renovated. It wasn't very nice when I was here in 1990, but, by 2018, visitors were able to enjoy good food, music and theater, or even a baseball game at Petco Park. Now, in 2030, the neighborhood near my favorite hotel is completely transformed!

There are new roads, a park, and new traffic lights. There wasn't so much traffic in 2018, but now traffic lights on every corner are essential. There were some good grocery stores downtown before, but now there are three new ones on my block where you can send your robot to do the shopping. And there's more! When I was here in 2018, there was a movie theater next to the bank. I went there often. But now, there's an enormous movie complex with six large theaters! And there are security cameras everywhere, but there weren't any in 2018. Maybe that's because there's a new school across from the movie complex. In 2018, there weren't any schools in this area.

My recommendation: This is a great city! Beautiful weather, clean, too, and there are a lot more cars in Los Angeles!

C ▶7.12 **Read the article again and complete the chart about the neighborhood near Bill's hotel. Listen to check.**

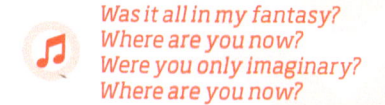

Was it all in my fantasy?
Where are you now?
Were you only imaginary?
Where are you now?

Back then, 2018	Today, 2030
1 There _____ so much traffic.	There _____ a lot of _____ lights.
2 There _____ some good grocery stores.	There are _____ new ones on the block.
3 There _____ a movie theater _____ _____ the bank.	There _____ a movie complex with _____ theaters.
4 There _____ no _____ cameras.	There are a lot of _____ cameras.
5 There _____ any _____ in the area.	There _____ a _____ across from the _____ _____.

D 🔘 **Make it personal** **Imagine that you live in San Diego in 2030. In pairs, say which city you prefer, San Diego in 2018 or San Diego in 2030.**

San Diego was great in 2018. It was so quiet!   *Yes, but there were no ...*

③ Listening

Shanghai Then and Now

A **In pairs, use the photos of Shanghai, China, in 1992 and 2018 to find two things that are the same and two that are different.**

There is a big lake in both photos.

B ▶7.13 **Listen to a conversation about Shanghai then and now. Which changes are mentioned that you can see in the photos in A?**

C ▶7.13 **Listen again. Complete the chart on Shanghai. Write + (a lot), - (not much / many), or a number.**

	1990	Today
Traffic		
Population		
Pollution		
Tall buildings		
Famous sights		

🔘 **Common mistakes**

many
There were ~~much~~ more low buildings.

was
I ~~~~ born in Quito.

D 🔘 **Make it personal** **Find out about your own city or town.**

1 Google your hometown or another place you're interested in. Find five ways it was different 20 years ago. (Try to read online texts in English!)
2 In pairs, describe the changes. Mime what you can't express in English.
3 Share your information with the class. Who found the most interesting changes?

Twenty years ago, Curitiba was / wasn't very clean / big / busy.

There was / were / wasn't / weren't a lot of malls / traffic / people.

7.5 Do you enjoy weddings?

ID Skills Predicting from context

A **Match the events to photos 1–5. What do you know about the five events?**

☐ The 1985 Live Aid Concert
☐ The 1970 World Cup
☐ The first Oscars in 1929

☐ Prince Harry and Meghan Markle's wedding in 2018
☐ The 2016 Olympic Games in Rio

B ▶7.14 **Read and listen to check your answers to A.**

Dream tickets

It was at the Hollywood Roosevelt Hotel in Los Angeles, California, on May 16, 1929, and was a private dinner with 36 tables, and only 270 people. Believe it or not, tickets were only $5. Actors and actresses arrived at the hotel in luxury cars, and there were many fans waiting to greet them. It was not on radio or television. Douglas Fairbanks, president of the Academy of Motion Picture Arts and Sciences, was the host, and the ceremony was just 15 minutes long.

There were 600 people at the "small" ceremony and reception, but 1,200 guests came to greet the happy couple at Windsor Castle. An incredible 18 million people watched the event live on TV in the UK and 29 million in the U.S. The location of the honeymoon was secret!

It was the first World Cup in North America and the first outside South America or Europe. The Brazilian team were fantastic. Brazil beat Italy 4–1 in the final. It really was a great competition – the third World Cup victory for Brazil. It was Pelé's fourth and final World Cup. Pelé is about 80 years old now, but he's still considered the best player of all time.

This spectacular charity event was organized to raise money for the terrible famine in Ethiopia. There were two simultaneous concerts, one at Wembley Stadium in London, the other at JFK Stadium in Philadelphia. There were 72,000 people at the concert in London, and 100,000 in Philadelphia. On the same day, the event also inspired concerts in Australia and Germany. About 1.9 billion people, in 150 countries, watched it all live on TV. Artists included Queen, U2, David Bowie, and Paul McCartney.

C **Cover the text. Uncover only line 1 and guess the word that comes next. Uncover line 2 to check, then guess the first word in line 3. Continue like this until the end. How many of your guesses were right?**

D ▶7.15 *Race the Beep!* **Listen to 12 numbers from the text in B. You have only 10 seconds to find the number and say what event it refers to.**

E **Make it personal** **In pairs, follow these steps. Then change roles.**

A: Imagine you were at one of the events. How was it? Tell your partner. You can add any information you want!

B: Ask your partner questions. What do you want to know?

I was at the ... It was amazing! There was a lot of great music and dancing.

Were there a lot of people?

7.5 **How about a barbecue on Sunday?** ♫

This is an invitation across the nation, A chance for folks to meet, There'll be Dancing in the streets.

ⒾⒹ in Action   Making invitations

A Read the invitations. What kind of event is each one for?

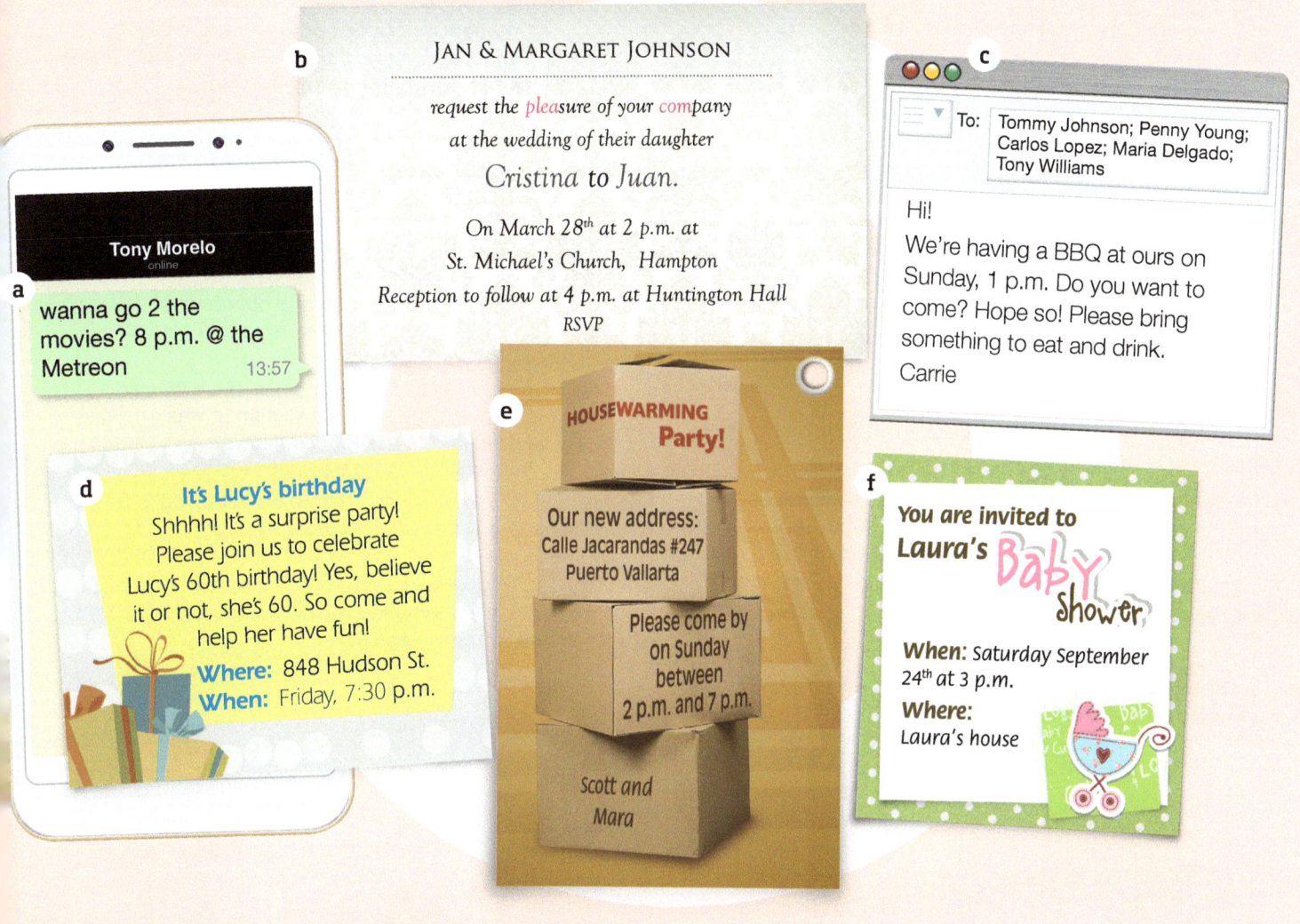

a

Tony Morelo
online

wanna go 2 the movies? 8 p.m. @ the Metreon
13:57

b

JAN & MARGARET JOHNSON
⋯⋯⋯⋯⋯⋯⋯⋯⋯
request the pleasure *of your* company
at the wedding of their daughter
Cristina to Juan.

On March 28ᵗʰ at 2 p.m. at
St. Michael's Church, Hampton
Reception to follow at 4 p.m. at Huntington Hall
RSVP

c

To: Tommy Johnson; Penny Young; Carlos Lopez; Maria Delgado; Tony Williams

Hi!
We're having a BBQ at ours on Sunday, 1 p.m. Do you want to come? Hope so! Please bring something to eat and drink.
Carrie

d

It's Lucy's birthday
Shhhh! It's a surprise party!
Please join us to celebrate Lucy's 60th birthday! Yes, believe it or not, she's 60. So come and help her have fun!
Where: 848 Hudson St.
When: Friday, 7:30 p.m.

e

HOUSEWARMING Party!
Our new address:
Calle Jacarandas #247
Puerto Vallarta
Please come by on Sunday between 2 p.m. and 7 p.m.
Scott and Mara

f

You are invited to
Laura's Baby shower
When: Saturday September 24ᵗʰ at 3 p.m.
Where: Laura's house

B ▶7.16 Listen and match conversations 1–6 to invitations a–f.

1 _____   2 _____   3 _____   4 _____   5 _____   6 _____

C ▶7.16 Listen again and choose the expression you hear. Is the person making an invitation (M), accepting an invitation (A), or refusing an invitation (R)?

1 Can you and Sandy come? / Do you and Sandy want to come?
2 Sure. Sounds good. / Sure. Sounds great.
3 I'm sorry. We already have plans. / I'm sorry. We can't.
4 Great. I'd love to. / Sounds great.
5 Are you free on Friday? / Can you come on Friday?
6 Of course we can! What time? / Yes, we can! What time?

🔥 Common mistakes

                    I'm going
I~~go~~ to a wedding this weekend.

                    I'm taking
Sorry, I can't go. I~~go take~~ my mom to the hospital.
Use the present continuous, NOT the simple present for future plans.

D 👤 **Make it personal** In pairs, imagine an event and write the invitation. Go around the class and invite others. Note if they accept or refuse. Who has the most people going to their event?

We're having a Halloween party next weekend. Can you and your partner come?

We'd love to! What time?

Writing 7 An online review

A Read the ad and <u>underline</u> the positive features of this city-center apartment.

Beautiful luxury apartment, with garage.

👤 2 guests   📶 Wi-Fi   🚗 Parking

Ideal for a weekend city break. In quiet location, only 10 minutes from city center and close to transportation. All modern conveniences, including superfast Wi-Fi, well-equipped kitchen, terrace with great views. Sheets and towels provided. $300 per night for two people.

B Read the review and circle the features in the ad that weren't good or weren't true.

Review by Alisha2001

●○○○○

Apartment sounds great, but was terrible – don't stay there!

My mom and I wanted a relaxing city break, but we were very disappointed. Yes, it's beautiful inside, but …

The first problem was car parking – the garage is over 100 meters away across a busy street!

Secondly, the ad says "close to transportation." That's true – kind of! There was a huge highway in front of the building, and a busy subway station at the back, too! Also, the apartment was not 10 minutes from the city center. Walking fast, it was over 30 minutes.

Then there were the "modern conveniences." There was a refrigerator and a microwave but no dishwasher or washing machine … not even a toaster! Plus, the sheets weren't clean, and the Wi-Fi was really slow.

Finally, there was the noise. Unbelievable! Thousands of cars, and trains passing all night so we never opened the terrace doors!

C Read **Write it right!** and <u>underline</u> the connectors in the text in **B**.

> ✅ **Write it right!**
>
> In a review, start with a statement summarizing your feelings / opinion. Use connectors to:
> - sequence – *the first problem was, secondly, another thing was, then there was / were, finally.*
> - add information – *also, too, plus.*

D Use connectors from **Write it right!** to complete the review. Circle the eight problems.

My friends and I rented a camper van from ZZ Rentals last weekend – it was a disaster!

(1) _____ there was no record of our reservation.
(2) _____, there was only one very small camper available, so we had to take that.

(3) _____, because it was so small, there was no bathroom, and there wasn't a kitchen. It was (4) _____ dirty, and we had to ask for clean towels and sheets (5) _____, when these were supposed to be included.

(6) _____ the insurance. There was an extra $100 per person to pay because we were all under 24. (7) _____, there was a deposit of $1,000 in case of damage!

(8) _____, when we were on the road, we realized there was no gas in the tank! I will never rent a camper van from this company again.

E 🔘 **Make it personal** Write a review of a bad experience at a hotel, in a restaurant, or on vacation.

Before	Use ideas from **B** and **D**, or your own experience.
While	Use a variety of connectors.
After	Check your review carefully and exchange it with a partner. Think of two questions to ask your partner about their experience.

7 House rules

① Before watching

A 🎙️ **Make it personal** In pairs, describe your home. Find six differences.

> *Bea lives in a new apartment block, but I live in an old house.*

B Match photos 1–5 to these words.

- ☐ antique furniture
- ☐ an attic
- ☐ a cellar
- ☐ an indoor pool
- ☐ a lake house

C Complete 1–6 with the prepositions.

at	behind	in	in front of	next to	on

1. August has a computer _____ his lap.
2. Andrea has a cell phone _____ her hand.
3. August's sitting _____ Andrea on the sofa.
4. The window's _____ the sofa.
5. Andrea and August are _____ home.
6. The sofa's _____ the window.

② While watching

A Check (✓) the correct answer.

1. Andrea says they'll be the best ever ...
   - ☐ students ☐ owners ☐ renters.
2. Andrea and August are going to a lake house ...
   - ☐ on the ocean ☐ in the mountains
   - ☐ on the beach.

B Check (✓) or correct all the rules they mention.

1. Don't sit on the furniture in the huge sitting room.
2. Don't go in the cellar.
3. You cannot go in the attic.
4. You can sleep in the master bedroom.
5. Don't swim in the lake.
6. Absolutely no parties.

C True (T) or False (F)? Correct the false sentences.

1. There are ten rules on the list.
2. August's status update doesn't mention the party.
3. Daniel says "My holiday is over."
4. Lucy says she'll clean the downstairs bedroom.
5. Andrea is sad because now they can't go to the beach.
6. Daniel says he'll put the dining room furniture back and vacuum.

③ After watching

A In pairs, describe the photo. Then complete 1–6 with was(n't) / were(n't).

> *Three of them are sleeping. Andrea is ...*

1. It obviously _____ a small, quiet party.
2. There _____ probably a lot of people there.
3. There _____ probably a lot of food and drink.
4. Lucy _____ at the party, but Genevieve _____.
5. After the party, everyone except Andrea _____ sleeping.
6. All the rooms _____ very messy.

B Order the events, 1–6.

- ☐ The cleaning crew arrives.
- ☐ The crew goes upstairs.
- ☐ August sends an email to someone.
- ☐ August says he is selling his car.
- ☐ Everyone goes to the beach.
- ☐ They all start cleaning except August.

C 🎙️ **Make it personal** In pairs, describe the last party you went to. Were your parties similar?

> *My last party was at a hotel. It was my cousin's 15th birthday.*

8.1 When did you start school?

① Reading

A Name someone famous from the past. Your partner says something they know about that person. If they are correct, they get a point. Take turns.

Pablo Picasso.   *He was an artist. I think he was Spanish.*   *That's right!*

B ▶8.1 Match pictures 1–10 to a–j. Complete with *in*, *to*, or ~~0~~. Listen to check.

a   marry _____ him
b   learn how _____ tattoo
c   want _____ go out with her
d   stop _____ work (n.)
e   be born _____ 1877

f   die _____ 1961
g   work _____ the circus
h   agree _____ see him
i   start _____ tattoo lessons at nine
j   study _____ hard

IN LOVING MEMORY OF MAUD WAGNER, 1877 - 196

C ▶8.2 Read and listen to Maud's biography. What were her two professions?

MAUD STEVENS WAGNER Famous ... as a tattoo artist!

Maud Stevens was born in 1877 in Kansas in the United States. She was a circus performer who **worked** in the circus for many years, but that's not all. She was also a tattoo artist, the very first female tattoo artist in the U.S.

In 1909, Maud **married** Gus Wagner, who was a tattoo artist, too. His body was completely covered – there were tattoos all over it! When Gus first **wanted** to go out with Maud, she **didn't want** to go out with him. She only a**greed** to see him in exchange for a tattoo lesson. Maud **studied** hard, and soon she **learned** how to tattoo.

Maud **didn't stop** working in the circus, but she **covered** her body with tattoos. Soon, everyone wanted a tattoo from Maud. Maud and Gus's daughter Lotteva **started** tattoo lessons when she was only nine years old. They **toured** the U.S., giving tattoos to people everywhere. Finally, they **moved** to Lawton, Oklahoma, where Maud **died** in 1961 at the age of 84.

D ▶8.2 Write the verbs in the correct group, according to the pronunciation of their *-ed* endings. Read and listen again to check. Any surprises?

| agreed | covered | died | learned | married | moved |
| started | studied | toured | wanted | worked | |

/t/	/d/	/ɪd/
stopped	lived	needed

⚠ Common mistakes

/askt/

I asked ~~/askɪd/~~ my teacher a question.

E In pairs, decide if 1–5 are True (T) or False (F). Then cover each paragraph in turn, and remember all you can from it.

1 Gus was a tattoo artist, but he didn't have any tattoos.
2 Maud wanted to go out with Gus, but Gus didn't want to go out with Maud.
3 She didn't learn how to tattoo before she married him.
4 Maud and Gus's daughter Lotteva didn't learn how to tattoo.
5 There were no female tattoo artists in the U.S. in 1877.

F 🔘 **Make it personal** Choose a famous person from the past. Research their life and write five sentences about them. Share your information with a partner.

So wake me up when it's all over, when I'm wiser and I'm older. All this time I was finding myself, And I didn't know I was lost.

8.1

⚠ Common mistakes

worked
Maud ~~work~~ in many places.
didn't live
She ~~no lived~~ in Mexico.

> *Avicii was a Swedish musician, DJ, and record producer. He died in Oman in 2018 when he was only 28. He didn't have any children. I loved his music, especially "Wake Me Up" and "Hey Brother".*

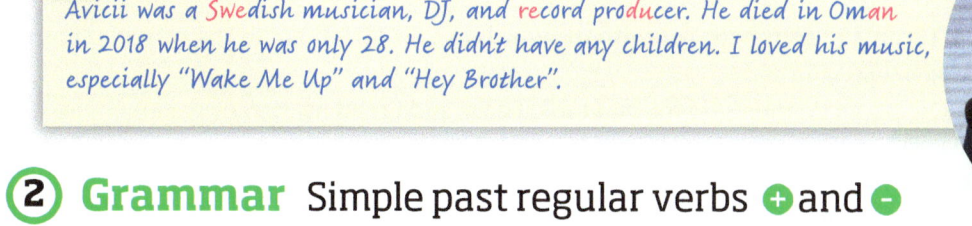

② Grammar Simple past regular verbs ➕ and ➖

A Complete the grammar box. Does the simple past in your language have more or fewer forms?

> Study the bold verbs in Maud's biography (and the negative verbs in **1E**). Complete the rules.
>
> 1 Positive and negative forms have **more than one / only one** form for all persons.
> 2 For negatives, use **doesn't / don't / didn't** + the infinitive.
> 3 To form the simple past tense:
>   the usual ending is _____.
>   when a verb ends in *-e* (*agree, live, like*), add only _____.
>   when a verb ends in *-y* (*study, marry*), change the *y* to _____ and add _____.
> 4 For positive *-ed* endings, there are three possible pronunciations: /t/, /d/, or /_____/. The most common is _____.
>   Only add an extra syllable for *-ed* endings with verbs ending in the letters *d* and *t*.
>
> ➜ **Grammar 8A** p. 152

B ▶8.3 Write the simple past verbs. Then listen to information about the Mexican painter Frida Kahlo, and match the information to the dates.

1928	*was born* in Coyoacán, Mexico City (**be born**)
1907	_____ in Casa Azul with her family (**live**)
1920s and 1930s	_____ to be a doctor (**want**)
1954	_____ to be a painter after a bus accident (**decide**)
1907 to 1928	_____ Diego Rivera, the world famous muralist (**marry**)
before 1925	_____ to the U.S. (**travel**), and _____ a unique style (**develop**)
childhood to 1954	_____ her entire life, and was famous for her self-portraits (**paint**)
1925	_____ in bed at the Casa Azul in Mexico City (**die**)

C ▶8.3 Listen again. Choose the correct answer.
Frida **enjoyed / didn't enjoy** her time in the U.S., but she **liked / didn't like** some aspects of American society. She **didn't travel / traveled** outside North America.

D In pairs, take turns telling Frida's story. Try to help each other with pronunciation.

E 🔘 **Make it personal** Write your own short biography using six of these verbs. Tell your story to the class.

be born   decide   learn   live   marry   move   start   study   travel   work

> *I was born in Bogotá, Colombia. I lived there for five years before we moved to Baranquilla. I started school in 2009.*

8.2 Did you go out last weekend?

① Listening

A In pairs, guess which question goes with each picture.

How was your …?

| day off | day yesterday | summer | Sunday | Thanksgiving | weekend |

I think "How was your day off?" is "b."   *Really? I think it's "e."*

B ▶8.4 Listen and complete 1–6 with the words in **A**. Match them to the correct picture.

1 **A:** How was your _____ _____?
   B: Oh, perfect! I didn't do much. I **took** it easy and I **read** my book.
2 **A:** How was your _____ _____?
   B: I **slept** late. Then I **made** brunch and **had** a good time with my friends.
3 **A:** How was your _____?
   B: Great! My sister and her family **came** over, and we **ate** a lot!
4 **A:** How was your _____?
   B: Slow! I **didn't get up** until midday. Then I **met** some friends, and we **saw** a movie.
5 **A:** How was your _____?
   B: Fantastic! We **got up** late every day and then we **went** to the beach.
6 **A:** How was your _____?
   B: Saturday, I **went** shopping and **bought** some new jeans. I **did** chores all day Sunday.

C ▶8.5 Listen to the pronunciation of 14 common past tense irregular verbs and repeat.

buy – bought /ɔ/
come – came /eɪ/
do – did /ɪ/
get – got /ɑ/
give – gave /eɪ/

go – went /ɛ/
have – had /æ/
know – knew /u:/
make – made /eɪ/
meet – met /ɛ/

say – said /ɛ/
see – saw /ɔ/
take – took /ʊ/
think – thought /ɔ/

D 🎧 Make it personal   Tell the class at least two things you did last weekend.

I met some friends and we decided to go to a nightclub. We had a great night.

② Grammar   Simple past irregular verbs ➕ and ➖

A Complete the grammar box.

1 Complete the sentences with the simple past ➕ form of the verbs in parentheses.

	Subject	Verb	
1	I		my homework last night. (**do**)
2	You		me a really nice gift. (**give**)
3	He		really late after his final exam. (**sleep**)
4	She		good-bye at the airport. (**say**)
5	We		your parents at the mall. (**meet**)
6	They		some expensive clothes last weekend. (**buy**)

In the simple past, ➕ irregular verbs only have one form for all persons.

2 Complete the rule for ➖ sentences.

We saw Vero but she **didn't see** us.   Leo **didn't play** soccer because he **didn't feel** well.
Use the auxiliary _____ + infinitive for ➖ regular and irregular simple past verbs.

➡ **Grammar 8B** p. 152

⏱ Common mistakes

~~have~~
We didn't ~~had~~ a class yesterday.

B Complete Laura's email to her friend Barbara with the simple past form of these verbs. Use each verb only once.

8.2

I knew it when I met him,
I loved him when I left him.
Got me feelin' like, ooh, and then I
had to tell him, I had to go, Havana.

buy	come	get up	give	go ➕	go ➖
know	make	meet	relax	see	sleep

To: **Barbara**   Monday at 09:23
Subject: Hello!

Hi Barbara,

How was your weekend? Mine was pretty good! Saturday I _____ _____ early and _____ shopping downtown with my brother. You _____ him at my party, remember? I _____ some new sandals, and I'm wearing them now! Then we _____ a really good movie. In the evening, my old school friend, Bill, _____ over, and I _____ dinner. And guess what? He _____ me a gift! I _____ he liked me! I _____ to the beach Sunday because I _____ until noon, and then it started raining 😣. So, I just _____ at home. Perfect!

Call me! Let's get together soon.

Laura xx

Common mistakes

Did you know my father?

Not really. I only ~~knew~~ *met* him once.

C 🔊 **Make it personal** List three things you did yesterday. Go around the class. Find at least two people who did the same things.

I ate pizza yesterday.   *Me, too!*   *Oh, I ate fish.*

③ **Vocabulary** Ordinal numbers

A ▶8.6 **In pairs, read the rules and practice saying the dates. Listen to check.**

June 1st, 1996	March 2nd, 2001	December 3rd, 2018
February 4th, 1988	May 5th, 2016	August 6th, 2005
September 7th, 1803	January 8th, 1943	July 9th, 1994

> 1–3 are irregular: *first*, *second*, *third*. Other numbers add *-th*: *fourth, fifth, sixteenth*.
> Over 20: *twenty-first, thirty-seventh*.

B Add three family members to the chart. In pairs, share your information.

	Born on	Died on
My great grandmother	October 14th, 1861	April 3rd, 1961

My great grandmother was born on October 14th, 1861, and died on April 3rd, 1961.

Wow! She was nearly 100 years old!

C 🔊 **Make it personal** Make a class birthday line. Which month and date have the most birthdays?

1 Stand up and ask "When's your birthday?" to form a class birthday line, from January 1st to December 31st.
2 Tell five classmates what you did on your last birthday. Any unusual celebrations?

What did you do on your last birthday?   *I had a big party.*   *Lucky you! I didn't do anything special.*

Common mistakes

Miley Cyrus was born in 1992, ~~in~~ *on* November 23rd.

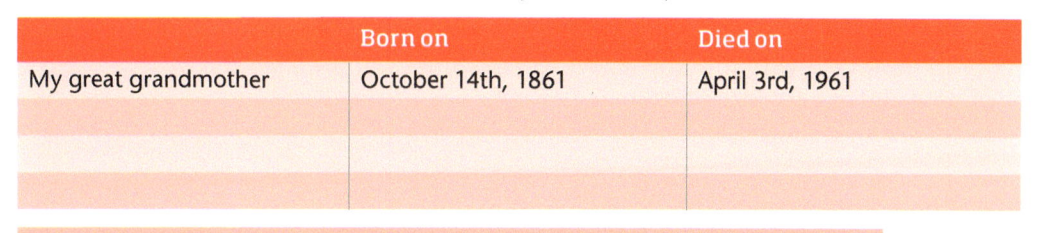

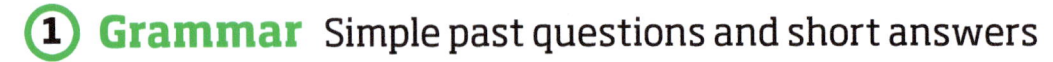

8.3 Where did you go on your last vacation?

① Grammar Simple past questions and short answers

A ▶8.7 **In pairs, make sure you know the simple past of these verbs. Listen to the conversation, then complete David's blog about his vacation.**

be   drink   eat   go   have   meet   see   stay   take   travel   visit   walk

On my last vacation, my girlfriend and I _traveled_ to Ilha Grande – that's Big Island in English! We _____ by car and then _____ the ferry. There are no cars there, so we _____ a lot! The island's incredible, the forest is really beautiful, and the smell of nature is absolutely fantastic. We _____ lots of beautiful beaches, too, and I _____ three dolphins! We _____ fresh fish every day. It _____ very hot, so I _____ a lot of cold soda, too! We _____ in a tiny hotel right across from the beach, and _____ some cool tourists from Argentina. We _____ a wonderful time, and I can't wait to go back.

B ▶8.7 **Listen again. Which word is missing in these questions? How is it pronounced? Now complete the grammar box.**

How _____ you get there?   What _____ you do?

What _____ you eat?   _____ you stay in a hotel?

Yes / No questions (ASI)			Short answers		
Auxiliary	**Subject**	**Infinitive**		**Subject**	**Auxiliary**
Did	you	enjoy your vacation?	Yes,	I	did.
	she	go to Brazil?		she	
	we	buy water?	No,	we	didn't.
	they	have a car there?		they	

Wh- questions (QASI)			
Question word	**Auxiliary**	**Subject**	**Infinitive**
When	_____	you	go?
What	did	he	see?
Where	_____	she	stay?
	did	we	eat dinner?

To form simple past questions, use the auxiliary _____ . To answer *Yes / No* questions, use _____ ➕ or _____ ➖.

➜ **Grammar 8C** p. 152

⏺ Common mistakes

~~did~~ go
Where she ~~went~~?

She went to Miami.

C ▶8.8 **Listen and point to the four questions you hear. Which has more emphasis – *did you* or the verb after it?**

What did you do on your last vacation?

I went out of town.   I stayed here.

Where / go?
Who / go with?
How / get there?
Where / stay?
/ meet anyone interesting?
/ do a lot of shopping?
/ take many pictures?
/ have any problems?

/ eat well?
/ drink a lot of soda?
/ have a good time?

Why / stay here?
/ relax?
What time / wake up?
What / do every day?
/ visit anybody?
/ watch a lot of TV?
/ go out a lot?
/ do anything unusual?

What did you do on your last vacation?

I traveled. / I stayed at home.

D ⏺ **Make it personal** In pairs, ask and answer about your last vacation.

② Reading

A Quickly read a radio show interview and put the pictures a–e in order 1–5.

A BAD TRAVEL EXPERIENCE? Not really!

Travel the World: Next call, please.

Ms. Riggs: Hi! My name's Pamela Riggs.

TtW: Hi, Ms. Riggs. So, can you tell us about a bad experience you had on a trip?

Ms. R: Well, I don't usually have big problems on my trips, but here's an interesting story for you. Two years ago, I went to Turkey. It's a fantastic country – half European, half Asian!

TtW: Yes, it's amazing. Who did you go with?

Ms. R: Nobody. It was a business trip. Anyway, I got to Istanbul airport early in the morning, and I had a connection to Cappadocia, but the airline canceled the flight because of bad weather.

TtW: Really?

Ms. R: Yes, there was no flight until the next day!

TtW: Oh no! And what did you do?

Ms. R: Well ... at first, I just cried! But then I saw a familiar face. It was Semir, my lovely neighbor from New York!

TtW: That's an incredible coincidence! What did he say?

Ms. R: He said, "I also had a ticket on that flight. But I need to get to Cappadocia tonight, so I rented a car. Do you want to come with me?"

TtW: So did you accept his offer?

Ms. R: Of course! But the trip took us around 13 hours.

TtW: But why did it take so long?

Ms. R: Well, Cappadocia is about 740 kilometers from Istanbul by car. And Semir knew the way very well, so we stopped a few times, and I saw some really interesting places. We also had a delicious Turkish meal at a fantastic restaurant in Ankara. We ate and talked for hours. It was great!

TtW: Wow ... So the airline canceled the flight, but your trip to Cappadocia wasn't bad after all.

Ms. R: Not at all. On the contrary, I thought it was fantastic! It was one of the best trips of my life. And, um ... I don't think I told you, I'm now married to Semir. Thanks to that bad weather!

B ▶8.9 **Read and listen to the interview, and then complete 1–5 with two words. Do you know of any similar travel stories with a happy ending?**

1 She arrived in Istanbul to _get a_ flight.
2 She cried because the airline _____ the _____ to Cappadocia.
3 Semir _____ a ticket for the same _____.
4 The trip to Cappadocia took around _____ _____.
5 She _____ a delicious Turkish _____ with Semir in Ankara.

C Circle the past tense verbs in the interview. In pairs, think of five past tense questions to ask Pamela Riggs in an interview.

D 🔴 **Make it personal** In pairs, role-play the interview with Pamela Riggs.

So, Ms. Riggs, where did you go for this trip? *I went to Turkey.* *I see. Did you fly to the capital, Ankara?*

⏱ **Common mistakes**

~~to~~ *at*
She arrived ~~to~~ the hotel late.

③ Pronunciation *Did you*

A ▶8.10 **Read the explanation. Then listen to six questions. Are they present or past? Compare in pairs. Then listen again to check.**

> In rapid, informal speech, *did you* is often pronounced /dʒə/, but *do you* is pronounced /dəjə/. Can you hear the difference?

1 Where did you go?
2 Do you watch a lot of TV?
3 Did you relax?
4 Where did you stay?
5 Do you eat well?
6 When did you go on vacation?

B 🔴 **Make it personal** In pairs. A: tell B about a trip. B: ask questions about it using *do / did you*. Then change roles.

Last year I went to see my grandmother. *Oh, when did you go?*

8.4 When do you listen to music?

① Listening

A ▶8.11 Listen to an interview with Jay De La Fuente, a young songwriter. Order his actions yesterday 1–13.

1	He got up at about 6 o'clock.	☐	He had lunch.
☐	He took a shower.	☐	He turned on the computer.
☐	He played the keyboard and wrote a song.	☐	He ran a mile.
☐	He ate breakfast.	☐	He answered the rest of the emails.
☐	He answered 30 emails.	☐	He went to sleep.
☐	He brushed his teeth.	☐	He went to visit friends.
		☐	He made coffee.

B ▶8.11 Listen again. In pairs, try to remember Jay's day.

> *What was the first thing he did?*   *He got up at about 6 o'clock.*   *What did he do next?*

C ▶8.12 Listen to excerpts and number the "How to sound impressed" phrases in the order you hear them, 1–4.

D ● Make it personal Interview role-play. **A**: interview **B**, a famous person, about yesterday. Sound very impressed! Then change roles. Who has the funniest interview?

> *What did you do first yesterday?*   *I got up at about 5 o'clock.*   *Wow! So early. That's amazing!*

How to sound impressed
- ☐ You're kidding! That's incredible.
- ☐ Wow! That's amazing.
- ☐ That's fantastic!
- ☐ That's great!

② Grammar Subject questions vs. object questions

A ▶8.13 How much do you know about music? Take the ID Pop Quiz and find out!

B ▶8.14 Listen to check. How many did you get right?

C Complete the grammar box. Choose the correct options. Is your language similar?

Object questions (QASI)

Who	does	Jay	live with?	He lives alone.
What	did	he	say?	He said he loves his job.
Where	did	he	go?	To a friend's house.

Subject questions (QV)

Who	sings	that song?	Michael Jackson.
Who	wrote	it?	Michael Jackson.
What	happened to	him?	He died in 2009.

1 In **subject** / **object** questions, you know the subject and want information about the action.

2 In **subject** / **object** questions, you know the action and want to discover who or what is responsible.

3 **Subject** / **Object** questions need an auxiliary.

4 Quiz questions 1-8 are **subject** / **object** questions.

→ **Grammar 8D** p. 152

ⓘ Common mistakes
What ~~did~~ happen^ed on Sunday?

What ~~said~~ our teacher ^say?

*Right now, I'm in a state of mind
I wanna be in like all the time,
Ain't got no tears left to cry.*

8.4

🅳 Pop Quiz

1 Who sold more than 100 million records and recorded the most songs?

a Elvis Presley
b The Beatles
c Michael Jackson

2 Who became the first artist to surpass 50 billion streams worldwide in 2018?

a Drake
b Coldplay
c Justin Bieber

3 Who sang "Let it Go" in Disney's movie *Frozen*?

a Celine Dion
b Idina Menzel
c Demi Lovato

4 Who wrote the first rap song to win an Oscar?

a Eminem with "Lose Yourself"
b Kanye West with "Stronger"
c Jay-Z with "Run this Town"

5 Who made a massively popular music video in which the singer(s) walk and sing in the street, wearing colored suits?

a Mark Ronson and Bruno Mars
b Ed Sheeran
c Maroon 5

6 Who had the first song in Spanish to surpass a billion views on YouTube?

a Ricky Martin ("Livin' la Vida Loca")
b Enrique Iglesias ("Bailando")
c Luis Fonsi featuring Daddy Yankee and Justin Bieber ("Despacito")

7 Who was born when and where? Match the singer to their birthday and birth place.

a Ariana Grande
b Justin Bieber
c Rihanna
d Shawn Mendes

- March 1st 1994; London, Canada
- February 20th, 1988; St. Michael, Barbados
- August 8th 1998; Toronto, Canada
- June 26th 1993; Florida, the U.S.

8 Who didn't sing at President Barack Obama's inaugurations?

a Beyoncé
b Kelly Clarkson
c Lady Gaga

9 Where did Reggaeton begin in the late 1990s?

a Brazil
b Colombia
c Puerto Rico

10 What did Bob Marley say to his son, Ziggy, just before he died?

a "Love one another"
b "No woman, no cry"
c "Money can't buy life"

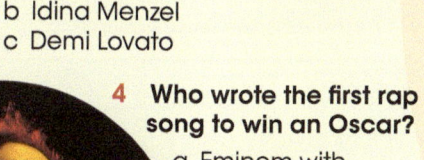
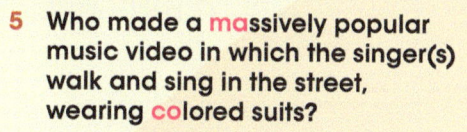
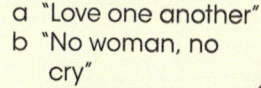

In pairs, take turns asking and answering subject and object questions about facts 1–5.

INTERESTING FACTS!

1 _____ landed on the moon in _____.
2 _____ directed *The Shape of Water* in _____.
3 _____ won their second soccer World Cup in Russia in _____.
4 _____ became U.S. President again in 2012.
5 _____ won five gold medals and one silver medal at the Rio Olympic Games in _____.

Who landed on the moon in ... I think ... 1968?   *No, it was 1969, and I think it was Buzz Aldrin and ....*

🅜 Make it personal In groups, write five questions for a class quiz. Include at least three subject questions. Exchange with another group and take their quiz. Which group got more answers right?

Which driver won the 2018 Formula One Championship?

8.5 Can I use your phone?

Skills   Understanding a story

Five common phone questions

1 I can't talk right now. Can I call you later?

2 Can I borrow your charger?

3 Can I use your phone? I left mine at home.

4 Is your phone working? I can't get a signal.

5 Can you tell me the Wi-Fi password, please?

A Do you remember the last time you asked 1–5?

I asked number 5 at a café last night.

B ▶8.15 Listen to the dialogue. Who's talking? Where are they? What's the problem?

C ▶8.15 Listen again and complete the dialogue. Predict what happens next.

Salesclerk: Hello, can I *help* you?
Customer: Yes, I _____ so. There's a _____ with my new phone.
Salesclerk: OK. I'll try to help. What _____ is the problem?
Customer: Well, I _____ to transfer the data and all my _____, but only _____ of them are here.
Salesclerk: Hmm … OK, _____ you have a _____ in the Cloud?
Customer: Yes, I _____ so.
Salesclerk: OK, just a _____ please.

D ▶8.16 Listen to the end of the dialogue. What does the customer do?

E In pairs, role-play the dialogue.
A: You're the salesclerk. B: You're the customer.

F ▶8.17 Number the pictures 1–5 to make a story. Then listen to check.

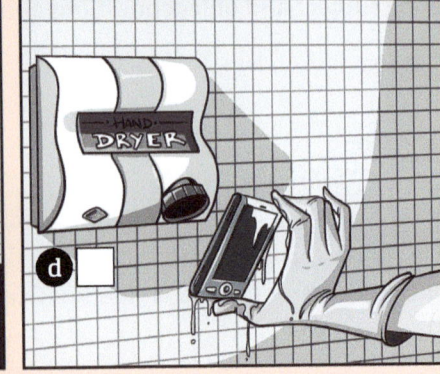

G ▶8.17 Listen again. What four questions does Mike ask Chris?

H 🔾 **Make it personal** Do you know any cell phone stories? Tell a story about something that happened to you or someone you know.

I left my cell phone in a taxi one day and …

8.5 Could you help me, please?

♫ Help! I need somebody,
Help! Not just anybody
Help! You know I need
someone, help!

ⒾⒹ in Action   Asking for favors

A ▶8.18 **Match pictures 1–5 to favors a–e. Listen to five dialogues to check. Which favors did not happen?**

B ▶8.18 **Listen again and complete requests 1–7. Then match them to the responses.**

Requests	Responses
1 Could you _____ who it _____?	☐ I'm really sorry. I have two parties to go to …
2 Could you _____ the _____ for me, please?	☐ Sure. There you go.
3 Can you please _____ the _____?	☐ Come on, I can do it tomorrow.
4 Could you please _____ the _____, Jim?	☐ Don't worry. I'll get it.
5 Could you _____ _____ this afternoon, please?	☐ Sorry, it's Brian's turn today.
6 Could I _____ you a _____?	☐ That depends. What do you want?
7 Can _____ _____ my son with you this weekend?	☐ OK, I'll do it now.

Common mistakes

Could you ~~to~~ help me?
Could you ~~make~~ *do* me a favor?

C **Read the requests and responses in B again and complete the rules with the words.**

can	could	'll	will

1 Use _____ or _____ to ask for favors. _____ is a little more polite.
2 Use _____ + verb for unplanned responses or decisions. The contraction is _____.

D 🧑 **Make it personal** **Role-play. A: Ask a favor 1–4. B: Respond and ask questions. Then change roles.**

1 You're having a party next week, but you don't have any good music.
2 You can't read French, and you got an email from a customer in French.
3 You bought a new dog, but you're going away for the weekend.
4 You have to go to the airport really early tomorrow morning.

Hey, I'm having a party next week. Could you put some good music on my phone?

Sure, I'll do that, no problem. What type of music do you want?

Writing 8   A vacation message

 This is my message to you-ou-ou. Singin' Don't worry about a thing. 'Cos every little thing gonna be alright.

A   Use the photos to guess where Tom went on vacation. Quickly read his email to check.

To: **Mom**   Today at 16:03
Subject: Hello!   All Mail

Hi Mom and Dad,

This is just a short email to tell you I'm OK. Monica and I are having a great time – there are so many things to do. The hotel is pretty basic, and there's no air-conditioning, but it's very cheap! The food's great, too – very hot and spicy! And the weather's excellent – it's much hotter than back home.

Last weekend, we visited a Buddhist temple in the jungle. We had to walk for two hours through the rainforest before we arrived. There were trees growing on the ruins and there were monkeys everywhere, too – it was beautiful. I took some fantastic photos – you can see them on my blog. After that, we rode an elephant – that was really cool.

Tomorrow, we plan to go kayaking in the bay – one of the most beautiful places in Vietnam … maybe the world! There are thousands of islands and secret beaches to explore – it's awesome and we're really excited!

Anyway, I have to go. Please say "Hi" to everyone, and don't forget to walk Toby!

Lots of love and see you soon,

Tom XXX

B   Read again and answer 1–6.
1. Is their hotel comfortable?
2. What did Tom and Monica do last weekend?
3. Was it easy to get to the temple?
4. Did they see any animals?
5. How do Tom and Monica feel about kayaking tomorrow?
6. Who do you think Toby is?

C   Which paragraphs answer 1–6? Complete the chart.
1. What are your plans for tomorrow?
2. What's the place / food / weather like?
3. Are you having fun?
4. What did you do before now? / How was it?
5. Where can we see your photos?
6. Do you have any other things to say?

Paragraph 1	Paragraph 2	Paragraph 3	Paragraph 4
		1	

D   Read **Write it right!** How does Tom start and end his email? How does he start paragraphs 1 and 4? Underline five added comments.

> ✓ **Write it right!**
>
> Try to remember short phrases to start and end emails, or start paragraphs.
> Use — to add opinions or comments to a sentence.

E   **Make it personal**   Write an email home in 150–180 words.

Before	Research a location for your vacation. Use the questions in **C** to help and imagine your answers.
While	Use starting and ending phrases, and write in paragraphs.
After	Check your email, then send it to a classmate to check again. Then send it to your teacher.

8 The favor

Café

① Before watching

A 🔘 **Make it personal** In pairs. Do friends sometimes ask you for favors? Do you ask, too? Any good stories?

> *My friend asked me to help him with his homework.*

B What's August doing? Then watch to check.
- ☐ He's waiting to be connected.
- ☐ He's listening to music.
- ☐ He's checking his voicemail.
- ☐ He's working on his in**ven**tion.

② While watching

A Complete with the simple past of the verbs.

Genevieve: Hi, Rory. What's up?

Rory: Oh, hey, Genevieve. It's Rory. Oh, but right. You just _____ (**say**) ... Sorry, I _____ (**not / know**) you _____ my number. (**have**)

Genevieve: I'm a little busy here. Is there anything I can help you with?

Rory: August just _____ (**call**) me. He _____ (**say**) maybe you need help? With a music program or something?

Genevieve: Oh, I see. Yeah, I do need computer help.

B Order 1–7 to make sentences and questions. Some are two sentences / questions.
1. maybe / need / said / help / August / he / called / you / me / just
2. my / go / can't / I / day / there / it's / off
3. OK / anywhere / to / don't / you / need / go / it's
4. I / exercised / thanks / just / anyway / but
5. I / can / I / can / your / it / from / computer / here / fix / screen / and / see
6. weird / kind / of / sounds / safe / that / is / it
7. me / on / cup / and / your / first / coffee's / of

③ After watching

A Number the phrases in the order you hear them, 1–8.
- ☐ Call me back, OK?
- ☐ Could you do me a favor?
- ☐ Could you do something for me?
- ☐ He said maybe you need help?
- ☐ I need a favor.
- ☐ I really need your help.
- ☐ Is there anything I can help you with?
- ☐ What do you need me to do first?

B Who said it? August (A), Genevieve (G), or Rory (R)?

	A	G	R
1 Oh, sorry, yeah.			
2 Everything's fine.			
3 Tell her I'm sorry.			
4 Sounds simple!			
5 Put me on speaker phone.			
6 Oh, I see.			
7 What do you mean?			
8 That's all it was.			
9 Thank you so much.			
10 I really appreciate your help.			
11 You did me the favor!			

C Now check (✓) the things they did.

	A	G	R
1 asked for a favor			
2 called someone back			
3 fixed a computer			
4 listened to a voicemail message			
5 needed computer help			
6 thanked a friend			
7 didn't want to see Rory			

D In pairs, take turns asking and answering about what the characters did and said.

> *Who said "..."?*   *Who asked ...?*

E 🔘 **Make it personal** Help! Choose a situation and call a friend for help.
1. You don't know how to use your new phone.
2. You need a babysitter for tonight.
3. You're in bed sick with no food at home.
4. You have a job interview today and your best suit is dirty.

> *David? Help! I have a big problem. Could you do me a favor?*
>
> *What is it Marta? How can I help?*

R4 Grammar and vocabulary

A **Picture dictionary.** Cover the words on these pages and use the pictures to remember:

page	
86	9 rooms and 19 furniture words
88	15 party items
91	13 prepositions of place
97	5 more *house* words
98	10 verb phrases
103	Ms. Riggs' story
107	5 favors
159	16 picture words for lines 3 and 4 of consonants

B Circle the correct alternative to complete 1–7.

1 Forty years ago, _____ no cell phones.
   a there were   b there was   c was

2 How many people _____ at the party?
   a were they   b there were   c were there

3 It _____ my sister's birthday yesterday.
   a is   b were   c was

4 _____ you at school last week?
   a Are   b Were   c Was

5 When was she _____?
   a born   b is born   c was born

6 Who _____ the Mona Lisa?
   a did paint   b painted   c was painted

7 What _____ Leonardo da Vinci paint?
   a did   b was   c is

C Complete stories 1 and 2 using the simple past of the verbs in parentheses. In pairs, compare. Do you know any similar stories?

1 I love Beyoncé, so when I _____ (**read**) about a writing competition to win tickets for her show I _____ (**be**) really excited. I _____ (**write**) about how her songs make me happy or sad and I sent the letter. I ____ (**not think**) about it anymore, but imagine my surprise when, two weeks later, a letter _____ (**arrive**). I couldn't believe it! I _____ (**win**) two tickets to the show. I _____ (**take**) my sister and we ____ (**have**) a really good time. She _____ (**give**) an unforgettable show.

2 I _____ (**see**) BTS about two years ago when they _____ (**visit**) my city, and the best thing was – I _____ (**have**) a VIP pass! The band _____ (**come**) on and they _____ (**start**) with a song from their new album. Not everybody _____ (**know**) the words, but I _____ (**do**) and I _____ (**sing**) really loudly. They _____ (**finish**) with an old song. After the show, I _____ (**go**) backstage and _____ (**meet**) the band. They _____ (**be**) fantastic. I _____ (**get**) all their autographs.

D It's Monday morning. Put expressions 1–8 in the timeline.

1 the day before yesterday
2 tomorrow afternoon
3 Tuesday evening
4 last Friday
5 tonight
6 next Thursday
7 yesterday morning
8 last Thursday

○—○—○—○—●—○—○—○—○→

Monday morning

E Complete the questions for the answers given.

1 Who _____ a famous second world war diary?
   Anne Frank.

2 Where and when _____ born?
   On June 12, 1929, in Frankfurt, Germany.

3 When _____ die?
   In March 1945.

4 Who _____ these sunflowers?
   Van Gogh.

5 When _____ this picture?
   He painted it in 1888.

6 How many sunflower pictures _____?
   He painted five of them.

F Play *Past tense tennis!* Take turns "serving" a verb for your partner to "return" in the simple past.

> Agree.   Agreed.   Correct – well done!

G Correct the mistakes. Check your answers in units 7 and 8. What's your score, 1–10?

1 Some years ago, had two movie theaters in my town. (2 mistakes)

2 You was at school today? (2 mistakes)

3 A: Was your dad on vacation the last week? (1 mistake)
   B: No, wasn't. He was sick all the week. (2 mistakes)

4 Five years behind, there were a lot trees here. (2 mistakes)

5 I finished the school when I had eighteen years. (3 mistakes)

6 I no went to college. I get married and had children. (3 mistakes)

7 What did Ms. Riggs saw from her trip to Turkey? (2 mistakes)

8 What did happen to her there? (1 mistake)

9 With who did she traveled? (2 mistakes)

10 Could you to open the door for me? (1 mistake)

Skills practice

You're everything I need and more, It's written all over your face, Baby, I can feel your halo, Pray it won't fade away.

A Read the fact files. True (T) or False (F)?

The Olympics

The first modern Olympics were in Athens, Greece, in 1896, but there are many differences between the early days of the games and the Olympics today. In the first games, there were 245 sportsmen from only 14 countries, only nine different sports, and 43 events. Nowadays, the whole world participates and there are approximately 17,000 competitors from 205 countries, and 306 events – that's an enormous change! Another big social change is in the number of women involved. In 1896, there were no women at all. Today, there are sportswomen in all the Olympic sports.

The soccer World Cup

The first World Cup was in 1930 in Uruguay. There were only 13 teams and all of the games were in Montevideo. There were four European countries, eight came from South America, plus the U.S. In the final, Uruguay beat Argentina 4-2. These days, over 200 teams try to qualify, but only 32 teams get through to the finals of the competition. There are other differences, too. Until 1970, there were no red or yellow cards. Nowadays, teams that don't get many cards can win the Fairplay award, and there are other awards, too. In 1930, there were only the winner's cup and the Golden Ball for the best player. Today, there are also the Golden Boot for the top goal-scorer and the Golden Glove for the top goalkeeper.

1 There weren't any women in the first Olympics. _____
2 There were more sports than countries in Athens, in 1896. _____
3 In 1930, there weren't World Cup games in different cities. _____
4 Argentina won the first World Cup. _____
5 The winner's cup is the only award teams can get in the World Cup. _____
6 There is the same number of countries in the World Cup finals as in the Olympics. _____

B ▶R4.1 Read the blog about a visit to Amsterdam and number the paragraphs 1–5 in the correct order. Listen to check.

C Read again and complete 1-6. Which attraction would you like to visit most?

1 It *wasn't* cheap to rent a _____.
2 The bike tour _____ perfect because the bike _____.
3 They thought the Anne Frank museum _____.
4 They _____ to check out of the hotel before _____.
5 The journey to the airport was _____.
6 Their visit to Amsterdam _____ more positive than _____.

At last we were in Amsterdam! We were really excited to see everything the city has to offer, even though we were there for only a few days. We saw a lot! Here's what we did:

____
The next day, it rained all day and we got very wet in the morning! So, in the afternoon, we avoided the rain and went to some of the fabulous art galleries and museums in the city. My favorite was the Van Gogh Museum, where we saw hundreds of original Van Gogh paintings and learned a lot about his life. It was fantastic. After that, we ate in a tourist restaurant near the museum. It was a bad choice – the food was terrible, and it was very expensive, too.

____
First, we took a bike tour of the city. Amsterdam is famous for its bikes – people ride bikes everywhere, and it's definitely the best way to see the sights. It was more expensive to rent a bike than we expected, though. We had a great time riding around on the bike paths and narrow streets along the canals. But then I got a flat tire! We were a long way from the place where we rented the bikes, and we couldn't fix the tire, so we walked all the way back. It took ages and it wasn't the best way to end our first day.

____
We had to check out of our hotel at noon on our last day, so we left our bags there and found a cheap Vietnamese restaurant close to the hotel for lunch. It was great! There were lots of locals eating there, as well as tourists. Then we walked around and did some shopping for souvenirs, before collecting our bags and getting the train to the airport. It's a really easy journey by train.

____
I recommend Amsterdam for a visit. There were a couple of disappointments, but overall it was a really good experience.

____
On our second day, we got tickets for a canal cruise. This is a great way to see the city from the water. In the old part of the city, the canals are lined with amazing tall, narrow houses that are hundreds of years old. We stopped at different places and went to Anne Frank House, which is where she hid with her family in World War II and where she wrote her diary. The house is now a really interesting museum, but we all felt a little sad thinking about what she and her family suffered during the war.

D How many stars (from 1–5) do you think the blogger gave the visit? In pairs, compare and say why.

I think it was probably 3 stars because ...

E 🔴 **Make it personal** Question time.

In pairs, practice asking and answering the 12 lesson titles in units 7 and 8. Use the book map on p. 2–3. Where possible, ask follow-up questions, too. Can you comfortably ask and answer all the questions?

Do you live in a house? *No, I don't. I live in an apartment.*

How many bedrooms do you have? *Just two, but there's an enormous terrace!*

9.1 How did you get here today?

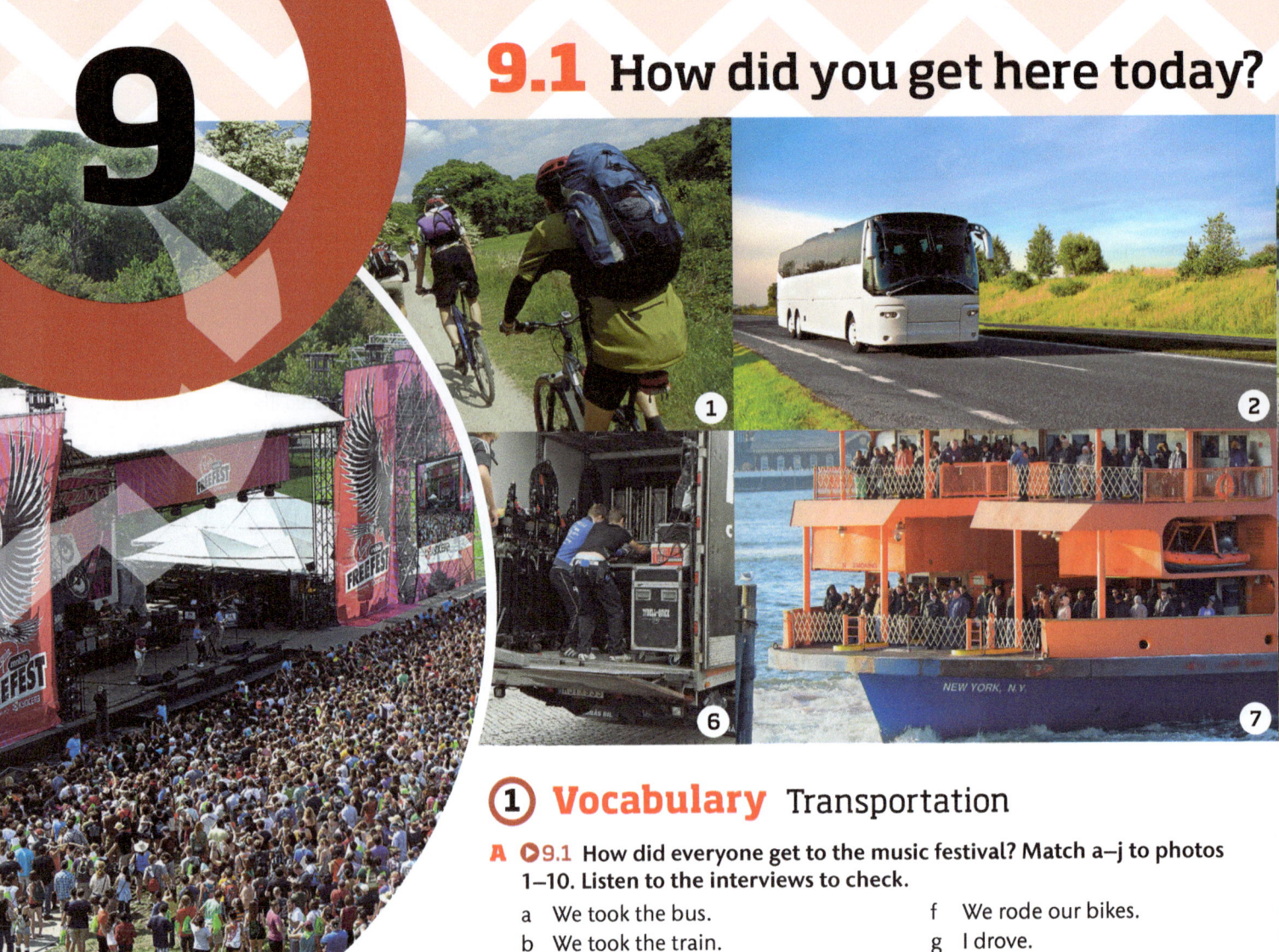

① **Vocabulary** Transportation

A ▶9.1 **How did everyone get to the music festival? Match a–j to photos 1–10. Listen to the interviews to check.**

a   We took the bus.
b   We took the train.
c   We took the ferry.
d   They took a helicopter.
e   I rode my motorbike.

f   We rode our bikes.
g   I drove.
h   I drove the band's truck.
i   I flew.
j   We walked.

B **In pairs, take turns asking and answering about the photos.**

A: Point at a photo and ask "How did (they) get there?"
B: Answer.
A: Confirm and rephrase.

> He went by motorbike.   That's right, he rode his motorbike.

Common mistakes

did you get / come
How ~~you arrived~~ here?
                on
I came ~~by~~ foot.

C **Make it personal** **In pairs, ask and answer the questions.**

1   What's the best way for you to get to:
   a   the nearest shopping mall?
   b   this English class?
   c   your favorite restaurant?
   d   your local airport?
   e   a good beach?
   f   a place with snow?

2   How did you get:
   a   here today and how are you getting home?
   b   to school when you were a child?
   c   to your last vacation destination?

> What's the best way for you to get to the nearest shopping mall?

> By car. I live 20 kilometers away, so I always drive.

② Listening

A ▶9.2 **Guess which transportation problems a–f go with sentences 1–6. Listen to check. Were you right?**

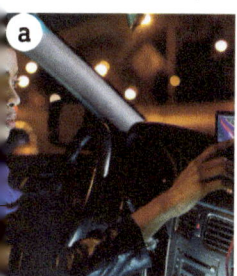

1 The train was late.
2 My plane was delayed.
3 My bus had a flat tire.

4 There was a traffic jam.
5 I made a wrong turn.
6 I had an accident.

B ▶9.3 **Listen to two conversations at a party. Which problems in A does each person have? Which ones have you experienced?**

Conversation 1   Conversation 2

_____ _____   _____ _____

C ▶9.3 **Match the questions to the answers. Listen again to check.**

1 Did you just get here?
2 Where do you live?
3 How did you get here?
4 How's it going?
5 What happened?

a Pretty good, thanks. How about you?
b I had an accident. Nothing serious.
c Yes, actually.
d Right now? In Chicago.
e I took the bus.

D 🔴 **Make it personal** **Imagine you're at a party. Invent a character. In pairs, role-play a "problem" conversation. Then change partners. Who had the biggest problem?**

Hi Bob! Great to see you! How's it going?   *Hi Jane! Sorry I'm late ... I lost my car keys.*

▶ **Common mistakes**

Where are you working these days?
Right now?
Actually? In New York.

9.2 What do you do?

① Reading

A **Guess the answers to questions 1–4. Then read the article quickly to check.**

1 What's the man in the photo doing?
   a He's going to work.   b He's training for a marathon.
2 What's his job?
   a He teaches sports.   b He's a doctor.
3 How far is his commute to work and home?
   a eight miles   b two miles
4 Why does he commute like this?
   a He can't drive and is afraid to ride a bike.   b He wants to stay in shape.

An Unusual Commute

Most people commute by bus, or they drive, but not Ted Houk, from Towson, Maryland. For five years, Dr. Houk rode his bike to work, but then he decided to run, instead, because he wanted even more exercise. Then, for 15 years, Dr. Houk always ran to his internal medicine practice from his home in Lutherville, and back again every day. It's about four miles (around six and a half kilometers) there and four miles home, but he ran when it was sunny, when it was raining, and even when it was snowing. He ran if it was hot or cold, and if it was light or dark.

He always ran with a big bag in his hand. In the bag were his clothes, his stethoscope, his phone, and about two pounds of fruit and vegetables. His full bag weighed about ten pounds (around four and a half kilograms). When Houk got to work, he always rubbed alcohol on his body to remove perspiration. But sweat is not really a problem, he says, because "your sweat is clean."

Then, in 2013, Dr. Houk had a serious accident as he ran. He was seriously injured when a car hit him, and he was in the hospital for two months. Fortunately, he recovered and now works – and runs – again.

B ▶9.4 **Listen and read again. True (T) or False (F)? Do you agree with Ted's ideas?**

1 Dr. Houk lives next to his workplace.
2 He takes the bus to work if it rains or snows.
3 The bag he carried was empty.
4 He went by bike to work before he started running.
5 He thought the sweat on his body was a problem.
6 Dr. Houk started to run again after his accident.

C 🎧 **Make it personal** **Do you know anyone with an unusual commute or way to exercise? What do your classmates do to keep in shape?**

My aunt swims five kilometers every day.   *I never use elevators.*

② **Vocabulary** Jobs

♫ *I'm too hot, Call the police and the fireman, I'm too hot.*

A ▶9.5 **Match photos a–j to the jobs. Which words are easy for you to recognize? Listen to students discussing the photos to check.**

a

b

c

d

e

1 David
2 Chris
3 Brian
4 Valerie
5 Amelia
6 Jane
7 James
8 Martina
9 Robert
10 Larry

f

k

g

h

i

j

a cab driver	a firefighter	a photographer
a computer programmer	a flight attendant	a police officer
a cook	a hairdresser	
a dentist	a personal assistant	

B ▶9.6 **Look at picture k. What job do you think each person has today? Listen to two of the friends talking about the group to check.**

C **In pairs, decide which sentences 1–7 apply to the jobs in A. Which are the best professions? Why?**

1 You can / can't make a lot of money.
2 It's interesting / boring / dangerous work.
3 You work with other people / alone.
4 You work / don't work long hours.
5 You help / don't help a lot of people.
6 It's a job of the past / future.
7 It's a job I'd like / I wouldn't like to do.

> *I think computer programmer is the best job because you can make a lot of money, and it's interesting.*

D 🔴 **Make it personal** **What's your occupation? What do you like about it? What don't you like? What's your dream job?**

> *What do you do?*

> *I'm a student. I enjoy it because my teachers are good, but I don't have any money!*

⚠️ **Common mistakes**

~~a~~ **a** ~~in~~ **at**
I'm student in City College.
~~win~~ **earn / make**
Doctors win a lot of money.

9.3 Where are you going to be in 2025?

① Listening

A ▶9.7 **Listen to Kelly and Michael discussing future plans and check (✓) the correct answers.**

	Profession interested in?	Need to go to grad school?
Michael	☐ financial advisor ☐ pet psychologist	☐ yes ☐ no
Kelly	☐ financial advisor ☐ pet psychologist	☐ yes ☐ no

B ▶9.7 **Listen again. Who says 1–8, Michael (M) or Kelly (K)?**

1 That sounds boring. _____
2 You can make a lot of money. _____
3 You help people. _____
4 You can be your own boss. _____
5 Your parents are going to be happy. _____
6 I don't want to be a veterinarian. _____
7 It's going to be fun. _____
8 Tell me what that dog is thinking. _____

C 🔘 **Make it personal** **Which job do you prefer? Why?**

> *I think I prefer the pet psychologist because I love animals, too.*

② Grammar *going to* for future

A ▶9.8 **Listen to these sentences from the conversation in 1A and complete 1–7. Then complete the grammar box.**

1 What are you _____ to do?
2 I'm _____ to _____ a financial advisor.
3 Your parents _____ going to _____ happy.
4 _____ going _____ be a pet psychologist.
5 It's _____ going to _____ easy, but it's what I want.
6 You can meet lots of people. _____ going _____ be fun.
7 I know I'm _____ going _____ be rich, but that's OK.

⏺ **Common mistakes**

~~to~~
It isn't going be easy.

are you
Why ~~you are~~ going to do that?

Subject	A	➖	*going to*	I	
I	'm			go	to grad school.
You	're	(not)	going to	like	it.
She / He / It	_____			make	a lot of money.
We / They	_____			study	psychology.

Q	A	S	*going to*	I		➕➖ Short answers
What	are	you	going to	do?		Yes, I am.
	Are			go	to grad school?	No, I'm _____.

Use *going to* to talk about predictions and future intentions. In ➖ sentences, use contractions.

1 I _____ not going to like the movie.
2 She _____ going to be late.
3 My parents _____ going to be happy.

➡ **Grammar 9B** p. 154

B Order these questions. Then find someone who has the same answers.

9.3

♫ I'm gonna swing from the chandelier, from the chandelier, I'm gonna live like tomorrow doesn't exist.

1 you / are / going / what / evening / do / this / to / ?

_____

2 you / going / tonight / are / TV / watch / to / ?

_____

3 year / going / you / to / go / vacation / are / on / next / ?

_____

4 are / where / celebrate / next / birthday / going / you / to / your / ?

_____

C ⬤ Make it personal Where are you going to be in 2025? Discuss your answers in groups. Who has the most original answer?

> I'm going to be in space. I want to be an astronaut.

> Wow! How do you learn to do that?

③ Reading

A ▶9.9 Read the article and write the name of the person who talks about these topics. There's one extra topic.

1 buildings _____	4 space travel _____	7 shopping _____
2 education _____	5 conservation _____	8 technology _____
3 politics _____	6 transportation _____	

THE FUTURE?

What is work going to be like for young people? We asked some high school graduates for their plans and predictions for the world of work. This is what they told us.

"I'm not going to be like my parents. They have an online movie rental business. I want to open a physical store like in the old days!" **Saul, 17**

"We're all going to live on the moon, so I'm going to be a space pilot and fly people to the moon and back." **Mariana, 16**

"We're not going to educate our kids in the same way in the future. We're going to use video games to teach kids. I'm going to be an educational video-game designer." **Laisa, 18**

"Humans are not going to use cars forever. I think we're going to be able to teleport pretty soon." **Margarita, 17**

"I'm not going to work in an office. With technology, everyone can already telecommute, and more people are going to do it." **Chris, 19**

"Politics is a career that's not going to change. Even if you don't like politicians, this is an important job and it's what I'm going to do." **Javier, 16**

"Because we can print in 3D now, soon we're not going to need construction workers, and we'll be able to "print" new houses. I'm going to work in this business." **Marco, 18**

④ Pronunciation

A ▶9.10 Listen to the sentences. Check (✓) the ones that are pronounced "gonna" /gənə/ in rapid speech. Then listen again and repeat.

1 a ☐ b ☐   2 a ☐ b ☐   3 a ☐ b ☐   4 a ☐ b ☐

⚠ Common mistakes

I'm
I̶ not going to be rich.
Are you gonna to be famous?

B ⬤ Make it personal Which predictions in **3A** do you agree / disagree with? In pairs, compare answers.

> I don't agree with Mariana. We're not gonna live on the moon in the future.

> I'm not so sure. The future is a long time, and the population is growing fast!

9.4 What are you going to do next year?

① Vocabulary Life changes

A ▶9.11 Listen to Mr. James and complete phrases 1–11. Match six of the phrases to pictures a–f.

1 leave c_ollege_.
2 find a g_____.
3 get e_____.
4 get m_____.

5 leave h_____.
6 start a (new) j_____.
7 start a f_____.
8 get d_____.

9 m_____.
10 lose a j_____.
11 retire (from a j_____).

B ▶9.11 Listen again to check. In pairs, what is one mistake that Mr. James made?

C 🔴 Make it personal In groups, discuss at what age people usually do these things in your country. Do you all agree?

learn to drive   leave home   go to college   get married   start a family

We usually go to college when we're 17 or 18.   *People usually start a family when they're about 30.*

② Reading

A Quickly read Alex's blog. What eight changes is he going to make?

New Year's Resolutions!

Well, I had a long talk with my dad the other day, and he convinced me. We're very different, but I love him. So, I'm going to make a few changes in my life. And, anyway, today is a new year, so time for a new start!

First, I'm going to exercise more. I ate too much over the holidays! Then I'm going to get a new job. I'm a server in a restaurant, and I hate my boss. He makes me stay late and keeps my tips! I want to be a web designer, so I'm going to go back to school, get my bachelor's, and show them all! I'm going to learn a new language, too. I want to learn to speak Mandarin.

I'm also going to move out of my mom's house and get an apartment with some friends. I think it's time, don't you? And I'm going to buy a new car. Then I'm going to find a new girlfriend – I'm so lonely! So … "How are you going to do all this?" I hear you asking.

Here's my plan: Well, after lunch, I'm playing basketball with my friend, Carl, and then tonight, I'm having dinner with my mom to tell her I'm leaving home. Next week, I'm talking to a career specialist, and I'm starting a class in Mandarin. And … I'm going on a date tomorrow night. Wow! Wish me luck! What do you think of my plan? Thanks for reading!

comment:

Hi Alex! I think this is a good plan. But why are you going to learn Mandarin? Why don't you learn Spanish or Portuguese?

B ▶9.12 Listen to and read the blog again and complete the chart.

⚠️ Common mistakes

are you doing
~~What do you do~~ after class?
I'm going   I'm working
~~I go~~ home. ~~I work~~ tonight.

Intention	Reason
1 do more exercise	*he ate too much over the holidays*
2 get a new job	
3 go back to school	
4 move from his mom's house	
5 get a new girlfriend	

C 🔴 Make it personal What do you think of Alex's plan? Follow the models above and below, and write a blog comment to encourage him.

Hi Alex! I think your plan sounds great! I studied Mandarin, too, last year. It's not easy, but I really enjoyed it

♫ *Ooh, love, no one's ever gonna hurt you, love. I'm gonna give you all of my love. Nobody matters like you. So, rockabye baby, rockabye.*

③ Grammar *going to* vs. present continuous

A Are 1–4 in the present continuous (PC) or do they use *going to* (GT)?

	PC	GT
1 I'm going to leave this job when I find a better one.		
2 After lunch, he's meeting his teacher.		
3 Tonight, he and his mother are having dinner.		
4 I think we're going to win tonight.		

B Answer the question in the grammar box.

I'm going to do all my homework this weekend.	= an intention in the future
I'm starting a new job tomorrow.	= a fixed plan in the future

Use the present continuous to talk about a fixed plan in the future. For intentions or predictions, use *going to*.

Which sentences in **A** are intentions / predictions or fixed plans?

→ **Grammar 9C & 9D** p. 154

C In Alex's blog in **2A**, find four examples of intentions and four examples of fixed plans.

D Complete 1–5 with the present continuous or *going to*.

1 I'm _____ (**travel**) to Rio next week to see my mom. I got my ticket online yesterday.
2 They say it _____ (**rain**) tomorrow. I hate the rain!
3 My brother says he _____ (**save**) for a new car next year. He wants an electric one.
4 I think they _____ (**win**) the election.
5 Sofía _____ (**not / go**) to the movies with us on Saturday. She has a dance class.

Common mistakes

~~*going to go to sleep*~~
I'm ~~sleeping~~ early tonight.
When *go* is the main verb or is part of an expression, always include it.

E 🔒 **Make it personal** In pairs, talk about:

1 your plans for the weekend.
2 things you intend to do next year.
3 predictions for your future (jobs, marriage, retirement).

I'm meeting my friends on Saturday. We're having a party at the beach.

I'm taking my grandmother out for dinner. It's her birthday!

④ Listening

A ▶9.13 Listen to four phone messages. What are these people going to do? Match 1–4 to the correct answers.

1 Carla's brother — move to a warm place ☐
2 John's parents — get engaged ☐
3 Julia — go back to school ☐
4 Martin — live in France ☐

B ▶9.13 Listen again and choose the main reason why each person is calling. Who do you think is going to be most surprised?

1 Carla wants Ronnie ... ☐ to cook dinner. ☐ to help with packing.
2 John wants Melissa ... ☐ to give him information. ☐ to move to Costa Rica.
3 Julia wants to tell her mom ... ☐ that she graduated. ☐ some important news.
4 Martin wants Lucy ... ☐ to go to work. ☐ to celebrate with him.

🔒 **Make it personal** Imagine it's New Year's Eve. Write a post about the changes you are going to make in your life next year.

Well, next year I'm going to ...

9.5 Would you like to be a nurse?

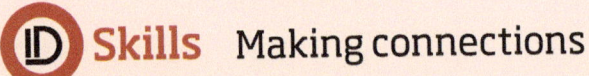

ID Skills Making connections

Reading

A ▶9.14 **Match jobs 1–6 to their area of work a–f. Listen to the talking dictionary to check.**

1 a civil engineer
2 a dentist
3 a financial advisor
4 a market research analyst
5 a nurse
6 a software developer

a computers
b money and finance
c teeth
d health and medicine
e bridges and roads
f what people buy

B Read the article and match the jobs to the paragraphs 1–6.

computer specialists   engineers   nurses
dentists   financial advisors   market research analysts

THE BEST JOBS FOR THE FUTURE

What professionals are we going to need in the future? Here are predictions for the six jobs that are going to be in demand in the U.S. in 10 years.

 1 _____

We will need more people to help the millions of workers who are going to retire in the next 10 years. Many people are going to ask experts to help them plan what to do with their money.

 2 _____

People over the age of 65 are going to keep more of their own teeth, so there are going to be more professionals to show them how to keep their teeth healthy.

 3 _____

What are we going to do about all the cars and buses? With more traffic, we need more roads and bridges, for example. We need more people who can build these large structures.

4 _____

Companies need people to help them understand what people want to buy. They want people who can analyze what customers want and tell them what products to make.

 5 _____

People with IT (information technology) degrees and extensive computer experience are going to be in high demand, to make new software.

 6 _____

There are going to be a lot more people over the age of 90 because of progress in medicine. This means we are going to need more people to help to look after them.

C ▶9.15 **Listen and read again and circle the best answer.**

1 When people retire they **don't need / need** help with their money.
2 People **always / don't always** know how to take good care of their teeth.
3 We need to build roads because of more **traffic / people.**
4 Companies want information about why people **buy / sell** things.
5 You will need a degree **or / and** experience to make software.
6 Medicine is going to be **good / bad** for people over 90.

D 🔴 Make it personal   In pairs, do you agree with the six predictions? Which of the jobs would you most / least like to do?

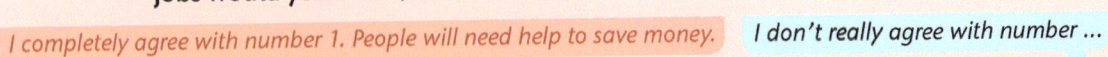

I completely agree with number 1. People will need help to save money.   _I don't really agree with number …_

9.5 Could I borrow your pen?

Lend me your ears and I'll sing you a song, and I'll try not to sing out of key. Oh, I get by with a little help from my friends.

ID in Action — Asking for permission

A Guess what the people in photos a–d are asking for. Use these ideas.

to borrow the car
to borrow some money
to close a window
to leave work early
to take the day off
to turn on the air conditioning

I think in photo "a" the man is asking to …

B ▶9.16 Listen to dialogues 1–4 to check, and match them to photos a–d.

1 ☐   2 ☐   3 ☐   4 ☐

C ▶9.16 Listen again. Complete the questions and circle the responses you hear.

Common mistakes

Can I borrow ~~you~~ a pen?   *from you*
Could you ~~borrow~~ me a pen?   *lend*

Asking for permission	Giving permission	Saying no
Can I ask you something?	That's fine.	No, I'm busy.
Could _____ take the day off?	Sure. Go ahead.	Maybe next time.
Can I _____ the car?	Of course. No problem.	No, I'm sorry, you can't.
Could _____ lend me some _____?	Help yourself.	I'm sorry, but …
Do you mind if I turn _____ the _____ conditioning?	Not at all.	I'm sorry, but it's too cold.
		Sorry, I'm meeting a friend.

D Role-play conversations for photos 1–4. Change roles. Be difficult sometimes!

Do you mind if I borrow your laptop?   I'm sorry, but I'm going home. And I'm working tonight.

E 👤 **Make it personal** Choose something you could ask for permission to do. Go around the class and ask. How many positive responses did you get?

Could you lend me your phone for a minute?   I'm sorry. I left it at home.

Can I borrow some money for a coffee?   Sorry, I only have my credit card with me.

Writing 9 A reply to a blog post

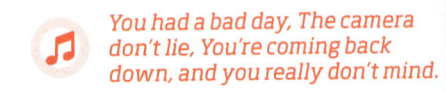

You had a bad day, The camera don't lie, You're coming back down, and you really don't mind.

A Read Michael's blog entry and answer 1–3.

1 Why did Michael have a bad day? (3 reasons)
2 What does he want people to do? (2 things)
3 What advice can you give him?

Michael's Blog

Today was terrible, seriously, one day to completely forget! I got to work a little late. OK, it wasn't the first time, so, of course, my boss didn't believe a word I said, and he fired me immediately. Yes, I actually lost my job! Can you believe it? Well, I hated that job anyway, but the thing is – what am I going to do now? I'm 25, I'm a smart guy (I graduated from college two years ago), I'm getting married next year, but I just don't know what to do. Come on blogosphere, give me some advice and tell me your plans! I need to make some money! Maybe I can get a few ideas from you guys.

B Read three replies. Which advice do you agree with?

Hi, Michael. What a horrible day – are you OK? I think you need to find your dream and work hard for **it**! **That**'s what I'm doing. I want to go back to college to study medicine. I'm working as a personal assistant and living with my parents so I can save for **it**. When I graduate, my dream is to work as a doctor for a charity in Africa. Why not go back to college?
Megan, 20

Sorry to hear about your job. I don't like **mine**, either. Why don't you take a course in your free time? I'm taking **one** in the evenings so I can get a promotion or do something different. You see, I work in a bank and I spend all day, every day **there**. But I want to work with customers in other countries, and for **this** I need to improve my English. **That**'s why I'm not going out until I pass this course! Go for it, Michael!
Jorge, 23

Man, that is bad luck. I know how you feel, I really can't decide what I'm going to do, either. My teachers say I'm good at most school subjects. **They** say I'm ready to go to college, but I don't want to go right now. I'm going to Europe in the summer! I want to travel **there** and try lots of different jobs so I can see which **ones** I like, then … who knows? Do you want my advice? Take a break and go traveling, too.
Leon, 19

C Reread the replies. Circle the words or phrases that the **bold** words refer to.

D Complete the rules with the **bold** words in **B**.

1 *This*, *that*, and *it* all refer back to a thing or a situation.
2 _____ refers back to more than one person or thing.
3 _____ refers back to a place.
4 _____ or _____ replace countable singular or plural nouns.
5 _____ replaces *my* + noun.

✓ Write it right!

Use pronouns to avoid repetition.
I like red apples, but I don't like green ones.

E ▶ Make it personal Write a reply to Michael.

Before	Use your ideas from **A**. Include your own experience, what you're doing now, and your future plans.
While	Use the highlighted phrases to introduce your advice. Use pronouns to refer back to nouns and ideas.
After	Send your ideas to your classmates. Which is the best advice?

9 The sky's the limit

iD Café

① Before watching

A Complete 1–4 with the words in the box.

> climatology   internship
> meteorologist   tornado alley

1 A _____ is a person who researches weather patterns.
2 In the Midwest of the U.S. they call the states of Iowa, Kansas, and Nebraska _____ because of all the strong wind storms.
3 He's applying for an _____ in a science department.
4 The study of the Earth's climate is called _____.

B In pairs, guess what Daniel is looking at, doing, and thinking in the photo. Write a thought bubble for him. Watch the start of the video to check.

> I think he's …   I don't think so. I think he's …

② While watching

A Order the phrases 1–10 as you hear them. Complete the missing words.

☐ I think this is g_____ t_____ b_____ an important program for climatology.
☐ I wanna invent a m_____ or a p_____ that can tell people when a storm is coming.
☐ I'd like to go to grad school and then w_____ a_____ an environmental reporter.
☐ I'll s_____ y_____ the program as soon as I can. Express mail.
☐ So where do you s_____ y_____ in five years?
☐ Thank you for a_____ t_____ this interview.
☐ That's incredible. Could you let me k_____ h_____ that goes?
☐ Can you tell me a l_____ m_____ about your Storm Tracker?
☐ You a_____ n_____ a paid intern of the Foundation for Environmental Advancement.
☐ You'll be part of my r_____ s_____.

B Complete with the *going to* form of the verbs. Which ones would also be correct in the present continuous?

1 Daniel _____ (**talk**) on the phone in a few minutes.
2 Dr. DiChristina _____ (**track**) a tornado in Kansas.

3 His storm tracker _____ (**be**) useful for scientists.
4 Dr. DiChristina _____ (**recommend**) Daniel for a full, paid internship.
5 She _____ (**email**) him the address.
6 Daniel _____ (**start**) his internship after the semester ends.

C True (T) or False (F)? Correct the false sentences.

In the video …
1 Daniel is waiting nervously to make a call.
2 Daniel and the doctor are meeting for the first time.
3 Only the doctor is asking questions.
4 Daniel is giving a video presentation of his Tracker.
5 Daniel talks about his past and his future dreams.
6 She asks him to send her his invention to test it.
7 She offers him a job.
8 He sends her his address.
9 He says he's going to contact her again soon.

③ After watching

A Cover the photo of Dr. DiChristina. In pairs, describe her office.

> On the left, there's a window and some …   Is there a plant?

B Make five *Wh-* questions using the words in 1–5.
1 you / plan / after school
2 time / start / she / the interview
3 he / wait / for the phone call
4 they / do / after / their conversation
5 you / talk to / this evening

C ⬤ Make it personal In pairs, ask and answer the questions in **B**. Add some follow-up questions.

> Where are you planning on going after school?
>
> First, I'm going home, and then …

D ⬤ Make it personal In groups, speculate about your lives in 10 years. Any big differences?

> In 10 years' time, I'm going to be married with a baby!
>
> Really? Who are you going to marry?

123

1
2
3
4
5
6
7
8
9
10

① **Vocabulary** The body and face

A ▶10.1 **Label the photos with these words. Listen to a sports science class to check. Point to the part(s) of your body as you hear each word.**

arms	back	chest	fingers	foot / feet
hands	head	legs	stomach /k/	toes

B **In pairs, say which parts of the body you use to do activities 1–8.**

1 to think
2 to run
3 to swim
4 to ride a bicycle
5 to play soccer
6 to write
7 to do yoga
8 to learn English

You need your legs and your feet to run.   *And you need your arms, too.*

C ▶10.2 **Look at the photo and label these parts of the face. Listen to check.**

ears
eyes
eyebrows
hair

lips
mouth
nose
teeth

♪ I feel it in my fingers, I feel it in my toes, Love is all around me, And so the feeling grows.

10.1

1
2
3
4
5
6
7
8

D **What part(s) of the face do you associate most with these verbs?**

- [ ] eat
- [ ] listen
- [ ] look
- [ ] kiss
- [ ] read
- [ ] see
- [ ] smell
- [ ] speak
- [ ] watch

E 🔴 **Make it personal** In pairs, think of more activities you can do with the parts of the body and face in **A** and **C**. Which pair has the most activities?

You need your arms to get a taxi in the street.

You have to have fingers to use a cell phone.

② **Listening**

A ▶10.3 **Listen to descriptions of three suspects. Write the name, Adam, Charlie, or Mark, under the correct person.**

B ▶10.3 **Write the number of the suspect 1–3 for each item. There are four items for each suspect. Then listen again to check.**

Weight
- [ ] average build
- [ ] overweight
- [ ] slim

Height
- [ ] average height
- [ ] short
- [ ] tall

Eyes
- [ ] blue eyes
- [ ] brown eyes
- [ ] green eyes

Hair
- [ ] long dark hair
- [ ] short dark hair
- [ ] short fair hair

2.00 m
1.90 m
1.80 m
1.70 m
1.60 m
1.50 m
1.40 m
1.30 m
1.20 m
1.10 m
1.00 m
0.90 m
0.80 m
0.70 m
0.60 m
0.50 m
0.40 m

C Spot the suspect! **A:** Describe one of the suspects. **B:** With your book closed, say who it is. Change roles.

He has ... hair and he is ...

🔴 **Common mistakes**

What does he look like?
~~How is he?~~
's
He~~ ~~tall.
He has ~~the~~ long hair.

D 🔴 **Make it personal** Describe a "suspect" in the class. Use "this person," not "he" or "she." Can your classmates guess who it is?

This person is tall with long, dark hair. This person is wearing ...

10.2 Are you like your dad?

① Reading

A ▶10.4 Read the article and complete the information about Kelly. Listen and read again to check.

An extraordinary athlete

Kelly Bruno is tall and slim with long dark hair and brown eyes – she loves sports and she's an excellent athlete. She looks like a lot of young women, but Kelly is different. Born in North Carolina on March 23, 1984, Kelly was six months old when doctors amputated part of her leg. Three months later, she got a prosthetic leg and she began to walk at the age of only 13 months. She was very athletic in school and was good at sports, especially baseball, soccer, and running. She was also courageous and determined, and wanted to succeed. Now she is a champion triathlete. In a triathlon, she has to swim 1,500 m, ride a bike for 40 km, and run 10 km. She won the New York City Triathlon in 2008, and she also competes in ultramarathons – races of over 160 km.

Kelly became a doctor in 2017. Her father was a doctor, and he inspired Kelly to study medicine before he died in 2010 in an earthquake in Haiti. He was working there for an organization called "Food for the Poor."

What does Kelly think about her leg? "It's just an obstacle," she says. "Everyone has their own obstacles. Whatever yours is, just don't quit."

Full name:
Kelly

Description:

Hobbies:

Occupation:

B ▶10.5 Read again and complete Kelly's timeline. Listen to a conversation to check.

6 months old	9 months old	13 months old	2008	2010	2017
doctors amputated part of her leg					

C In pairs, match words 1–3 to definitions a–c. Then take turns miming a word from the article for your partner to say.

Is that thin? No, I know, slim!

1 to quit
2 an earthquake
3 to succeed

a when the ground shakes
b stop, give up, abandon
c be successful

⊘ Common mistakes

is
What ~~does~~ she like?

D 🔊 **Make it personal** What do you think of Kelly's experiences and attitude? Choose three words to describe her. Compare your choices in groups. Do you know anyone like her?

active	athletic	courageous	determined	extraordinary
energetic	heroic	ordinary	strong	

Which words did you choose?

I think she's strong, determined, and heroic. My grandfather is like her.

What doesn't kill you makes you stronger, Stand a little taller, Doesn't mean I'm lonely when I'm alone.

10.2

② **Grammar** Comparatives with -er and *more*

A ▶10.6 **Listen to Maggie and Steve. Then match photos 1 and 2 to the adjectives.**

☐ boring ☐ happy ☐ interesting ☐ sad ☐ short ☐ tall

B ▶10.6 **Listen again and complete 1–4 with the word(s) you hear.**

happier   interesting   sadder   shorter   taller

1 Scott is _____ than Jake.
2 Jake is _____ than Scott. Scott's _____.
3 It doesn't matter that he's _____ than Scott.
4 Scott is more _____ than Jake.

C **Complete the grammar box.**

1 Jake   2 Scott

> **Match 1–4 to a–d to make rules.**
>
> 1 Adjectives of one syllable:
> 2 Adjectives of two or more syllables:
> 3 Adjectives of two syllables (ending in -y):
> 4 Irregular comparatives:
>
> a *good → better; bad → worse*
> b use *more* plus adjective
> c change -y to -i and add -er
> d add -er.
>
> Spelling adjectives that end consonant + vowel + consonant (CVC), double the final consonant:
> "Russia is bigger than Canada." "It was hot yesterday, but today it's _____."
>
> **→ Grammar 10A** p. 156

D **Write eight comparative sentences with your opinions. Choose from the adjectives below or others of your own.**

bad   friendly   happy   interesting   relaxed
expensive   good   hard   nice   sad

1 work / school   *School is more relaxed than work, I think!*
2 summer / winter
3 museums / movies
4 evenings / mornings
5 shoes / sandals
6 my mother / my father
7 the news in [country] / the news in [country]
8 rock music / hip hop music

⊘ Common mistakes

~~*worse*~~
My writing is ~~more bad~~ than my speaking.

~~*bigger*~~
Our apartment is ~~more big~~ than Sheila's new house.

E  **In groups, share your opinions in D and give reasons.**

I think winter is nicer here because there aren't a lot of tourists.   *Yes, but it's cold!*

③ **Listening**

A ▶10.7 **Listen and identify Brad's sisters Zoe and Rebecca in the pictures.**

B ▶10.7 **Listen again. Complete these sentences with Zoe (Z) or Rebecca (R). Are you more similar to Zoe or Rebecca?**

1 _____ is friendlier than _____.
2 _____ is more generous than _____.
3 _____ is more timid than _____.
4 _____ is calmer than _____.
5 _____ is more intelligent than _____.
6 _____ is more organized than _____.

Make it personal **Use adjectives from 2A, 2D, and 3B (and others that you know) to compare yourself with someone in your family.**

My dad is friendlier than me. He likes to go to parties and meet people. I'm a little shyer.

Do you look like him?   *Not really. He's a lot shorter.*

① **Reading**

A ▶10.8 What is an enneagram, definition 1 or 2? Read the introduction to the website and choose the best answer. Then read and listen. Pause after each type and repeat the pink-stressed adjectives.

1 A new system to label positive and negative people.
2 A diagram that represents nine personality types.

Which type are you?

The enneagram is an ancient symbol used to describe personality types. It is a circle with nine points. Each of them represents a different personality type with both negative and positive characteristics. The enneagram says that we move between these negative and positive characteristics. All of us have one of nine basic personality types. Here is an example of each type:

 I'm **type 1**. I'm a perfectionist and I'm idealistic. My negative side is that sometimes I'm very critical of other people.

 **Type 4** people are romantic and want to understand other people. That's me! I like to understand how people feel, but sometimes I can be moody.

 I love to have fun and be spontaneous. I'm **type 7**, and I'm usually happy, but I can be disorganized when I'm trying to have fun!

 I love to help people and I'm very generous, but if you're my friend, I don't want to share you! I can be very possessive. I'm **type 2**.

 I'm a solitary person, and I want to try to understand what's happening in my world. That's **type 5**. Sometimes I feel depressed and that's my negative side.

 **Type 8** people are strong, and they want to do important things for the world – that's me. My negative side is that I can get angry when you don't agree with me!

 Well, I'm **type 3**. I am ambitious and good at things. If I do things well I can become more arrogant – this is my negative side.

 I'm very loyal to my friends, and I'm very responsible. My negative side is that I can be suspicious. This is **type 6**.

 I'm **type 9** and I hate conflict, so I always try to be calm. The negative part of this is that I'm a little passive and accept things, just because I don't want any problems.

B Work in groups of three. Each student reads three personality types from **A** and completes their part of the chart with adjectives.

Student	Type	Positive side	Negative side
A	1	idealistic	
	2		
	3		

Common mistakes

Don't stress suffixes *-ive*, *-al*, *-ous*, or *-ic*.
po**sse**ssive, **pa**ssive, **cri**tical, **loy**al, am**bi**tious, **ge**nerous, i**dea**listic, ro**man**tic

C ▶10.9 Listen to a conversation to check your answers. Which type(s) do you like best?

D ⊙ **Make it personal** What enneagram type are you? In groups, describe yourselves using adjectives from **A**. Similar or different?

Well, I think I'm type 1. I'm idealistic, but I'm also critical.

Me, too. I think I'm more critical than you.

2 Grammar Superlatives with -est and *most*

A ▶10.10 **What can you see in the photos? Read the quiz and answer the questions. Listen to check. Is the suffix -est pronounced /ɪst/ or /est/?**

Well, the highest is … so the second highest has to be …

Who came second?

We always remember the winner, but what about second place?

1 **What's the second highest mountain in the world?** ☐
  a Kilimanjaro b Everest
  c K2

2 **What's the second most-spoken language in the world?** ☐
  a English b Spanish
  c Mandarin Chinese

3 **What's the second most populated city in the Americas?** ☐
  a São Paulo b New York City
  c Mexico City

4 **What's the second most successful movie of all time?** ☐
  a *Star Wars* (1977) b *Avatar*
  c *Gone with the Wind*

5 **What is the second closest planet to the sun?** ☐
  a Venus b Mercury c Earth

B Complete the grammar box.

---

*Their **Greatest** Hits* by The Eagles is the **best**-selling album in history. 6 ☐
The **most successful** national soccer team is Brazil. 7 ☐
Salzburg is **the prettiest** city in the world. 8 ☐

Match the halves of the rules.

When an adjective …
  a has one syllable,   good → the best, bad → the worst, more → the most
  b has two or more syllables,   put *most* before the adjective.
  c ends in -y,   change -y to -i and add -est.
  d is irregular,   add -est.

Spelling adjectives that end consonant + vowel + consonant (CVC), double the final consonant: "The **biggest** airport is in Atlanta, Georgia."

Which rule a–d do the superlatives in the quiz questions in **A** and the three examples above follow?

→ **Grammar 10B** p. 156

Common mistakes

nicest
Home is the ~~most nice~~ place in the world.
She is the ~~most~~ happiest person I know.

C Put these words in order to make questions. Then, in pairs, take turns asking and answering as many as you can.

1 the / what / largest / your / is / city / country / in / ?
2 the / in / expensive / are / what / most/ your / restaurants / town / ?
3 highest / what / the / town / your / is / building / in / ?
4 most / in / country / popular / beaches / your / what / the / are / ?
5 mountain / what / the / is / country / highest / in / your / ?
6 most / world / people / famous / the / in / are / who / the / ?
7 youngest / your / in / who / the / is / class / person / ?

Make it personal In pairs, write five questions for a trivia quiz. Then find someone who can answer each question correctly.

What age is the oldest person in the world?

I really don't know, but it's definitely over 100.

10.4 What's the best place in the world?

① Reading

A Do you know the places in photos 1–9? Find examples of these things in the photos.

> a canyon   a cave   a forest   an island
> a lizard   a mountain   a river
> an underground river   a volcano   a waterfall

B ▶10.11 Quickly scan the article and match the places to photos 1–9. Then listen and read. Any pronunciation surprises?

C In pairs, try to answer 1–9. Then read again to check. Which place:

1 is in nine different countries?
2 has many different flowers?
3 has caves and lakes?
4 has an underground river?
5 is in two countries?
6 contains a volcano?
7 is a very deep canyon?
8 is home to a famous animal?
9 is a mountain over five kilometers high?

D 🔘 **Make it personal** Do you agree with the choices? Which of the places do you most want to visit? Why?

> *I want to visit Table Mountain. I really want to go to South Africa, plus I love flowers.*

② Pronunciation Sentence stress

A ▶10.12 Watch the video and say which two of the nine places in the photos are not mentioned.

B ▶10.12 Watch again and number the places 1–7 in the order you hear them. Notice the most stressed words. Then read the pronunciation rules.

> We normally stress words that carry the message. Other words are often unstressed, reduced, and said faster. If you don't hear them, you can still understand the meaning.
>
>   •   •   •   •
> The <u>Pacific</u> is the <u>largest</u> <u>ocean</u> on <u>Earth</u>.

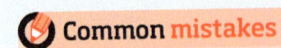

🖊 **Common mistakes**

> ~~the most common language in~~
> English is ~~the language most common of~~ the world.

C ▶10.13 In pairs, listen and <u>underline</u> the stressed words in each sentence.

1 The biggest lizard in the world is in Indonesia.
2 The Amazon rainforest is the largest in the world.
3 The River Nile is longer than the Amazon.
4 The Arctic is the world's smallest ocean.
5 The Amazon River goes through six countries.

D 🔘 **Make it personal** In pairs, search the Internet to find five surprising facts and say them, stressing the most important words. Then share the facts in groups. Which are the most interesting?

> *Look at this one! An astronaut wrote his daughter's initials on the moon!*

> *You're kidding!*

The NEW Seven Wonders of Nature

In 2007, Bernard Weber started a project to find the seven most beautiful places in the world. People from all five continents voted for their favorite place. Here are nine of the finalists.

☐ **Komodo National Park** is in Indonesia. It opened in 1980 to protect the Komodo dragon, the largest lizard in the world. ___

☐ The **Amazon rainforest** is the largest in the world. It's located in nine different countries, and it's home to one of the world's longest rivers, the Amazon River. ___

☐ The **Grand Canyon** in the U.S. is more than 1.6 km deep. It has many canyons and caves. ___

☐ **Halong Bay** in Vietnam has thousands of rocks and islands in different sizes and shapes. It also has beautiful caves and lakes. ___

☐ **Table Mountain** in Cape Town, South Africa, got its name because it's flat on the top. More than 1,470 types of flowers grow there. ___

☐ The **Iguazú Falls** is one of the largest groups of waterfalls in the world. There are 275 different waterfalls there. The Falls are on the border between Brazil and Argentina. ___

☐ **Jeju** is the largest island in South Korea. It's home to Hallasan, a dormant volcano that's also the tallest mountain in South Korea. There are 360 other volcanoes around Hallasan. ___

☐ **Mount Kilimanjaro** in Tanzania is one of the highest mountains in the world. The top of Kilimanjaro is 5,895 m above sea level. ___

☐ The **Puerto Princesa National Park** in the Philippines has one of the world's longest underground rivers. ___

10.5 What's your blood type?

ID Skills Understanding facts

Vocabulary

A Match these words to pictures a–g. Which two words rhyme?

- [ ] a beard
- [ ] blood
- [ ] a brain
- [ ] a heart
- [ ] a lung
- [ ] fingernails
- [ ] a tongue

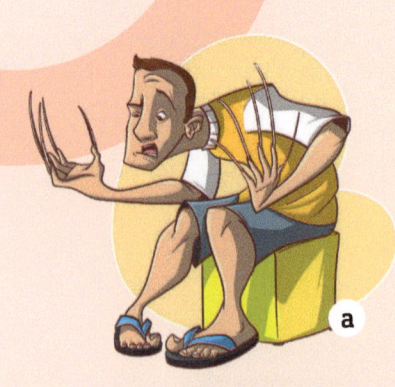

a

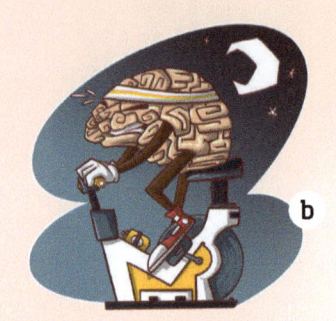

b

c

e

f

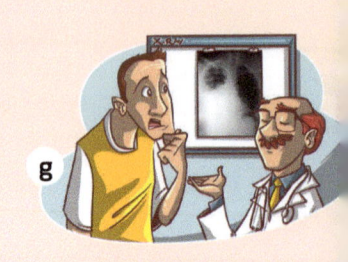

g

True or false?

How much do you know about the human body?

1. The brain is more active at night than during the day.

2. Hair grows faster on your face than on other parts of your body.

3. Toenails grow faster than fingernails.

4. On average, women's hearts beat faster than men's.

5. Your right lung is smaller than your left lung.

6. Food is more important to humans than sleep.

7. The tongue is one of the strongest muscles in the human body.

8. The most common blood type in the world is Type A.

B ▶10.14 In pairs, take the quiz. Listen to check. Which fact is not illustrated?

C ▶10.14 Listen again and complete the words in 1–8. Which is the most interesting fact?

1. Your b_____ is very a_____ when you s_____.
2. It says that if m_____ don't shave, a b_____ can g_____ to more than 10 meters long!
3. Your t_____ grow slower than your f_____.
4. Women are s_____ than men, so their h_____ needs to move the blood f_____.
5. The h_____ needs a lot of s_____.
6. The l_____ time a person can go with no s_____ is 11 d_____.
7. When you eat or t_____, you are using your t_____.
8. The most c_____ blood type is _____.

For me, the most interesting fact is ...

D 🔒 **Make it personal** *Memory test!* **A:** Ask a question from the quiz. **B:** Cover the quiz, answer, and give a reason. Google another fact of your own.

Is the brain more active at night than during the day?

Yes, it is. The brain is very active when we dream.

ID in Action   Making choices

A ▶10.15 Listen and match conversations 1–3 to three of the photos a–d. Check (✓) the option they choose. Which of the three was the easiest to understand?

a

☐ Strawberry
☐ Chocolate
☐ Vanilla
☐ Coconut

b

Penguins of Madagascar: The Movie
★★★★★ 2014 PG 1h 32m HD CC
A mad-genius octopus uses a snack machine to kidnap a crew of courageous penguins. Things just get werder from there.

New Releases

Trending Now

NETFLIX

c

d

B ▶10.15 Listen again and read AS 10.15 on p. 168 and try to remember all you can.

C In pairs, look only at the photos in **A** and practice the three conversations from memory. Create a similar one for the fourth picture.

So, which movie do you want to watch?

Hmm, the actors in the comedy are much better than in the others …

But the action movie looks so much more exciting!

D 🔘 Make it personal   In pairs, discuss which of the three options in each of the situations below you'd like to do. Use any adjectives from this unit and make a decision.

Go and see Ed Sheeran, Taylor Swift, or Drake.
Continue studying English, start learning Chinese, or give up learning languages.
Go for a coffee, go home, or go out to dance.

Let's go see Ed Sheeran. He's the best.   *No, I prefer Taylor Swift. She's a better singer.*

Writing 10 A family profile

You're simply the best, better than all the rest, better than anyone, anyone I ever met.

A Read the family profile and complete Karina's family tree.

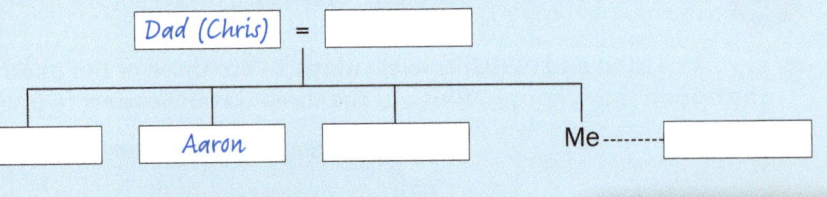

Dad (Chris) = [ ]

[ ] = [ ]   Aaron   [ ]   Me ------- [ ]

[ ]

We're a close family. My dad, Chris, is an engineer. He's a big guy, a little taller than both my brothers. He's around 50, with gray hair and a beard, and he's strong and very calm. My mom, Kathy, works at the hospital as a nurse. She's quite short, with dark hair, and she's always busy – she's far more energetic than anyone I know.

My sister Rachel is the oldest. She's tall and slim with long dark hair, and she's the most athletic one in the family. She does triathlons – that's how she met her husband, Victor. He's a firefighter. They've been together for about five years and have a little girl, Salma. She's 15 months old and very cute.

My older brothers are twins. They look almost identical and are both very tall, approximately 1.95 m. In fact, Aaron is a little taller, and Ben is a bit heavier. Aaron is serious, ambitious, and idealistic; he can be moody and critical, but he's the most intelligent person I know. Ben is more spontaneous and very disorganized. He's less ambitious than Aaron, but a lot more fun.

Finally, there's Max the dog. He's 10 years old, which is around 70 in dog years! He has big brown eyes and long ears. He's very loyal and he's my best friend.

B Which member of the family:
1. is 10 years old?
2. is always busy?
3. is the most athletic?
4. is the tallest?
5. is fun to be with?
6. is the most intelligent?
7. is the youngest?
8. has the most energy?

C Read **Write it right!** and underline the connectors in the text in **A**.

✓ Write it right!

To show approximation, you can use: *approximately, around*.
To make a comparison more accurate, you can use: *a lot, much, a little*.

D Order these words to make sentences.
1. much / me / brother / heavier / my / than / is / .
2. know / I / he's / person / the / ambitious / most / .
3. romantic / think / boyfriend / far / is / more / than / her / people / her / .
4. a little / than / expected / exam / that / was / easier / I / .
5. her / than / Anya / much / is / ambitious / sister / less / .
6. men / stronger / is / a lot / some / than / she / .

E Answer the questions in **B** about your family, or a family you know.

F 🎧 Make it personal Write a family profile.

Before	Use your notes from **E**. Think of two more pieces of information about the family.
While	Use words / expressions to show approximation and more comparisons.
After	Check your writing carefully. Give it to your partner to check. Then email it to your teacher.

10 Geminis

 **ID Café**

1 Before watching

A Complete 1–5 with these words.

| attitude | genius | horoscope |
| tattoo | twins | zodiac sign |

1 My sister has a bad _____. She thinks she doesn't have to work hard.
2 She has a _____ on each arm.
3 I read my _____ online every morning.
4 My _____ is Leo. My birthday is in August.
5 August is Gemini, and he thinks he's a _____.
6 I don't know any identical _____. Do you?

B 🔘 **Make it personal** In pairs, modify the sentences in A so they are true for you. Any similarities?

My son has a positive attitude to school. He's never late.

C Complete the song lines with the comparative or superlative of the adjectives.

1 I'm your _____ (big) fan, I'll follow you until you love me, paparazzi. (Lady Gaga)
2 It seems to me, that sorry seems to be the _____ (hard) word. (Elton John)
3 Never mind, I'll find someone like you, I wish nothing but the _____ (good) for you. (Adele)
4 Just like a pill instead of making me _____ (good) you keep making me ill. (Pink)
5 Today this could be, the _____ (great) day of our lives. (Take That)

D Look at the photo. In pairs, predict four topics Lucy and Andrea will talk about. Watch to check.

I think they'll talk about their plans for the weekend.

Yes! Or … the celebrities in their magazines.

2 While watching

A Check (✓) the words you hear in the first part of the video.

- ☐ a beauty salon
- ☐ fashion and design
- ☐ your horoscope
- ☐ hair
- ☐ magazines
- ☐ pictures of celebrities
- ☐ outfit

B Complete with the comparative or superlative you hear.

Andrea: Can you believe her? That is _____ (ugly) outfit. No, no, this is _____ (ugly) outfit. And this is _____ (bad) nose job ever!

Lucy: Or, look at this one.

Andrea: No, no. That's ridiculous. She looked way _____ (good) before.

Lucy: I know. Her lips were already big and now she has _____ (big) lips in Hollywood.

C Watch the next part of the video. In pairs, remember what they say about:

1 the actress   3 Zoey
2 the girl   4 August

D Watch the final part of the video. True (T) or False (F)? Correct the false sentences.

1 Marlena was really nice to August at school.
2 She worked as an actress in scary movies.
3 She had the most wonderful voice and really positive attitude.
4 She wasn't mean to anyone.
5 The girls thought they saw Marlena in the salon.
6 Lucy's impressed by Andrea's love for her brother.
7 Andrea and August got their Gemini tattoos after the science fair.
8 August won the fair but then Marlena broke his experiment.

3 After watching

A In pairs, remember what these superlatives refer to.

1 the ugliest   3 the biggest
2 the worst (x 2)   4 the most annoying

B 🔘 **Make it personal** In pairs. Do you know anyone who has made changes to their physical appearance (cosmetic surgery, tattoos, piercings, etc.)? What do you think about them?

Lady Gaga has lots of tattoos.

Yes, you're right. My cousin has one of a dragon! I think it's cool.

R5 Grammar and Vocabulary

A **Picture dictionary.** Cover the words on these pages and use the pictures to remember:

page	
112	10 methods of transportation
115	10 jobs
118	6 life changes
121	4 short dialogues for photos a–d
124	10 parts of the body
125	8 parts of the face
125	descriptions of the 3 suspects
132	7 more parts of the body
159	16 picture words for lines 5 and 6 of consonants

B Read the chart and circle the correct alternatives in 1–5.

	Canada	China	Russia
Size in km²	9,984,670	9,598,086	17,098,242
Population	37 million	1,415 million	144 million
Life expectancy	82 years	76.5 years	71 years
Highest point	Mount Logan, 5,959 m	Mount Everest, 8,848 m	Mount Elbrus, 5,642 m

1 Russia is **smaller** / **larger** than China.
2 China has a **bigger** / **smaller** population than Russia.
3 Canada is **more** / **less** populated than Russia.
4 People live longer in China than in **Russia** / **Canada**.
5 Mount Logan is higher than **Everest** / **Elbrus**.

C **Make it personal** In pairs, ask and answer 1–4 with superlatives about your country.
1 Which country is the _____ (small / big)?
2 Which country has the _____ (large / small) population?
3 Where do people live the _____ (long / short)?
4 Which is the _____ (high) mountain?

D In pairs, ask and answer 1–6 about the picture.
1 What is Mark saying? And the chef's answer?
2 Are Fred and Rory honest? Why (not)?
3 What's Scott going to do? What's Laila going to say?
4 Is the floor going to get messy? Why?
5 Are Rachel and Owen happy? Why (not)?
6 Which character do you like best? Why?

E ▶R5.1 Order requests 1–6, adding a verb to each. Listen to check.
1 you / mind / / do / your / if / bike / I / ?
Do you mind if I borrow your bike?
2 a / / could / pen / me / you / ?
_____
3 door / I / / the / can / ?
_____
4 mind / I / / pizza / this / you / do / if / ?
_____
5 your / can / / laptop / I / ?
_____
6 earlier / home / / I / could / today / ?

F In pairs, practice 1–6 in **E**. Vary your questions and answers.

Could I borrow your bike this afternoon?

No, sorry. I'm doing a triathlon next week. I need to train!

G Play *Describe it!* In groups of three, take turns describing an item from units 9 and 10 for your partners to guess. How many can you describe and guess in four minutes?

It's the opposite of (thin).

It's what you say when (you meet somebody).

H Correct the mistakes. Check your answers in units 9 and 10.
1 My mom is great cooker. (2 mistakes)
2 I'm student in UCLA and I'm an unemployed. (3 mistakes)
3 Sales assistants don't win a lot money. (2 mistakes)
4 I don't do anything special next weekend. (2 mistakes)
5 Are you gonna to go to the party? (1 mistake)
6 Could you borrow me your charger? (1 mistake)
7 We run the New York marathon the next week. (2 mistakes)
8 She looks like slim with the long curly hair. (2 mistakes)
9 I'm more big then my father. (2 mistakes)
10 It's the most old city of the country. (2 mistakes)

Skills practice

A In teams, play **Give us a clue!** Team A: cover card 2. **Team B:** cover card 1. Give one clue at a time. You score three points for a correct answer after clue a, two after clue b, or one after clue c. Write one extra question with three clues.

OK, number one.   *The first clue is …*

Uh, we don't know. Give us the next clue.

CARD 1

1 **People in this job:**
  a studied a lot for their job.
  b usually wear a white coat to work.
  c work with animals.
2 **People in this job:**
  a wear a uniform.
  b have a dangerous profession.
  c look for criminals.
3 **This type of transportation is:**
  a common in big cities.
  b a kind of train.
  c under the streets.
4 **This type of transportation is:**
  a good for you.
  b free.
  c faster than walking.
5 a You have two of them.
  b They're part of your head.
  c You listen with them.

CARD 2

1 **People in this job:**
  a wear a mask.
  b are often unpopular with children.
  c care for our teeth.
2 **People in this job:**
  a serve people.
  b travel a lot.
  c work on a plane.
3 **This type of transportation:**
  a is large.
  b carries people.
  c travels on the road.
4 **This type of transportation:**
  a travels on the road.
  b is dangerous.
  c in heavy traffic, is faster than a car.
5 a You have lots of them.
  b They are part of your legs.
  c They are shorter than your fingers.

B 🎧 **Make it personal** In pairs, ask and answer 1–3. Do you agree?
1 Which profession in **A** is the best paid / the most interesting / the most difficult / the most dangerous? Why?
2 Do you use the methods of transportation from the quiz? Which do you prefer? Why?
3 Which is more important to you: your eyes, ears, or hands?

C 🎧 **Make it personal** In pairs, use the chart to ask and answer ten superlative questions. Do you agree?

Who / What is the	(bad) (delicious) (exciting) (famous) (funny) (good) (interesting) (young)	food restaurant singer actor writer student model cook politician	in the world? in this country? in this neighborhood? in our class?

D Read Laila's email. True (T), False (F), or Not mentioned (N)?

Hi Jenna!

All good with you? I hope so! Well, me, I'm finishing grad school soon and I have to start making plans now! I'm taking a vacation first. I'm going to Thailand with Scott for two weeks, I can't wait! But, before that, I'm moving out of my apartment, so right now I'm busy packing everything. I'm actually looking for a new apartment at the moment. Do you know anywhere I could stay? Fingers crossed! 🙂 Then when we get back from vacation, I'm going to find a job. Wish me luck!

Love, Laila

1 Laila left grad school recently. _____
2 Scott is Jenna's boyfriend. _____
3 After her vacation, she's leaving her apartment. _____
4 She's going to find a place to live alone. _____
5 She has a job to go to when she gets back. _____

E ▶R5.2 **Listen to Laila and Jenna and answer 1–3.**
1 Which room does Jenna offer to Laila?
2 When is Laila going to fly to Thailand?
3 How long does she need the room for?

F 🎧 **Make it personal** Question time.
In pairs, practice asking and answering the 12 lesson titles in units 9 and 10. Use the book map on p. 2–3. Where possible, ask follow-up questions, too. Can you comfortably ask and answer all the questions?

How did you get here today?   *I came by car.*

Did you drive?   *No, I came with a friend.*

Grammar Unit 6

6A Countable and uncountable nouns

Countable (C) nouns

Singular	Plural	Singular	Irregular plural
an apple	ten apples	a child	two children
a banana	three bananas	a foot	two feet
a bottle	two bottles	a man	five men
a box	eight boxes	a mouse	ten mice
a baby	four babies	a person	three people

C nouns can be singular or plural, regular, or irregular.

Most plurals are formed with *-s*, but also *-es* or *-ies*. There are a few irregular plurals.

Singular C nouns need an article (*a, an, the*), or quantifier (*some, any*, etc.)

Uncountable (U) nouns

U nouns have only one form.

Food-related: beer, bread, butter, cheese, chocolate, coffee, coke, ice, meat, milk, oil, pasta, pepper, rice, salad, salt, soup, sugar, tea, water, wine, yogurt.

Substances, materials: alcohol, deodorant, detergent, gasoline, gold, paper, perfume, plastic, metal, money, oil, wood.

1 To count U nouns use *a / an / number* + **portion** + *of*: *a piece* of bread; *two bottles* of water; *four spoons* of sugar.
2 Some U nouns have only a plural form and take a **plural verb**: *glasses, gloves, jeans, pants, shoes, shorts*, etc.
 ▸ *My jeans are new. This is a new pair of jeans.*

6B Quantifiers: *some* and *any*

Countable ➕	Uncountable ➕
We have **some** apples on our tree. (unspecified number)	I have **some** money for a tip. (enough to pay)

Countable ➖	Uncountable ➖
There aren't **any** children in the playground. (zero)	There isn't **any** water in the bottle. (zero)

Countable ❓	Uncountable ❓
Do you want **any** potatoes? (a portion)	Do you want **any** meat? (a portion)

Use **some** in questions when you expect the answer "yes":

Countable ❓	Uncountable ❓
Do you want **some** apples?	Do you want **some** cake?

Use **any** in questions when you expect the answer "no" or aren't sure:

Countable ❓	Uncountable ❓
Are there **any** tomatoes?	Is there **any** milk?

Use:

any with C nouns and the verb in the negative.
 ▸ *There aren't any pens on the table.*
no with C nouns and the verb in the affirmative.
 ▸ *There are no pens or pencils on the table.*
any with U nouns and the verb in the negative.
 ▸ *There isn't any information on their website.*
no with U nouns and the verb in the affirmative.
 ▸ *There's no gas in the car.*

6C Quantifiers: *a little, a few, a lot of*

Countable ➕	Uncountable ➕
I only eat a few fries on weekends.	There's a little cereal in the box.
There are **a lot of** donuts.	They eat **a lot of** pasta in Italy.

Countable ❓	Uncountable ❓
Do you eat **a few** cookies a day?	Can we eat **a little** ice cream?
Does he have **a lot of** tomatoes in his garden?	Does she eat **a lot of** bread for breakfast?

Countable ➖	Uncountable ➖
There aren't **a lot of** tickets available.	There isn't **a lot of** news online today.

6D *How much* and *how many* ❓

Question (*how much*)	Answer ➕
How much **time** do you have?	There was **a lot of** information on the web.
How much **sugar** do you want?	Just **a little**, please.
How much **exercise** do you get?	I work out **a lot**.

Question (*how many*)	Answer ➕
How many **dresses** does she have?	I know she has **a lot of** dresses. More than 20.
How many **eggs** do we need?	Only **a few**.
How many **people** are in the class?	**A lot**. Over 15!

Question (*how much / how many*)	Answer ➖
How much **meat** do you want?	I don't want **any** meat. / want **no** meat.
How much **homework** do you get?	**Not much.**
How many **apps** do you use?	I use **no** apps. / I don't have **any** apps.
How many **friends** do you have?	**Not many.**
How many **watches** do you have?	**None.** I use my phone.

Use:

how many to ask about **plural C nouns**.
how much to ask about **U nouns**.
any with a ➖ **verb**, and *no* with a ➕ **verb** in ➖ answers.
any and *no* with the noun in the **plural (C nouns)**.

6A

1 **Circle the correct words in 1–5.**

1 I'm buying some **cookies** / **cookie** for dessert.
2 I need some **information** / **informations** before I can go.
3 Remember to buy some **cheeses** / **cheese**, please.
4 Can you put some **breads** / **bread** in the toaster?
5 I'd like some **egg** / **eggs** for breakfast.

2 **C or U? Cross out the odd word.**

1 bread water ~~apples~~ milk
2 information books computers magazines
3 paper metal children rice
4 men women perfume bananas
5 eggs money dollars euros
6 news information paper ideas

6B

1 **Complete 1–5 with *some* or *any*.**

1 I'm looking for organic pasta, but I can't find _____.
2 There isn't _____ cheese for our sandwiches, so we're cooking _____ eggs instead.
3 There isn't _____ information about the restaurant online, so let's stay home and order _____ pizza.
4 I can't see _____ healthy dishes on the menu.
5 I don't eat meat, but I do eat _____ fish occasionally.

2 **Complete questions 1–5 using *some* or *any*.**

1 Is there _____ chocolate?
 No, of course not!
2 Do you want _____ of this delicious chicken?
 Yes!
3 Are there _____ tomatoes in this pie?
 No! It's a banana pie!
4 I know you don't like pasta, but do you want _____?
 No way, you can have it all.
5 It's your favorite cake, do you want _____?
 Yes, of course I do!

6C

1 **Circle the correct quantifier.**

1 I'm buying **a few** / **a little** sugar because I don't have **many** / **much** left.
2 Dad wants to cook **some** / **any** pasta, but he has **no** / **none**, so we're having potatoes instead.
3 There's **many** / **a lot of** meat, but not **much** / **many** milk in the refrigerator.
4 For breakfast, I like **a little** / **a few** eggs, but I don't drink **much** / **many** juice.
5 There's **no** / **any** fruit in the refrigerator for after dinner, just **a few** / **a little** chocolate.

2 **Correct the mistakes. Are 1–5 true or false about you?**

1 I don't eat a little meat, just once a week.
2 I drink a few juice for breakfast.
3 In my family, we eat a little bananas every week.
4 I don't drink a few coffee – about two cups a day.
5 I sometimes eat a few junk food, especially on weekends.

6D

1 **Circle the correct words in 1–5.**

1 How much **sugar** / **apples** do you want?
2 How many **pies** / **bread** is Mom cooking for dinner?
3 I don't know **how much** / **how many** coffee you drink, but I made a lot.
4 How much **money** / **dollars** did all this chocolate cost? You bought a lot!
5 He didn't know **how much** / **how many** eggs were in the refrigerator.

2 **Complete 1–5 with *how much* or *how many* and match them to pictures a–e.**

1 Please, tell the baker _____ cupcakes you'd like.
2 Let me know _____ people you're bringing to the party.
3 Look at this! _____ chocolate did you buy this time?
4 _____ slices of pie did they order?
5 _____ ice would you like in your drink?

a ☐
b ☐
c ☐
d ☐
e ☐

Grammar Unit 7

7A There was / there were ➕ ➖

	➕	➖
Singular	There **was** a car in front of the house.	There was **no** gas in the tank. There wasn't **any** gas in the tank.
Plural	There **were** two cars on the street.	There were **no** parking spaces. There weren't **any** parking spaces.

Use: *there was / there were* for "existence" in a place in the past.
Form: *there* + past tense *be* + quantifier + noun phrase.
There was an accident in my street. NOT ~~It was an accident ...~~
There weren't any police officers. NOT ~~Had no police officers.~~

There was / there were ❓

Past of *be* ➕ ➖		Object	Short answers ➕ ➖
Was / Wasn't	there	a gas station near here?	Yes, there was. / No, there wasn't.
Were / Weren't		a lot of people at the party?	Yes, there were. / No, there weren't.

Remember to invert in questions.
Were there any special offers? NOT ~~There were any special offers?~~
Note: Use *a lot of* + noun for large quantities.

7B Past of *be* ➕ ➖

Subject	Past of *be* ➕	Past of *be* ➖	Object phrase
I / She / He / It	was	was not / wasn't	at the party yesterday.
We / You / They	were	were not / weren't	

Be in the past tense has only two forms and two contractions.
Note: Be careful with *you* singular and plural.
- *You were late. Yes, I was. Sorry.*
- *You were late. Yes, we were. The traffic was horrible.*

Common past time expressions:
- *She **was** here **a few minutes ago**.*
- *I **wasn't** at home **last night**.*
- *We **were** at the concert **last Saturday**.*
- *They **were** in Italy **in 2017**.*

In time expressions, don't put *the* before *last* or *next*.
I was ill last night. NOT ~~the last night~~
See you next week. NOT ~~the next week~~

Yes / No ❓

Past of *be*	Subject	Phrase
Was / Wasn't Were / Weren't	I you	in your class? at the party?
Was / Wasn't	she he it	at the gym? in class? a good party?
Were / Weren't	we you they	in your class? in school? at work?

Short answers ➕ ➖

Yes, I was. / No, I wasn't.
Yes, you were. / No, you weren't.

he Yes, she was. it	he No, she wasn't. it

Yes, you were. / No, you weren't.
Yes, we were. / No, we weren't.
Yes, they were. / No, they weren't.

7C Prepositions of place

- *The armchair is **between** the window and the fireplace.*
- *The box is **on** the armchair.*
- *The cat's **in / inside** the box.*
- *The picture's **above / over** the TV.*
- *The skateboard's **under** the armchair.*
- *The sofa's **across from / opposite** the TV.*
- *The phone's **in front of** the TV.*
- *The fireplace is **next to** the armchair.*
- *The fan's **behind** the TV.*
- *The TV's **below** the picture.*

7A

1 Correct the mistakes in 1–5.

1 No had television when dad was a child.
2 In my last house, there wasn't any closets.
3 There no was food in that kitchen yesterday.
4 Were not there two bathrooms and a toilet downstairs?
5 No was there sofa or chair in that hotel room?

2 Order 1–5 to make sentences.

1 wasn't / furniture / any / her / in / apartment / there / .
2 balloons / there / no / at / party / his / birthday / were / .
3 snacks / table / the / on / were / there / .
4 was / kitchen / the / lemonade / there / in / .
5 napkins / any / there / on / table / the / weren't / .

7B

1 Order 1–5 to make questions and cross out the extra word in each.

1 were / at / park / on / you / last weekend / the / ?
2 yesterday / what / were / 6 p.m. / where / at / you / ?
3 there / who / with / you / where / was / ?
4 on / was / movies / there / any / were / last night / interesting / TV / ?
5 you / in / where / last Saturday / were / ?
6 in / your / country / family / this / were / last / the / summer / ?

2 Complete the dialogue with the past of verb *be*.

A: When _____ you in Seattle? I _____ there last year!
B: Wow! I _____ there in August. _____ you at the music festival?
A: No, I _____ . _____ there any good bands at the festival?
B: Yes, two local bands and one _____ from Australia.
A: Really? Cool. What _____ the name of the band?

7C

1 Look at the picture. True (T) or False (F)? Correct the false sentences.

1 The cell phone is under the desk.
2 The bed is opposite the desk.
3 There are shoes between the bed and the desk.
4 The night table is next to the desk.
5 There are books on the box.

2 Now circle the correct preposition.

1 The lamp is **in front of** / **behind** the alarm clock.
2 The poster is **above** / **on** the bed.
3 There are two boxes **under** / **behind** the desk.
4 The bed is **next to** / **opposite** the night table.
5 The socks are **on** / **under** the bed.
6 The light switch is **below** / **next to** the door.
7 The two shelves are **on** / **in** the wall, **over** / **below** the table.
8 There are lots of shoes **on** / **across from** the floor.

Grammar Unit 8

8A Simple past

Simple past ➕ ➖

➕	➖
Steve Jobs **lived** in California.	Jobs **didn't study** hard at school.
He **produced** the iPhone and iPad.	He **didn't finish** college.

Use the **simple past** to talk about completed past events. The simple past has only one form for all persons except *was / were*.

▸ *I / You / She / He / It / We / You / They* **lived** in Mexico City.
▸ *I / She / He / It* **was** born in Puebla.
▸ *You / We / You / They* **were** born in Cuernavaca.

Form the negative using *did not / didn't* + infinitive.

▸ *Jobs didn't live with his parents. He was adopted.*

Common past time expressions include:

▸ *a few moments / minutes ago, an hour ago*
▸ *last night / Monday / week / month / year / century*
▸ *yesterday evening / afternoon / morning*
▸ *in 2017, in 1974*

Simple past regular verbs – spelling rules

	Spelling rule
They **played** tennis yesterday.	Most verbs: verb + *-ed*.
She **danced** a lot at the party.	Verbs ending in *e*: + *-d*.
The car **stopped** at the traffic lights.	Verbs ending in consonant-vowel-consonant (**CVC**): double the final consonant + *-ed*.
They **tried** to talk to you last Monday.	Verbs ending in **consonant +** *y*: change *y* to *i* and add *-ed*.

8B Simple past irregular verbs

Irregular verbs don't end in *-ed*. They only have one form for all persons.

Most frequent irregular verbs

Infinitive	Past	Infinitive	Past	Infinitive	Past
become	became	hold	held	run	ran
bring	brought	keep	kept	say	said
buy	bought	know	knew	see	saw
do	did	leave	left	sit	sat
feel	felt	lose	lost	speak	spoke
forget	forgot	make	made	stand	stood
get	got	mean	meant	take	took
give	gave	meet	met	tell	told
go	went	pay	paid	think	thought
have	had	put	put	write	wrote
hear	heard	read	read		

Irregular verbs have no formation rules. For a complete list go to the Richmond Learning Platform.

8C Simple past ❓

Yes / No ❓

A	S	I	O
Did	she	go	to the concert?
Did	you	visit	your mom?
Did	they	call	him before the class?
Did	Fred	buy	a new laptop?

Did she call you this morning? NOT ~~She called you this morning?~~

To ask ➖ questions, use the contracted form *didn't*:

▸ ***Didn't he call** yesterday?*

Short answers are the same for all persons.

▸ *Yes, we did. / No, they didn't.*
▸ *Yes, she did. / No, he didn't.*

Wh- ❓

Q	A	S	I	O
Where	did	you	go	last weekend?
What	did	she	do	last night?
When	did	they	get up	yesterday?
Why	did	he	stay	there?

8D Subject questions

Question word	Simple past	Object
What	happened was	yesterday? that noise?
Who	broke wrote went	the glass? the book? with you?

Subject questions ask for / about the **subject of the answer**. Use *Wh-* words, but **don't** use the auxiliary *did*.
Who helped you? NOT ~~Who did help you?~~

8A

1 Complete with the verbs in parentheses.

Carmen Miranda was born in 1909, on February 9. She _____ (**live**) in Portugal until the age of one when she _____ (**move**) to Brazil with her parents in 1910.

In 1929, Carmen _____ (**record**) her first single and in 1932 she _____ (**appear**) in her first movie. She _____ (**arrive**) in the U.S. in May, 1939, and became a media sensation. She _____ (**become**) the most famous Latin American in the U.S. She _____ (**die**) at 46 of a heart attack on August 4, 1955.

2 Correct 1–5 by making them negative.

1 Carmen Miranda lived in Portugal all her life.
2 She moved to Brazil alone.
3 She recorded her first single in 1932.
4 She appeared in her first movie in 1939.
5 She arrived in the U.S. in 1955.

8B

1 Circle the correct forms in 1–5.

1 Bruce Lee **taught** / **teached** martial arts and **starred** / **stared** in movies in the 1970s.
2 His son Brandon Lee **didn't liked** / **didn't like** school and he didn't finish it.
3 Brandon **taked** / **took** a special test to get his high school diploma.
4 Brandon **studyed** / **studied** acting and **makes** / **made** a few movies.
5 Brandon **get** / **got engaged** just before he **dead** / **died**.

Complete the story with these verbs.

be   not buy   dance   eat
get   go   have   look   love
see / not see   rain   walk

I love London! On our first day it <u>rained</u> all day, and we _____ very wet! But, we _____ to the fabulous British Museum and _____ all types of amazing objects from around the world, including many from our country! I _____ the Egyptian mummies! It's huge, so we _____ more than 10% of what's there. After that, we _____ down Oxford Street and _____ in all the shops. I _____ anything as it was so expensive. That night, we _____ dinner in a pub. There _____ a cool band and we _____ for hours. A great day, even with the rain!

8C

1 Order 1–5 to make questions. Take turns asking and answering.

1 do / you / did / Saturday / last / what / ?
2 your / go / with / did / friends / you / ?
3 went / did / to sleep / what / do / you / before / you / ?
4 did / eat / last / what / you / night / ?
5 vacation / last / did / go / where / you / ?

2 Match answers 1–5 to questions a–e.

1 I went out of town last weekend for a few days.
2 I saw some old friends from college.
3 I really didn't spend any time in the city.
4 It rained all weekend, so we stayed in!
5 We watched TV and ate at the restaurant.

a What did you see downtown?
b What did you do at the hotel?
c Who did you meet up with?
d Where did you go for the holiday?
e What was the weather like?

8D

1 Complete dialogues 1–5 with the simple past of these verbs. Which are subject questions?

announce   give   go   happen   pay   tell

1 A: Hey, what _____? I heard they canceled your flight!
   B: Yes, they canceled it because of bad weather. Who _____ you that?
2 A: Sylvia saw it on TV. When _____ the airline _____ it?
   B: They didn't do it until 6:30 p.m. And my flight was at 7.
3 A: That's terrible. So, where _____ you _____ after that?
   B: I took a taxi back home with all my bags!
4 A: Gee … And who _____ for the taxi?
   B: Oh, at least the airline paid for it.
5 A: _____ they _____ you a new ticket?
   B: Yep, they gave me one for tomorrow morning.

2 Subject question (S) or object question (O)? Find the answers to the questions.

1 When did The Beatles start playing? _____
2 Who invented the name of the band? _____
3 What type of music did they play? _____
4 Why did the band finish? _____
5 Who composed the hit "Help!"? _____

Grammar Unit 9

9A Articles + jobs

Use an indefinite article in front of professions.
- *She's an engineer and he's a doctor.*

This becomes definite when we know who the person is.
- *The dentist I visit is very professional.*

Note: Don't use an article before adjectives with no nouns.
My father's retired. OR *My father's a retired firefighter.* NOT
My father's a retired.

9B Future with *be + going to* ➕ ➖

Subject	➕	➖		Infinitive + object
I	'm	'm not		win this game tonight.
You	're	aren't		sing with the band tonight.
She / He	's	isn't	going to	get engaged when he finds a job.
We	're	aren't		visit you next week.
They	're	aren't		study English next year.

Going to is the most common future form in spoken English.
Use *be* + (not) + *going to* + infinitive to talk about:
- general future plans: *I'm going to get married before I'm 30.*
- intentions: *We're going to study English next year, too.*
- predictions: *Look at those clouds. It's going to rain.*

Pronunciation of *going to* in informal speech is often *gonna*.

Be + going to – Yes / No ❓

Verb *be*	S		I + O	A
Am	I		finish my homework tonight?	Yes, I am. / No, I'm not.
Are	you		go out tonight?	Yes, I am. / No, I'm not.
Is	she	going to	find a job?	Yes, she is. / No, she isn't.
Are	we		travel to the U.S. next year?	Yes, we are. / No, we're not.
Are	they		work this weekend?	Yes, they are. / No, they're not.

Be + going to – Wh- ❓

Q	Verb *be*	S		I + O
What	are	you		do tonight?
When	is	she	going to	travel to Spain?
Why	are	they		study Mandarin?
How	are	you		get home?

9C Present continuous as future
➕ ➖ ❓

S	Verb *be* ➕ ➖	V + *-ing* + O
I	'm (not)	running the marathon next year.
You	're / aren't	leaving for Houston tomorrow.
She / He	's / isn't	taking a French class next semester
We	're / aren't	having fish for dinner tonight.
They	're / aren't	visiting their grandparents in Europe in June.

Q	S	V + *-ing* + O	Short answers
Am	I	coming to your birthday party?	Yes, I am. / No, I'm not.
Are	you	watching the game tonight?	Yes, you are. / No you aren't.
Is	she / he	taking the bus to Mexico City?	Yes, she / he is. / No, she / he isn't.
Are	we	doing our homework at your house later?	Yes, we are. / No, we aren't.
Are	they	driving to the beach in the morning?	Yes, they are. / No, they aren't.

9D *Going to* and present continuous as future

Use both *going to* and **present continuous** to talk about future actions / events which are already decided or planned.
- *We are **going to get** a new car.*
- *We are **getting** a new car.*

There's only a subtle difference in meaning.

Going to

Use *be* + *going to* + **infinitive** for predictions and intentions.
- *I think they're **going to win** the election.* (prediction)
- *I'm **going to do** all my homework this weekend.* (intention)
- *Ted's **going to try to take** the day off on Friday.* (intention)

Present continuous for future

Use the **present continuous** (**present of** *be* + **verb** + *-ing*) for fixed plans, or personal arrangements with other people. (e.g., things you put in your calendar)
- *I'm **leaving** on the midnight train tomorrow.* (fixed plan = I have a ticket)
- *She's **having** dinner with her mom tomorrow!* (personal arrangement with other people)
- *We're **buying** Terry's car next week.* (personal arrangement with other people)

To differentiate from actions that are happening now, use a **future time expression**.
- *I'm leaving.* (**now**)
- *I'm leaving in half an hour.* (**future**)

9A

Complete the sentences with a / an / θ (θ = no article).

1 Tina's _____ actor.
2 Charlie's _____ flight attendant.
3 I'm _____ unemployed, so I'm going to look for a job.
4 Jack's going to be _____ cook.
5 You're not going to be _____ artist!

9B

Look at the picture. Are predictions 1–5 True (T) or False (F)? Look at the example and write sentences about the people in the picture.

1 Charlie's going to cook dinner. _____
2 The cat's going to eat the fish. _____
3 Tina's going to have dinner. _____
4 The kids are going to play games. _____
5 Jack and Jane are going to sleep. _____

Charlie's not going to cook dinner. He's going to wash the dishes first!

Circle the correct form in 1–5. Mark intention (I) or prediction (P).

1 People **is / are** going to buy flying cars in 10 years. _____
2 I **am going to / am going** be a pilot. _____
3 Food **is not / are not** going to be more expensive in five years. _____
4 Politicians **are not going / are not going to** have a salary. _____
5 I heard Walter and Jen **is / are** going to travel to Europe. _____

9C & 9D

1 Look at Rob's diary for next week. True (T) or False (F)? Correct the false ones. Look at the example and write some more sentences about Rob's week.

MONDAY	TUESDAY	WEDNESDAY	THURSDAY	FRIDAY	SATURDAY	SUNDAY
Dentist 9 a.m.	Coffee with Juan	Work	Work	Sofia's party 7 p.m.	Gym	Lunch with Mom and Dad.

1 He's seeing the dentist on Tuesday. _____
2 He isn't working on Monday. _____
3 He's working out at the gym on Saturday. _____
4 He's having dinner with his parents on Wednesday. _____
5 He isn't having coffee with Juan next week. _____

He isn't seeing the dentist on Tuesday. He's seeing her on Monday at 9 a.m.

2 Complete the dialogue with *be + going to* or the present continuous of the verbs.

Jake: Hey, Sam! How _____ ? **(do)**
Sam: Fine, and you? So, _____ to Lisa's party on Saturday? **(come)**
Jake: I don't know. Do you think she _____ me? **(invite)**
Sam: Sure! Check your email. Lisa _____ invitations tonight. **(send)**
Jake: Well, OK. I _____ my email later tonight. **(check)**
Sam: Um, do you need a ride? Pat and Sue _____ us there. **(drive)**
Jake: No, don't worry. I _____ the subway. **(take)**

3 Look at the examples and write sentences about:

1 your arrangements for this week / weekend;
2 your plans for this week / weekend (not arranged yet);
3 predictions for your future (jobs / marriage / retirement).

I'm visiting my parents this weekend.
I think they're going to have a barbecue.

Well, I'm going out with my girlfriend on Saturday. And maybe we're going to eat out on Sunday.

Grammar Unit 10

10A Comparatives with *-er* and *more*

Comparative adjectives usually go before *than*.

- ▶ Her husband is **stronger than** mine.
- ▶ Quito is **hotter than** Buenos Aires.

English is **easier than** Arabic. NOT ~~English is more easy than Arabic.~~

One syllable adjectives + *-er*

high	higher
long	longer
short	shorter

- ▶ Mike's **taller than** his brother.

One syllable CVC adjectives double the consonant + *-er*

big	bigger
hot	hotter
thin	thinner

- ▶ Belo Horizonte is **wetter** than Rio.

One / two syllable adjectives ending *y* change *y* to *i* + *-er*

friendly	friendlier
heavy	heavier
pretty	prettier

- ▶ My mom is **funnier than** my dad.

Use *more* before two-syllable adjectives ending *-ed*, *-ing*

bored	more bored
boring	more boring

Adjectives ending *-ing* describe things or people.
Adjectives ending *-ed* usually describe feelings.

- ▶ I feel **more tired** today than I did yesterday.
- ▶ Swimming is **more tiring** than walking.

Use *more* before adjectives with more than two syllables

dangerous	more dangerous
relaxing	more relaxing

- ▶ New York is much **more interesting** than Boston.

The opposite of *more … than* is *less … than*.

- ▶ Boston is **less interesting than** New York.

Irregular adjectives

good	better
bad	worse
far	farther / further

- ▶ I think Game of Thrones is **worse than** Modern Family.

10B Superlatives

Superlatives usually go after *the* and before a noun.

- ▶ Asia's **the largest** continent in the world.
- ▶ Raquel's **the most intelligent** person I know.

One-syllable → use *the* … + *-est*

high	the highest
long	the longest
short	the shortest

- ▶ Suriname is **the smallest** country in South America.

One-syllable CVC → double the final consonant + *-est*

big	the biggest
hot	the hottest
thin	the thinnest

- ▶ The Lion King is **the saddest** movie ever!

One / two syllable ending *y* → change *y* to *i* + *-er*

friendly	the friendliest
heavy	the heaviest
pretty	the prettiest

- ▶ Finland is officially **the happiest** country in the world.

Use *the most* before adjectives with two or more syllables

difficult	the most difficult
important	the most important

- ▶ My mom is **the most courageous** person in my family.

The opposite of *the most* is *the least*.

- ▶ He is **the least** interesting person in the room.

Irregular adjectives

good	the best
bad	the worst
far	the farthest / the furthest
less	the least

10C *Like*

Like has different meanings and uses.
It can be:

  – a verb meaning *enjoy* or *want*.

- ▶ I really like ice cream. I would like an ice cream right now.

  – a preposition meaning *similar to*.

- ▶ Your phone's like mine.
- ▶ What's Stella like? Creative, just like her father.

10A

1 Complete 1–5 with a comparative and match to pictures a–e.

dangerous   friendly   large   small   tall

1   A whale's brain is about six times _____ than a human's brain.
2   Driving at night is _____ than during the day.
3   Dogs are usually _____ than cats.
4   Between the ages of 13 and 18, boys usually grow _____ than girls.
5   It's normal for one side of the body to be a bit _____ than the other.

2 Complete 1–5 with a comparative.

1   Sam is at math than other subjects. (**good**)
2   Carrie is than her classmates. (**organized**)
3   Their math teacher is than their science teacher. (**funny**)
4   Tomas thinks science is than English. (**inspiring**)
5   Marcus's mind is than his friend's. (**active**)

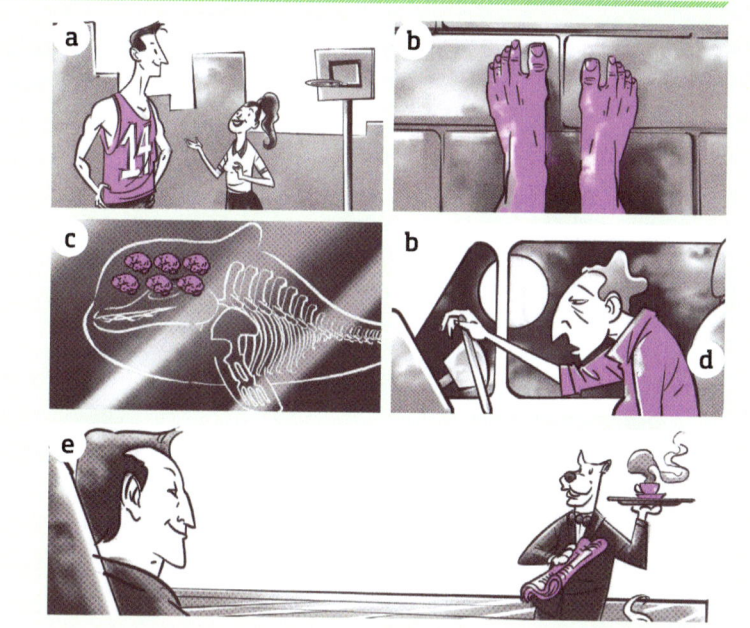

10B

1 Complete facts 1–5 with a superlative.

far   friendly   high   long   populated

1   Ojos del Salado, between Argentina and Chile, is _____ volcano on Earth.
2   Scientists believe Chimborazo in Ecuador is _____ place from the Earth's center.
3   The Andes Mountains in South America are _____ mountain range on the planet.
4   California is _____ state in the U.S.
5   The Abyssinian cat is _____ cat in the world.

2 In pairs, use *the most* or *the least* plus these adjectives to describe people a–d.

annoying   bored   interested
talkative   tired

3 Find the answers to these questions. In pairs, compare your answers. Are they the same?

1   What's the tallest building in the world at the moment?
2   Who's the most popular singer in your country?
3   Who are the fastest male and female athletes in the world?
4   Where are the hottest / wettest / coldest places on Earth?
5   Which is the highest captial city in the world?

10C

1 Add *like* in the correct place in questions 1–5. Then write the answers.

I look more like my mom than my dad.

1   What's the weather today?
2   Do your look your dad?
3   Is your mom you?
4   Would you a coffee?
5   What's your best friend?

Sounds and usual spellings

▶ To listen to these words and sounds, and to practice them, go to the pronunciation section on the Richmond Learning Platform.

Vowels

/iː/	three, tree, eat, receive, believe, key, B, C, D, E, G, P, T, V, Z
/ɪ/	six, mix, it, fifty, fish, trip, lip, fix
/ʊ/	book, cook, put, could, cook, woman
/uː/	two, shoe, food, new, soup, true, suit, Q, U, W
/ɛ/	pen, ten, heavy, then, again, men, F, L, M, N, S, X
/ə/	bananas, pajamas, family, photography

/ɜr/	shirt, skirt, work, turn, learn, verb
/ɔr/	four, door, north, fourth
/ɔ/	walk, saw, water, talk, author, law
/æ/	man, fan, bad, apple
/ʌ/	sun, run, cut, umbrella, country, love
/ɑ/	hot, not, on, clock, fall, tall
/ɑr/	car, star, far, start, party, artist, R

Diphthongs

/eɪ/	plane, train, made, stay, they, A, H, J, K
/aɪ/	nine, wine, night, my, pie, buy, eyes, I, Y
/aʊ/	house, mouse, town, cloud

/ɔɪ/	toys, boys, oil, coin
/oʊ/	nose, rose, home, know, toe, road, O

☐ Voiced
☐ Unvoiced

Consonants

TO MAKE THESE SOUNDS WE USE

our lips	p	b	m	w
our teeth + another articulator	f	v	θ	ð
the tip of the tongue	t	d	n	l
the front of the tongue	s	z	ʃ	ʒ
the back of the mouth	k	g	ŋ	h
the tooth ridge	tʃ	dʒ	r	j

/p/ pig, pie, open, top, apple
/b/ bike, bird, describe, able, club, rabbit
/m/ medal, monster, name, summer
/w/ web, watch, where, square, one
/f/ fish, feet, off, phone, enough
/v/ vet, van, five, have, video
/θ/ teeth, thief, thank, nothing, mouth
/ð/ mother, father, the, other
/t/ truck, taxi, hot, stop, attractive
/d/ dog, dress, made, adore, sad, middle
/n/ net, nurse, tennis, one, sign, know
/l/ lion, lips, long, all, old

/s/ snake, skate, kiss, city, science
/z/ zoo, zebra, size, jazz, lose
/ʃ/ shark, shorts, action, special, session, chef
/ʒ/ television, treasure, usual
/k/ cat, cake, back, quick
/g/ goal, girl, leg, guess, exist
/ŋ/ king, ring, single, bank
/h/ hand, hat, unhappy, who
/tʃ/ chair, cheese, kitchen, future, question
/dʒ/ jeans, jump, generous, bridge
/r/ red, rock, ride, married, write
/j/ yellow, yacht, university

Audio script

Unit 6

▶ 6.1 Notice /ə/.
Let's see. We need bananas and chocolate ... oil and salt ... uh... maybe some spaghetti? Yes, definitely some spaghetti and some tea ... oh, and I have to get tomatoes and vinegar.

▶ 6.2 Notice s = /z/ and /s/.
We need some bread, milk, fish, and chicken ... oh, and some apples and carrots, Sandra loves carrots! Then some eggs and lettuce. Oh, and butter and onions. Oh, finally, some cheese, oranges, potatoes ... do we need sugar? Oh, yes, and some sugar.

▶ 6.3 Notice the **silent letters** and /sh/.
J = Jeff S = Sandra
S Jeff! I'm home.
J Hi, Sandra.
S What's all this food on the table?
J What do you mean, all this?
S Well, to be precise, some chocolate, tomatoes ... uh, some spaghetti ...
J Oh, that?
S I'm not finished! There's also some salt, some tea, oil and vinegar here...
J I can explain ...
S ... and – eleven, twelve, no, thirteen bananas.
J There was a special offer on bananas. We can always freeze them!
S That's true – they make great smoothies! But, Jeff, we're leaving tomorrow. Why did you buy all this food for the refrigerator?
J Just some fruit: apples and oranges.
S I don't like apples.
J But I like apples ... and you like oranges. And I got some onions and potatoes, too.
S Potatoes? I don't eat them.
J I also got some chicken and fish.
S Well, we can freeze those. But what do we do with the milk, cheese, and butter?
J Sorry, Sandra ... I got some lettuce and carrots for salad, too.
S Hm, I guess I can make a salad for dinner. And all those eggs!!
J Well, I can make an omelet!
S You do make delicious omelets – good idea. So we can use the lettuce, carrots, and some of the eggs for dinner. But, wait – what are these doing in the refrigerator?
J Er ...
S Here! Look! You put bread and sugar in the refrigerator! What are they doing there?
J Uh, I don't know.
S You don't know?
J I always put sugar and bread in the refrigerator, I don't know why. My parents and my grandparents did it.
S OK, but it seems weird!

▶ 6.4 Notice the **stress in the phrases** and /ə/.
1 a **glass** of **juice**
2 a **cup** of **tea**
3 some **salad**
4 a **slice** of **bread**
5 a **piece** of **fruit**
6 a **bowl** of **rice**
7 some **meat**
8 some **fish**
9 some **eggs**
10 some **vegetables**
11 a **bottle** of **water**
12 a **piece** of **cake**
13 some **carrots** or **nuts**

▶ 6.5 Notice the links.
So, today is day one of eating more healthily. I eat too much junk food and sugar. For breakfast, I can have a cup of tea, a slice of wholewheat bread, and a piece of fruit! For lunch, it's a bowl of brown rice, some meat, some vegetables, and a bottle of water. In the afternoon, for my snack I get some carrots or nuts! Hmm ... or maybe a piece of cake. No, I don't think so. Carrots or nuts and that's it! Then for dinner, I get some salad, some protein again – some fish or eggs, and a glass of juice.

▶ 6.6 Notice /ʌ/, /ʊ/ and /uː/.
M = Maria T = Tony
M Hi, Tony. Want some potato chips?
T No thanks. I'm trying to cut down on junk food.
M Oh, OK – that's a good idea. How's it going?
T Great. I'm keeping a video diary. It really helps.
M So, what do you usually have for lunch?
T I have some brown rice for lunch – with vegetables and meat.
M That sounds pretty good.
T Uh huh, it is. And I can eat as much as I want. I'm never hungry!
M Now that's important!
T It's pretty easy, actually. I'm learning to cook, too.
M What about dessert?
T I never eat any sugar. But I eat a lot of fruit.
M Oh, come on. Never?!
T Well, OK not at home. I sometimes have a piece of cake in restaurants.
M Do you ever eat bread?
T Of course! I have a slice of bread with my lunch.
M And what about cheese?
T Well, sometimes for dinner. But usually I eat fish or eggs. And a glass of juice. Natural juice!
M Wow! That sounds great – I think I might try it! Forget about these potato chips! Do you want this bottle of water?
T Um ... no, thanks. I think I'll have a glass of juice, instead!

▶ 6.11 Notice the dark l vs. normal l.
J = Joe S = Sandra
J Hey, Sandra. Ready for lunch?
S Sure. I'm so hungry!
J Come on! Let's go to that Mexican restaurant on the corner. I'm dying for a burrito.
S I don't think that's a good idea. I want to eat something healthy today.
J Burritos are healthy! Look, I'm Googling the nutritional table. We can see what's in them.
S Oh, I hate those lists! They're so out of date!
J What do you mean?
S My grandmother counts calories! The ingredients are important, not the number of calories.
J Exactly! This chart doesn't even show calories. Let's look at the chicken burrito.
S I can't see anything without my glasses.
J Um, let's see. Well, it has five grams of fat.
S Aw! That's a lot.
J There's also a vegetarian burrito. It only has beans and cheese, and four grams of fat.

S Ugh! Beans! But my doctor told me to watch my cholesterol. How much cholesterol does the vegetarian burrito have?
J Only five milligrams.
S And the others?
J The chicken one has thirty milligrams and the meat one has thirty-five milligrams.
S Hmm ... that's a lot. Another reason to be a vegetarian! What about sodium? It's not good to eat too much salt.
J Well, let's see. The chicken one has 880 milligrams, the meat one 890 milligrams, and the vegetarian one only 730 milligrams. But they have a lot of protein! The chicken burrito has 18 grams and the meat burrito has 19 grams. That's important, too. And they all have fiber, especially the vegetarian one: 14 grams.
S You know what? I'm having the chicken burrito! I love chicken.
J And I'm having the meat burrito. "Everything in moderation." And they're so delicious. We'll have the vegetarian burrito another day.
S Great! Let's go. It's now one o'clock. I'm hungry!

▶ 6.14 Notice the the **alliteration**.
This is Wonderful Weekend at Fast and Fresh! Special savings on our fabulous favorites!
Our special starter is the Chopped Chicken: a salad made with fresh lettuce and tomato and topped with grilled chicken. We offer you two choices from our marvelous main courses: Fish Fillet, our delicious grilled salmon in orange sauce. It comes with a baked potato. Or the Special Steak, a succulent half-pound barbecued steak topped with a light cream and pepper sauce. Finally, there's nothing like a light, refreshing dessert: our Seasonal Fruit Salad, which includes strawberry, mango, melon, and pear topped with fresh fruit juice. All for a great price! Come to Fast and Fresh and check it out!

▶ 6.15 Notice /ɪ/ and /iː/.
Me = Melissa P = Phil Ma = Marie
Me Hi, my name's Melissa, and I'm your server today. Are you ready to order?
P Yes, please.
Me What would you like as a starter?
P I'll have the tomato soup, please.
Me OK. With croutons and parmesan cheese?
P No cheese, please.
Me OK. How about you, ma'am? What would you like?
Ma What's in the chicken salad?
Me The salad is lettuce, spinach, green peppers, red peppers, tomato, and onion. It comes with sliced grilled chicken.
Ma That sounds good. I'd like that, please – but no onion. I don't like onion!
Me Certainly. I'll be right back with your starters.

▶ 6.17 Notice /tʃ/ and the **connecting sounds**.
Me = Melissa P = Phil Ma = Marie
P Excuse me?
Me Yes, sir?
P Can_I have some decaf coffee, please?
Me Of course. And you, ma'am? What would_you like to drink?
Ma I'd like some tea, please. What kind_of tea do_you have?
Me Mint_or chamomile.
Ma I'll have chamomile tea, please.

Me Anything else?

Ma Uh, actually, I'd like some dessert. Can we have the Chocolate Chunk? It's to share.

Me Certainly. It's very good.

P Oh, and can you bring us the check, too, please?

Review 3

R3.1 Notice voiced th /ð/, and unvoiced th /θ/.

T = Tina C = Carl

T I'm thirsty. Is there any juice in the fridge?

C No, we didn't buy any juice this week. But, look, there are oranges. Do you want me to make you some juice?

T Yes, thanks. Uh, and did we buy any cookies?

C No, but there are still some cookies in the cabinet.

T Great, thanks!

Unit 7

7.2 Notice /eɪ/, and /æ/.

T = Tom A = Anna

T This is the living room.

A Hmm ... It's a little small.

T There's a fireplace and a nice TV with cable ... and, er, armchairs, and er, what else, ah, we love this sofa – it's the center of the house.

A Oh, but I never watch TV.

T Oh. This is the kitchen – it has a gas stove and a microwave and you can wash the dishes in the sink here. Here's the refrigerator. It's new. And, er, there's a table and two chairs here if you want to eat in the kitchen.

A Well, it's not very light in here.

T Here in the dining room we have this big table with eight chairs. Good for dinner parties!

A I don't really like to cook very much, though.

T Now for the bathroom – just a toilet and shower, there's no bathtub, I'm afraid.

A Oh ... I really like to take a bath. Especially in the winter.

T This is your bedroom – you can see it's large and it has a large bed and a table and a big closet and plenty of storage space and there is a fan so you don't get hot at night.

A Hmm ... But what's that smell?

T Here's the laundry room – there's more storage space on these shelves here. So, what do you think? Do you like it?

A Well, I need to think about it.

T Sure. Give us a call tomorrow.

7.3 Notice /ɔːr/ and the contractions.

This is my tiny house. Come on in. Just inside the front door I've got these two puffy chairs flanking this little faux fireplace. It's a very tiny fireplace, but it's a tiny house. Closet storage and cabinet space below this desk. Computer storage space and here's a little table down here. When I pull this table out, believe it or not, as long as I have tiny plates, it seats four people. Like that. Here in the kitchen I've got a bar sink, a double burner stove, a little refrigerator, and a toaster oven. The bathroom is the shower, so when I want to take a shower the nozzle's on the ceiling and everything would get wet except for I've got these little sliding doors that keep things dry and I can put this plastic curtain in here over the toilet which is right down here.

Above the kitchen I've got access to the loft – that's where I sleep. So the loft is nothing more than storage and sleeping. I've got all the storage at this end and then at this end I've got the sleeping – with the bed. It sleeps two really comfortably. So this is my bed and I've got a window at this end and a fan vent behind the shelves at the other so that if it ever gets hot I can just turn this whole thing into a wind tunnel.

7.5 Notice /ɛ/ and how /eɪ/ is usually stressed.

Hello, my name's Liz Marshall and I'm a party planner. Today, I want to talk to you about how to give a great party. Well, it all starts with the invitation. Send the invitations early – three weeks before the party – and include all the important information. Where? When? What type of party? Now ... what do you need for the party? First, food and drinks: Well, for drinks you need some soft drinks, and always have water. I like to keep it simple: just tea and coffee. You can have fresh juice too.

For food, I recommend chips and one or two other snacks, perhaps a healthy option like carrots. Don't forget the plates, glasses, and napkins too. If it's a birthday party, a cake is essential. And display your birthday cards! Next – decorations – again keep it simple with balloons. You can decorate the house with candles too – this gives a nice atmosphere. And if it's a special occasion, you can even give each guest a small present to take home.

Now for entertainment – music is essential for a good party – make sure there's space for people to dance. OK, so it's time to start planning. Have fun!

7.6 Notice the ↗ and ↘ intonation.

M = Martha R = Rob

M I was at a great↗ party yesterday, Rob!↘

R Oh, that's nice, Martha. Where was it?↘

M It was at Jane Foster's home. It was her birthday.

R Oh! Were there a lot of people?↗

M Yep, there were about fifty.↘

R Wow!↗ Was there a lot of food?↗

M Oh yes, and there was an enormous↗ chocolate cake.↘

R Hmmm ... And ... was Jane's boyfriend there?↗

M Yes, he was. Rick and Jane make a perfect↗ couple↘!! He's so attractive↘, they were so beautiful↘ together↘, and the music was great↗ – everybody was dancing, you know.↘

R He sounds nice↗. Were Jane's parents there?↗

M No, they weren't.↘ Do you know them? ↗

R Yes. Ummm ... I was Jane's boyfriend before Rick.↘

M Oh, I'm sorry↘ ... I didn't know that↘ ... in fact, the party wasn't that↘ great ... and her new boyfriend wasn't really that nice ...↘

R No problem. It's fine. Don't worry about it.↘

M Hey, there was a great show on TV last night. Did you see it?↗

7.8 Notice /oʊ/ and /aʊ/.

1 Is that ... Cheese? Mm. It is! Where is it? Is it in the box?

2 No ... Maybe under the table ... Hmmm. Where is it? ... People! Oh, no!

3 Now, quietly between the sofa and the table.

4 Slowly, next to the sofa ...

5 Where are the people? Where is the cheese?! OK, let's go! In the bed ...

6 Now on the bed ... and jump!

7 Ah! There they are! OK! I'm across from the people! I'm across from the people! Quick!

8 OK, concentrate, where IS that cheese? In front of the TV?

9 No. Behind the TV? No. Not here.

10 Ah, there it is! I see it. Now. How can I get above the TV? Hmmm.

7.9 Notice stress to emphasize change.

M See that?

W What?

M There was a mouse under the table.

W Oh no! Where?

M Over there!

W Oh now I see it! It's next to the sofa. It's moving!

M Where did it go?

W Ahhhh! It was in front of the TV now it's behind the TV.

M Let me see if I can get it.

W Ahhhh! It's on the bed. It was in the bed and now it's on the bed!

M There it goes. It was on the bed, but now it's in that box.

W Quick, close the box and take it out to the garden.

M Good idea!

7.16 Notice weak forms of to, at, for, and of.

1

Ma = Mara Mo = Morgan

Ma Hello Morgan!

Mo Hi Mara!

Ma Scott and I are having a housewarming party on Sunday. Can you and Sandy come?

Mo Oh, I'm sorry. We already have plans for Sunday.

Ma Oh, well, that's OK.

Mo Thanks for inviting us and I hope the party goes well.

Ma Thanks, Morgan.

Mo See you.

Ma Bye.

2

W = woman M = man

W Hi Tony! How about going to the movies tonight?

M Sure. Sounds good. What time?

W The movie starts at 8 p.m.

M Great!

3

C = Carrie T = Tommy

C Hi Tommy! It's Carrie. We're having a barbecue tomorrow. Do you want to come?

T Thanks for the invitation, but sorry, I can't. I'm away all weekend, not back until Monday.

C Oh, well. Maybe next time, then.

T Yes, definitely.

4

W = woman M = man

W Would you like to come to my sister's wedding with me?

M When is it?

W On March 28th.

M What time?

W It starts at 2 p.m.

M Great. I'd love to. Thanks.

5

M = man R = Roz

M Hey Roz! We're having a surprise party for Lucy's birthday. Are you free on Friday?

R What time?

M At about 7:30.
R Sounds great! What can I bring?
M Your favorite snack, maybe?
R OK – sure, see you there.

6
W1 = woman K = Kit
W Hello Kit! We're having a baby shower for Laura and Michael on Saturday. Do you think you can come?
K Of course we can! What time?
W 3 p.m. at Laura's.
K Great. See you there.

Unit 8

⏺8.1 Notice the silent e of most -ed endings, and the /ɪd/ after t.
1 Maud was born in 1877.
2 She worked in the circus.
3 Gus wanted to go out with her.
4 She agreed to see him.
5 She married him.
6 She studied hard.
7 She learned how to tattoo.
8 She stopped work.
9 Lotteva started tattoo lessons at nine.
10 Maud died in 1961.

⏺8.3 Notice -ed endings are /d/, /t/ or /ɪd/ (never /ɛd/).
Frida Kahlo was born on July 6, 1907, in an area of Mexico City called Coyoacán. Her full name was Magdalena Carmen Frida Kahlo y Calderón, something most people don't know. When Frida was a child, she lived in the famous Casa Azul, or blue house, with her family. It is now the Frida Kahlo museum and a fascinating place to visit! Frida painted her entire life, and was famous for her self-portraits. When she was young, she wanted to be a doctor, but in 1925, when she was only 18, she was in a bad bus accident. She then decided to be a painter, and in 1928, she married the world famous muralist Diego Rivera. Kahlo traveled to the U.S. with Rivera in the 1920s and 1930s, and she traveled in Mexico, too. She enjoyed her time in the U.S., but didn't like some aspects of American society. During this time, she developed her own unique style. Her first exhibition was in New York in 1938. In 1939, Kahlo went to live in Paris for a time. There, she exhibited some of her paintings, and met other artists, including Picasso. In 1943, she started teaching in Mexico City. Sadly, Frida was sick for most of her life. She died in 1954 at the age of 47 in her bed in the Casa Azul.

⏺8.8 Notice sentence stress.
What did you **do** on your **last vacation**?
Where did you **go**?
Did you **meet anyone interesting**?
What did you **do** every **day**?

⏺8.11 Notice and imitate the connections.
I = interviewer J = Jay
I So, what's your typical day like, Jay?
J Well, everyone thinks my life_is_exciting, but it can be pretty boring!
I Really? What did_you do yesterday?
J Yesterday? OK, I got_up_at_about 6 o'clock.
I Wow! So_early! That's amazing.
J That's when_I usually wake_up, you know.
I And then?

I I brushed my teeth, and then I made coffee. I absolutely can't start my day without_it.
I And did_you have breakfast?
J Yes, I had_a big breakfast. I love to cook, so then I made_an_omelet.
I That's great! And what did you do after that?
J After that, I turned_on the computer to check my email.
I Do you get_a_lot_of messages?
J I sure do! You have no_idea. I spent five hours_ on the computer yesterday. I answered 100 emails!
I You're kidding! That's_incredible.
J Well, not_all_at once. I_answered 30 messages, and then_around 10 a.m., I went out and ran_a mile. Then I came home and took_a shower. After that, it was time for lunch, so I had_a sandwich.
I And then?
J Well, I finished_answering all the emails. Then_at_about 2:30 p.m., I started to play the keyboard and_experiment with some ideas. I played for three hours ... and I wrote_a new song.
I That's fantastic! And what did you do after that?
J Well, then I went to visit some friends. My day_ ended_at midnight. That's when went to sleep.
I You had_a full day!

⏺8.14 Notice spellings of /ɑ/ and /oʊ/.
Q = quiz host M = man
Q So has everyone finished? Time for the answers. Number 1 was in fact The Beatles.
M Yes! We got that one!
Q OK, question 2. The first artist to surpass 50 billion streams in 2018 was Drake.
M Another one right!
Q Question 3. Idina Menzel sang "Let it Go" in Frozen.
M No!
Q OK, question 4. Eminem wrote the first rap song to win an Oscar.
M That is correct ...
Q A difficult one now. Question 5. Who made the video ...
M I know, I know, I've got it, I know the answer! It was Maroon 5!
Q Well, actually it wasn't ... it was Mark Ronson and Bruno Mars.
M I don't believe it. No. I'm sure it was Maroon 5 ...
Q Well I'm sorry. On to question 6. Enrique Iglesias sang the first song in Spanish to surpass a billion views.
M Hmm.
Q Now on to question 7. Ariana Grande was born on June 26th in Florida ...
M Oh.
Q ... Justin Bieber was born on March 1st in London, Canada, Rihanna was born on February 20th in Barbados, and Shawn Mendes was born on August 8th in Toronto. Now, question 8. Lady Gaga didn't sing at President Obama's inaugurations.
M Really?
Q Yes, really. Question 9. Reggaeton began in Puerto Rico.
M I was sure it was Brazil.
Q And finally ... question 10. Bob Marley told his son "Money can't buy life."
M Well, I got that one right ...

⏺8.16 Notice sentence stress.
S = sales clerk C = customer
S OK. So **when** did you **buy** this **phone exactly**?
C Er ... last week.
S And did you **buy** it in **this store** or **another one**?
C I **bought** it **here**.
S That's **good**! Well, did you **keep** the **receipt**?
C Yes, I **think** so ... Ah! **Here** it **is**!
S OK. **Great**. Can you **leave** your **phone** with **me**?
C Er ..., but, um ..., **how long**?
S You can **come back** in an **hour**. We **just need** to **take** a **look**.
C Phew! Thanks!
S Can you **give** me your **password**, **please**?
C Oh, well, **OK**. But the **password** is **only** for **you**!

⏺8.17 Notice h.
M = Mike C = Chris
M Hey Chris! How's it going? I tried to call you.
C Hi Mike, I'm not happy at all.
M Why? What happened?
C Well, I was at work at the hotel, right, and I had my phone in my jacket pocket. And my boss says, "Chris, can you clean the bathroom?" So OK, I went to clean the bathroom.
M Then what happened?
C I was cleaning the toilet when ... SPLASH! My cell phone fell in to the toilet!
M Oh no! Did you get it out?
C Yeah, but that phone cost $400!
M What did you do?
C Well, I put it under the hand-dryer, but it still doesn't work.
M Gee! That's bad luck. But at least the bathroom's clean now!

⏺8.18 Notice the connections.
1
M = Mom S = Sophie
M Oh no! Look at this mess. Sophie!
S Yes, Mom?
M Can_you please wash the dishes?
S Uh, sorry, it's Brian's turn today.
M OK, forget it. Brian!!!

2
M = man W = woman
M Excuse me. Uh, could_you open the door for me please?
W Oh, sure. There you go.
M Thank you so much.

3
W = woman D = Dan
W Dan, there's someone at the door.
D Could_you see who it is? I'm busy.
W Don't worry, I'll get it.

4
W = woman J = Jim
W Jim!
J Uh?
W Could_you please cut the grass, Jim?
J Er, but ... the game ... Come on, I can do it tomorrow.
W Could_you do it this afternoon, please? Your mother's coming to visit.
J Uh, OK, I'll do it now.

5
W = woman M = man
W Could_I ask you a favor?
M Hmmm, that depends. What do you want?

W Can_I leave my son with you this weekend?

M Oh. I'm really sorry, but I can't. I have two parties to go this weekend, so I can't be with your son. Sorry.

W Oh, no problem. Thanks anyway!

Unit 9

▶9.1 Notice /oʊ/, /ʊ/ and /ʌ/.

Hello and welcome to the Woodbury Music Festival! So, how did you all get here?

1 We rode our bikes. 30 miles!

2 We took the bus.

3 We walked. We live nearby.

4 I rode my motorbike.

5 By car. I drove.

6 I drove the band's truck! The other roadies all came the same way.

7 We took the ferry.

8 We took the train.

9 Some of the bands took a helicopter, I think.

10 I flew. I'm from Canada and my airplane landed this morning.

▶9.6 Notice /ə/ in articles and non-content words.

B = Brian J = James

B Look at this old picture from school, James! What's everybody doing now?

J Well, you know I'm a cab driver, Brian.

B Yes, you always loved driving!

J And Valerie is a hairdresser. She cuts and styles hair, you know – she loves it.

B And Martina is a firefighter. She was brave in high school.

J I know. What about Chris? What does she do?

B She's a flight attendant. She loves to travel.

J And I hear that Jane is a photographer.

B That's great! She always took fantastic pictures. What about Larry? Do you know anything about him?

J Yes! He's a police officer!

B What about David and Amelia?

J David's a cook ... no surprises there. And Amelia's a dentist.

B Wow, and Robert?

J He's a personal assistant to a famous singer! You know how he loves to organize people!

B Yeah! That's Robert! Nice job!

J I know – and I'm a computer programmer.

9.7 Notice the sentence stress.

K = Kelly M = Michael

K What are you going to do when you finish school, Michael?

M Well, first I'm going to go to grad school and then I'm going to be a financial advisor.

K Really? Why? That sounds boring.

M Well, you can make a lot of money as a financial advisor.

K I see!

M But seriously, you help people and you can be your own boss.

K That's cool. Your parents are going to be happy. You can give them financial advice. What about you?

M Promise you won't laugh if I tell you?

K Of course not. C'mon, tell me. What are you going do?

M I'm going to be a pet psychologist!

K What? How?

M Stop laughing! You promised not to laugh!

M Sorry!

K Yeah, I'm going to go to grad school and study psychology and then get a certificate in animal behavior. I want to be a pet psychologist. It's not going to be easy, but it's what I want.

M That's great! But, er, why, why do you want to be a pet psychologist?

K Well, first because I love animals, but I don't want to be a veterinarian. I want to work with animals. You can meet lots of people and make them happy. It's going to be fun!

M Maybe ...

K Well, I know I'm not going to be rich, but that's OK.

M OK then ... tell me what that dog's thinking.

K Don't be ridiculous!

▶9.11 Notice three pronunciations of o – /oʊ/, /ɑ/ and /ə/.

Well, Alex, maybe you can learn a few lessons from your dad. I left college in 1975, before graduating. I couldn't wait to get married, so I found a girlfriend immediately and got engaged after just three months! We got married only a month later, and I left home. At the same time, I started a new job as a photographer in a photography studio. And we started a family! But, as you know, things didn't work, and your mom and I got divorced when you were five. So I moved to a new house. Then I lost my job, because of digital photography, so I changed careers and became a computer programmer – boring, but it paid the bills. I finally retired from my job last week and now I think it's time for you to make a few changes in your life – I don't want you to make the same mistakes I did.

▶9.13 Notice the future verb forms.

C = Carla J = John Ju = Julia M = Martin

1

C Hi Ronnie! It's Carla. My brother's moving to Paris in July. He's going to fly there and he wants me to help him pack all his stuff. Can you help us too? it's going to take us weeks, but you're really good at packing. I hope you can! And I promise to buy you dinner! Thanks. Call me back.

2

J Hi Melissa, it's John. Listen, you know I told you that my parents are going to retire in February. Well, they've decided that they're going to move to a warmer place – so they're going to travel through Central and South America, and I wonder if you could help ... I know you lived in Costa Rica with your parents for a long time. We really value your opinion!

3

Ju Hi Mom! It's Julia. Uh ... Are you sitting down? We have some big news. Guess what! We're getting engaged! We're not going to get married until we finish school, so don't panic. So, uh, call me back when you get this message. Ciao!

4

M Hi Lucy, it's Martin. I got in! It's official! Yeah! I'm changing careers at last. I'm going to study nursing, and I'm going to be a nurse. A nurse! Woohoooo! I just got the news – they accepted me at the nursing school. I'm so excited! Call me back, because we need to celebrate. I'm going to be at work all afternoon, but then I'm going home, so give me a call and let's go out! Love you! Yeah!

▶9.14 Notice two pronunciations of e – /ɛ/, /iː/.

M = man W = woman

M A civil engineer: an engineer who builds public works, for example bridges or roads.

W A dentist: a person who takes care of other people's teeth.

M A financial advisor: a person who helps people invest their money.

W A market research analyst: a person who studies the reasons people buy certain products.

M A nurse: a person who helps doctors to take care of sick people.

W A software developer: a person who writes new computer programs.

▶9.16 Notice the connections.

1

L = Len J = Jane

L Excuse me, Jane. Can I ask you something?

J That's fine, Len. What_is_it?

L Could_I take the day_off tomorrow? I need to take my son to the doctor.

J Sure. Go ahead!

L Thanks, Jane. Phew! That's great!

2

S = son M = Mom

S Can_I borrow the car, Mom?

M No, I'm, sorry, you can't. I need_it this afternoon.

S Ooooooh! Why not? You never let me borrow the car ...

3

M = man W = woman

M Argh, do_you mind_if I turn_on the air conditioning?

W Not_at_all. It's really warm_in here.

M Phew, thanks.

4

A I hate to ask this, but could_you lend me some money? I left my money_at home, and_I need to get something to eat.

B I'm sorry, but_I don't have_any money with me_at the moment.

A Oh, OK, I'll_ask Jeff. Thanks_anyway.

Unit 10

▶10.2 Notice /aɪ/, /aʊ/ and /oʊ/.

Well, my job is to get people ready for the camera. I have to think about all these things: first, the hair, then the eyebrows and the eyes, then I quickly check the ears and the nose. Finally, I work on the mouth, and this means checking the teeth and working on the lips. I want people to look absolutely perfect!

▶10.3 Notice the connections.

P = police officer A, B and C = witnesses

1

P So, the man who took your bag. What did he look like?

A Hmm ... he wasn't short or tall. He was, um_ average height. And he wasn't overweight_or slim, he was_average build_I think.

P And can you remember the color_of his hair?

A Yeah, He, er ... He had dark hair.

P Long_or short?

A Er, long dark hair_and he had blue eyes, I think.

P OK. I think_I know who you mean. That's_ Adam. We know where he lives. Thanks! Let's go!

2

P OK, and what does the suspect look like?

B Well, he's short_and slim. And he said his name was Charlie, but, well, who knows.

P Uh-huh? What else do_you remember?

B Hmm, er ... he has short dark hair_and brown_ eyes. Like you!

P OK, thank_you. Oh, and don't worry. I'm not Charlie.

3

P OK, can_you describe the suspect, please? You said his name was Mark, right? What does_he look like?

C Well, he's tall_and very_overweight.

P Hmm, OK, and what color_is his hair?

C Er, I think he has short fair hair_and blue eyes.

P OK – thank_you, ma'am.

▶10.6 Notice /ə/.

M = Maggie   S = Steve

M I need some help, Steve.

S What's up, Maggie?

M Two people have invited me to parties on Saturday.

S Well, which one do you like better?

M They're both nice. Well, Scott is taller than Jake and you know I usually like tall men.

S Yes, so go with Scott to the party!

M But Jake is happier than Scott. Scott's sadder.

S So, go with Jake! That's more important. It doesn't matter that he's shorter than Scott.

M I know, but Scott is more interesting than Jake. Jake is a bit boring.

S Why don't you go to both parties? You can be friends with both of them.

M Good idea. I can go to the first party with Jake from seven to ten and then go to the second party with Scott at ten.

S Problem solved!

▶10.7 Notice word stress in the underlined words.

W What do your twin sisters look like?

M Those are my twin sisters, Zoe and Rebecca over there.

W Wow, Brad! They look identical.

M Yes, but they're very different.

W What's Zoe like?

M She's friendlier than Rebecca and she's more generous. She likes to be with other people and she's always giving people presents.

W What about Rebecca? What's she like?

M She's more timid than Zoe, and she's calmer. She likes to be alone, but she's more intelligent and more organized than Zoe.

▶10.9 Notice pronunciation of the suffixes.

A Type one is a perfectionist. They're idealistic but sometimes they're critical of other people.

B And what about type 2? What are they like?

A They're generous people but they're also possessive.

B And type 3?

A They're ambitious but they can become arrogant.

B Can you tell me about type 4? What are they like?

A Type 4. Umm, they're romantic, but sometimes they can be moody too.

B What about types 5 and 6?

A Type 5 people are solitary and they try to understand the world but sometimes they feel

depressed. That's type 5. Type 6 people are loyal and responsible but also suspicious.

B OK, the last three?

A Type 7 people are spontaneous, happy and fun. But they are very disorganized. Type 8 people are strong and try to do important things. The bad side is that they get angry. And the last one, type 9. They are calm and avoid conflict. The negative side is that they are passive and accept things because they don't want any problems.

▶10.14 Notice the sentence stress and the weak forms.

W = woman   M = man

W OK, so let's see how we did. Number **1** is **true**. **Scientists** don't know **why**, but your **brain** is **very** active when you **sleep**.

M OK – I **knew that** one – number **2**?

W **True**. It says that if men don't **shave**, a **beard** can grow to **more** than **10** meters long!

M **Wow! What** about number **3**?

W That's **false**. Your **toenails** grow **slower** than your **fingernails** because they get **less** sun.

M Hmm. **Interesting**. And number **4**?

W This is **true**, because **women** are **smaller** than **men**, so the **heart** needs to **move** the **blood faster** to the **different** parts of the **body**.

M Oh! I **didn't** know that. **What** about number **5**?

W **False**. The **heart** needs a **lot** of space, so the **left** lung is **smaller**.

M **Really**? OK, what about number **6**?

W That's **false**. We can **live** for a **month** or even **two** months without **food**, but the **longest** time a person can go with **no** sleep is **11** days. **Sleep** is **more important** than **food**.

M **Wow**, this is **really interesting**! And number **7**?

W This is **true**. When you **eat** or **talk**, you are **using** your **tongue** so it gets a **lot** of **exercise**.

M I suppose **so**. Blablabla! What about **8**?

W This is **false** – the **most common blood** type is **O**.

M I think **I'm** type **O**. How about **you**?

▶10.15 Notice the connections.

1

A So, what_do_you think?

B I'm not sure, Chinese_or_Italian?

A Hmm, I prefer the Chinese restaurant, but_it's_ more_expensive than the Italian.

B Yes, but the service_is faster in the Italian restaurant than_in the Chinese.

A I can't decide.

B Well, we're not_in_a hurry, so let's go to the Chinese restaurant.

A OK. Sounds good!

2

C Hmm, which one is best?

D Well, the strawberry is the sweetest and the coconut is more interesting. Chocolate is very popular!

C What do you recommend?

D I like the vanilla best.

C OK. I'll have the vanilla.

3

E So, where do_you want_to go? To the beach_or to the mountains?

F Well, the beach_is warmer than the mountains.

E Yes, but_it's_more peaceful_in the mountains.

F Well, I don't_know. I can't decide.

E OK, why don't we go to the beach? We need_to have some fun!

F That sounds great!

Review 5

▶R5.2 Notice voiced *th* /ð/ and unvoiced *th* /θ/.

L = Laila   J = Jenna

L Hi Jenna, how are you?

J Hi Laila. I'm great, thanks. Hey, I got your email. Great news about your trip.

L I know! I'm so excited!

J Listen, Laila. My brother went to work in Los Angeles and his room is empty. You can stay there until you go to Thailand.

L Your brother's room! Really? Oh, that's very kind of you. Are you sure he doesn't mind?

J No problem at all. But when exactly are you going on vacation?

L Well, I finish school on June 20th and I'm going to fly to Bangkok on July 16th.

J So you need a room for about two weeks, right?

L Umm, let me check ... No, about three and a half weeks actually.

J Three and a half weeks. No problem.

L Thanks so much, Jenna. OK, now tell me about you ... how are you?

PAUL SELIGSON

TOM ABRAHAM

CRIS GONTOW

2nd
edition

English
ID

Workbook
1

Richmond

6.1 What's in your refrigerator?

1 Write food items a–j and reveal the mystery sentence.

a ▢▢▢▢▢▢▢▢▢
   35 23 32   7 2

b ▢▢▢▢▢
  33 39

c ▢▢▢▢▢
  28 5 30   1

d ▢▢▢▢▢▢▢
     38 8 34 36

e ▢▢▢▢▢▢
  11 37

f ▢▢▢▢▢▢▢
  27 18 21 6 9

g ▢▢▢▢▢▢
   3 14 25 19

h ▢▢▢▢▢▢▢
  29 17 4 12 20 31

i ▢▢▢▢▢▢
  13 26   22

j ▢▢▢▢▢
  16 24 10 15

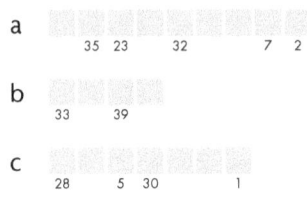

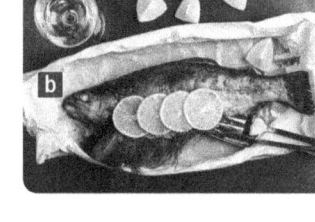

W__ W____ ____ _____ _____ Y____
1   2 3 4   5 6   7 8 9   10 11 12 13 14 15   16 17 18 19 20

____ D_ B_ _____ _____ _____
21 22   23 24 25 26 27 28 29 30 31 32 33 34 35 36 37 38 39

2 ▶ 6.1 Listen to the dialogue and write the shopping list.

3 ▶ 6.1 Listen again and complete a–e.
a They need tea because Hannah used _____ last night.
b They are going to eat _____ for _____.
c The mother is going to cook the _____ with _____ and _____.
d The mother wants some _____ because she likes to eat them for _____.
e Hannah wants some _____.

4 🎤 Make it personal Which of the food in exercise **1** do you like and which do you not like?
I like _____ and I like _____, but I don't like _____ .

5 Classify the food items in the pictures below as countable or uncountable.

Countable	Uncountable

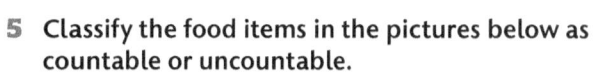
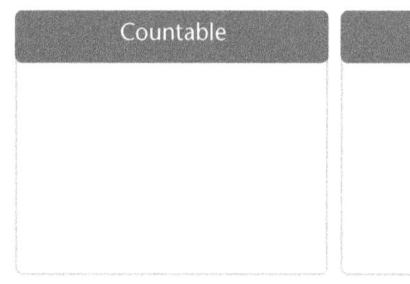

6.2 What do you eat for lunch and dinner?

1 Match photos a–i to these words.

☐ a bottle ☐ a can ☐ a glass ☐ a slice
☐ a bowl ☐ a cup ☐ a piece

a

c

e

g

b

d

f

2 ▶ 6.2 **Complete with *some*, *any*, or *a(n)*. Listen to check.**

Gina Hi, Mona. Would you like _____ cookies?

Mona No, thanks, Gina. I can't eat _____ cookies today.

Gina Why not? Are you on _____ diet?

Mona No, I'm not, but I have _____ test today and I can't eat _____ sugar or I get very nervous.

Gina Really?

Mona Yes. Last time I had a test I ate _____ chocolate before and my heart went crazy! And there was _____ information that I was sure that I knew but couldn't remember. So, I don't eat _____ sweets before tests anymore.

Gina Well, that's funny. That's what happens to me when I drink coffee before _____ important test. Hmmm, maybe next time I won't drink _____ coffee or tea and I will get a better grade!

3 Read about Jaime and Yolanda and answer a–f.

My daily diet: Jaime

I usually drink coffee with milk and I just eat bread and butter for breakfast. For lunch, I eat spaghetti with meat and sometimes chicken with potatoes. For dinner, I usually eat fish with rice or eggs. I sometimes eat an apple after dinner, but I never eat vegetables. I hate them!

My daily diet: Yolanda

I always drink orange juice for breakfast and sometimes I eat an apple. For lunch, I eat fish and some vegetables or salad. In the evening, I usually only have an egg and some fruit, and I often drink tea without milk with my dinner. I only eat chocolate on my birthday!

a What does Jamie normally have for breakfast?
b How often does Jaime eat fruit?
c What food doesn't Jaime like?

d What does Yolanda drink every day?
e What does Yolanda occasionally eat?
f How often does Yolanda eat vegetables or salad?

4 🔵 **Make it personal** Write a similar paragraph about your daily diet.

5 ▶ 6.3 **Look at the shopping list and talk about the things you have or don't have. Follow the model.**

Model: *eggs*
You: *I have some eggs.*
Model: *milk*
You: *I don't have any milk.*

eggs ✓   orange juice ✗
milk ✗   sugar ✓
lettuce ✗ pasta ✓
rice ✓   chocolate ✗
meat ✓   beans ✗

🔊 **Connect**

Get a classmate to make a video of you talking about your daily diet. Send each other your videos.

6.3 How often do you eat chocolate?

1 ▶ 6.4 **Read the blog post and circle the correct forms. Listen to check.**

My family
by Hannah King

My mom and dad have a very good diet and are very healthy. They only eat **a little / a few** red meat like pork or beef and they drink **a little / a few** coffee and tea each day. The problem is that my brother and I love fast food. We don't like healthy food and only eat **a little / a few** vegetables such as potatoes or beans. My parents say it is important that we eat fruit and vegetables because they are good for us, so I sometimes eat **a little / a few** apples or bananas. My brother thinks he is healthy because he only eats **a little / a few** chocolate daily and he never drinks coffee or tea, but he does drink a lot of soft drinks!! I don't like soft drinks very much, so I drink **a little / a few** water, but usually I drink tea or juice. I think my brother and I need to eat and drink more healthy food.

💬 **13 comments**

2 **Complete the sentences about the blog post.**

a Hannah's parents want her to eat a _____.
b Hannah and her brother love _____.
c Hannah sometimes eats _____ like bananas.
d Hannah's brother doesn't eat _____ chocolate.

3 **Match technical words a–e to their meaning.**

a calorie ☐ a substance that can block arteries
b cholesterol ☐ a chemical element found in salt
c protein ☐ a substance in foods such as meat, eggs, and milk that people need to grow
d sodium ☐ the parts of fruit, vegetables, and grains that our bodies cannot digest
e fiber ☐ a unit used to measure how much energy we get from food

4 **Complete extracts a–e from SB units 1–5 with *a few / a little*.**

a I need _____ information from you.
b No, I don't exercise. I'm _____ lazy.
c I need to ask you _____ questions.
d I speak _____ Spanish.
e Just _____ things to remember: When you come in ...

5 🔵 **Make it personal** **Complete a–e with *a few / a little / a lot of* so they're true for you. Add a frequency adverb when necessary.**

a I _____ eat _____ bread during the week.
b I _____ eat _____ calories at lunch time.
c There are _____ nice places to visit in our country.
d I _____ travel with _____ money.
e After lunch, I _____ eat _____ dessert.

6 ▶ 6.5 **Answer these questions about Mike. Follow the model.**

Model: *Does Mike buy a lot of potatoes?*   **Model:** *Does he buy a lot of coffee?*
You: *No, he only buys a few.*   **You:** *No, he only buys a little.*

6.4 How many meals do you cook a week?

1 ▶ **6.6 Steven is asking Becky about her diet. Listen. True (T) or False (F)?**

a Becky doesn't like any fruit. _____
b Becky only eats carrots and onions. _____
c Becky thinks fast food is good for you. _____
d Becky drinks a little tea every day. _____
e Steven thinks Becky has an unhealthy diet. _____

2 ▶ **6.6 Order the words to make questions. Listen to check.**

S Excuse me. My school is doing a survey to find out about people's diets. Can I ask you a few questions?

B Certainly. What do you want to know?

S ¹healthy / Do / ? / a / have / you / diet

B I think so.

S Well, ²fruit / how / do / every / eat / much / day / ? / you

B Not a lot, I'm afraid. I only eat bananas, I don't like other fruit.

S OK, so ³bananas / you / do / ? / many / every / eat / how / week

B Just a few – maybe two or three. But I do eat vegetables.

S ⁴like / you / all / ? / Do / vegetables

B Yes, carrots and onions are my favorite.

S ⁵vegetables / usually / week / you / ? / How / eat / do / many / eat / every

B Lots – I eat vegetables every day. But I don't eat a lot of meat.

S ⁶meat / How / ? / eat / do / much / you

B Well, I usually have a piece of chicken or fish on the weekend, but that's all.

S OK. What about fast food? ⁷food / ? / much / eat / fast / do / How / you

B I never eat any fast food. It's so unhealthy.

S Can I ask you about your drinks now? ⁸day / tea or coffee / many / cups / How / ? / of / every / have / you / do

B I have two cups of green tea every day, and then I drink water. I don't like coffee.

S Wow! You have a very healthy diet. ⁹eat / Do / unhealthy / you / ? / anything

B Well, I do like chocolate cake!

S And ¹⁰cake / eat / week / chocolate / how / of / ? / many / you / slices / do / every

B Oh, one every day.

S Seven slices of chocolate cake every week? That's not very healthy!

3 ▶ **6.7 Listen and complete the ingredients.**

Tasty Tomato Sauce

2 cans of _____ paste
1 tablespoon of _____
1 tablespoon of oregano
1 teaspoon of _____

Ingredients:
2 pounds of _____
1 _____
4 cans of _____

tablespoon   teaspoon

4 Jack and Tracy are going to make the sauce. Complete with *how much*, *how many*, *a few*, *a lot*, or *a little*.

J Tracy, I have a surprise for you. Tonight I'm making dinner!

T Sounds wonderful! What are you making?

J Spaghetti with tomato sauce.

T Uh, do you need help?

J Well, maybe you can read the recipe to me. _____ meat do I need?

T Two pounds.

J Hmm, we only have _____ meat.

T Well, how about we don't use meat this time?

J Good idea. OK. I have _____ cans of tomatoes. _____ cans do we need?

T Four.

J Four? That's a lot! I only have two.

T And _____ tomato paste do you have?

J Er ... I have _____ cans.

T OK, we only need two.

J OK, I have that. _____ onions do I need? I have _____ because I know you love onions.

T Well, we only need one.

J Ok, what else? Soup, right? _____ miso soup do I need?

T Hmm, no, Jack. You don't need any soup for this recipe. But you need _____ oil.

J Oh, no! I don't have any oil.

T You know what? Why don't we just call for pizza?

5 ▶ **6.8 Imagine you're going shopping for your family. Ask questions. Follow the model.**

Model: *sugar*

You: *How much sugar do we need?*

Model: *bottles of mineral water*

You: *How many bottles of mineral water do we need?*

6.5 What would you like for lunch?

1 Look at the pictures and complete the puzzle.

2 Put the words in the correct columns.

main courses	pureed	lettuce	grilled
barbecued	sautéed	steamed
starters	desserts	baked	lemon
melon	pears	carrots	onions

Courses	How it's cooked

Fruits	Vegetables

3 ▶ 6.9 Circle the correct forms. Listen to check.

Liv Hmm, I'm so hungry.

Ned Well, there isn't much in the fridge ... Let's see. **Would you / Do you** like an orange?

Liv Oh, no, thanks. I **wouldn't / don't** like oranges. Do you have any apples?

Ned I think so. **Would you / Do you** like one?

Liv Sure.

Ned Here it is.

Liv Uh, Ned, this apple looks really bad. I **would like / like** apples but not that much.

Ned Oops, sorry about that. Hey, **would you / do you** like some pizza? There's some in the freezer.

Liv No, thanks. I **wouldn't / don't** like any pizza now.

Ned Why not? I thought you really **would like / liked** pizza.

Liv Yeah, but not for breakfast!

4 ▶ 6.10 Order the words in the <u>underlined</u> phrases to complete the restaurant dialogue. Listen to check.

Gary Good evening. Welcome to Tom's Diner. My name is Gary and I'll be your server tonight.

April _I / menu / have / can / the_, please?

_____

Gary Sure. _you / to / a / like / starter / would / order?_

_____

April Yes, thanks. _the / have / chicken / I'll / salad_, please.

_____

Gary _drink / anything / to?_

_____

April Uh, yes. _I / like / soda / diet / a / would_, please.

_____

Gary _Just a minute, please._

April _Oh, excuse me?_

Gary _Yes?_

April _you / a / me / could / bring / plate / clean?_ This one is dirty.

_____

Gary Oh, sure. Sorry about that.

April No problem.

5 ▶ 6.11 Imagine you're at a restaurant. Order some items. Follow the model.

Model: _have – grilled chicken_
You: _I'll have the grilled chicken, please._
Model: _like – barbecued steak_
You: _I'd like the barbecued steak, please._
Model: _can – fish fillet_
You: _Can I have the fish fillet, please?_

🔊 **Connect**

Use the dialogue in **4** to practice a similar one with your partner. Record your dialogue and send it to your teacher.

Can you remember ...

➤ 22 food items? SB→p.72
➤ 10 uncountable food items? SB→p.73
➤ 9 countable food items? SB→p.73
➤ 7 portions of food? SB→p.74
➤ 3 quantifiers? SB→p.77
➤ 3 starters, 3 main courses, and 3 desserts? SB→p.80

7

7.1 Do you live in a house?

1 Circle the "different" item in each group. Write the room in the last column.

> basement   bathroom   bedroom
> dining room   garage   kitchen
> living room   office   laundry room

a (windows)	tools	storage space	*basement*
b sink	fireplace	bathtub	
c armchair	stove	microwave	
d shelves	computer	oven	
e closet	bathtub	shelves	
f TV	bed	sofa	
g car	bike	fan	
h table	chairs	shower	
i dryer	TV	washing machine	

2 Match a–i to a room in **1**.

a This is my _____. It's a little small, but I only come here to sleep.

b Welcome to my favorite room. It's the _____ I love sleeping on the sofa or watching TV here.

c I love cooking, so my favorite room is my _____.

d There's a _____ under the house with a lot of storage space.

e This is the _____. I only come here once a week to wash and dry my clothes.

f I work from home a lot, so I have an _____ with a computer.

g I don't have a _____, so my car is in front of my house.

h The _____ is really small, just a shower and a toilet.

i My parents have dinner parties in the _____, there's space for about eight people to eat.

3 ▶ 7.1 **Make sentences. Follow the model.**

Model: *A sofa. The living room.*
You: *There's a sofa in the living room.*
Model: *Some shoes. The bathtub.*
You: *There are some shoes in the bathtub.*

4 🔘 **Make it personal** Use the sentences in **2** to talk about your own house.

5 Read and answer a–c, True (T) or False (F).

Project Renovation is about individuals who take old, run down buildings and turn them into their ideal home. In tonight's episode, the host Kelly Fogarty visits an ambitious renovation project to talk with a young couple about their new house and film the progress.

> **a** Project Renovation is the name of a TV show.
>
> **b** It is about groups of people building new houses.
>
> **c** On tonight's show, the host goes to more than one project.

6 ▶ 7.2 **Listen and complete a–d with _was_ / _were_ ➕ ➖.**

> In the original house:
> a There _____ bathroom, or toilet, so this is a big part of the project.
> b The toilet _____ in the yard.
> c There _____ a big kitchen.
> d And there _____ windows in the kitchen.

7 ▶ 7.2 **Listen again and complete a–f with rooms or furniture.**

> Now:
> a Today, they are working on the _____.
> b The bathroom is above the _____.
> c The kitchen and the _____ are together in one room.
> d The _____ and the refrigerator are coming next week.
> e They are using the _____ to cook.
> f Phillip is excited about his new _____.

7.2 Where were you last night?

1 Add vowels to the incomplete words to make common party items.

How to plan the
perfect party!

a Make the _i_ nv _i t a t i_ _o_ ns and send them early.

b You can decorate the house with colored b___ll___ ___ns.

c If it's a birthday, make a c___ k___ and put c___ndl___s on it.

d Have lots of sn___ ___ks for people to eat.

e You also need drinks like l___m___n___d___ or c___l___.

f Some people like hot drinks so get some c___ff___ ___ and t___a.

g Remember to have lots of pl___t___s, n___pk___ns, and gl___ss___s.

h It's a good idea to have f___r___w___rks. Everybody loves them.

i A good party needs good m___s___c!

2 🅐 Make it personal Describe your perfect party.

3 ▶ 7.3 Add one word to questions a–h to make them correct in the past. Listen to check.

a When ˇwas Mari's party?
b How was?
c Where it?
d What the weather like?
e there a lot of food?
f there fireworks?
g there a cake?
h How many people there at the party?

4 ▶ 7.3 Listen again and repeat the questions.

5 ▶ 7.4 Listen to a conversation and answer the questions in **3**.

6 🅐 Make it personal Write a short note about your last party. Use the questions in **3** to help.

7 Take the music quiz. Match the song lines to the artists.

a "You **were** driving the getaway car."

b "I **was** just an only child of the universe. And then I found you."

c "Yesterday, love **was** such an easy game to play."

d "Listen to me when I say, I'm beautiful in my way because God makes no mistakes. I'm on the right track baby, I **was** born this way."

e "Cause I am whatever you say I am. If I **wasn't** then why would I say I am?"

f "When I **was** six years old, I broke my leg."

g "Look at the stars. Look how they shine for you, and everything you do. Yeah, they **were** all yellow."

h "Once there **was** a way to get back homeward. Once there **was** a way to get back home."

i "If I **were** a boy, even just for a day."

☐ Dua Lipa
☐ The Beatles
☐ Taylor Swift
☐ Coldplay
☐ Eminem
☐ Fall Out Boy
☐ Lady Gaga
☐ Beyonce
☐ Ed Sheeran

🔊 Connect

*Use the questions in **3** to interview a friend about his / her last party. Record your interview and send it to another pair to listen.*

7.3 Where were you last New Year's Eve?

1 Read the webpage about these events and answer a–c.

a Which event has the most people?

b Which event has music?

c Which event has food that people don't eat?

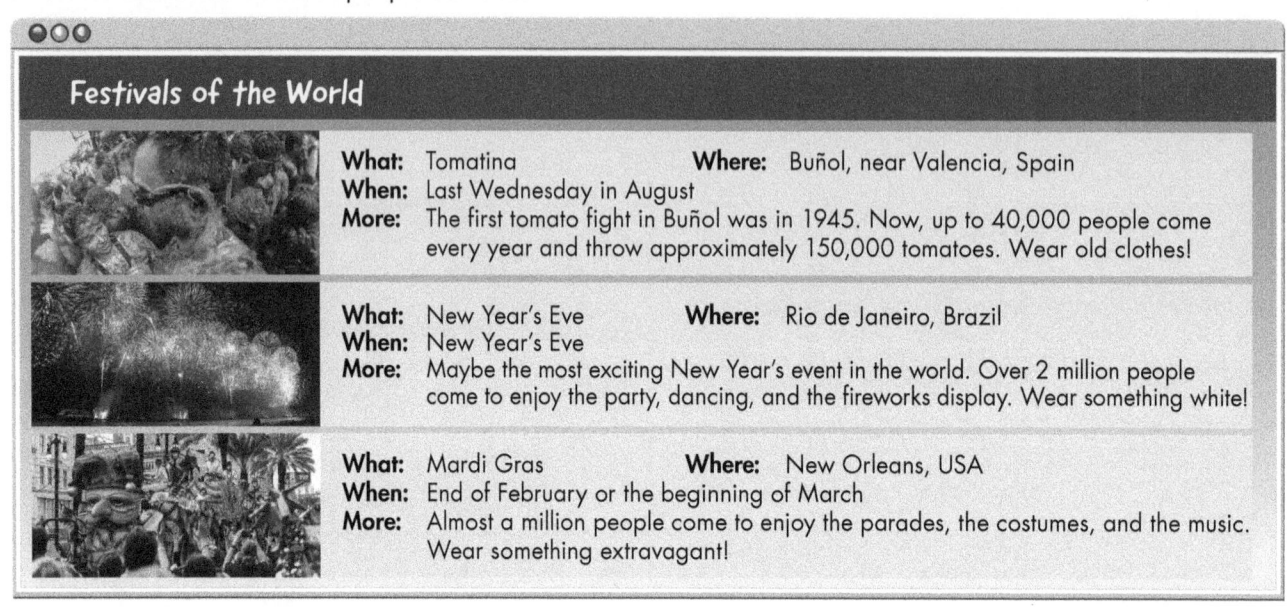

Festivals of the World

What: Tomatina **Where:** Buñol, near Valencia, Spain
When: Last Wednesday in August
More: The first tomato fight in Buñol was in 1945. Now, up to 40,000 people come every year and throw approximately 150,000 tomatoes. Wear old clothes!

What: New Year's Eve **Where:** Rio de Janeiro, Brazil
When: New Year's Eve
More: Maybe the most exciting New Year's event in the world. Over 2 million people come to enjoy the party, dancing, and the fireworks display. Wear something white!

What: Mardi Gras **Where:** New Orleans, USA
When: End of February or the beginning of March
More: Almost a million people come to enjoy the parades, the costumes, and the music. Wear something extravagant!

2 ▶ 7.5 Match the comments to two festivals, then complete them with *was* or *were*. Listen to check.

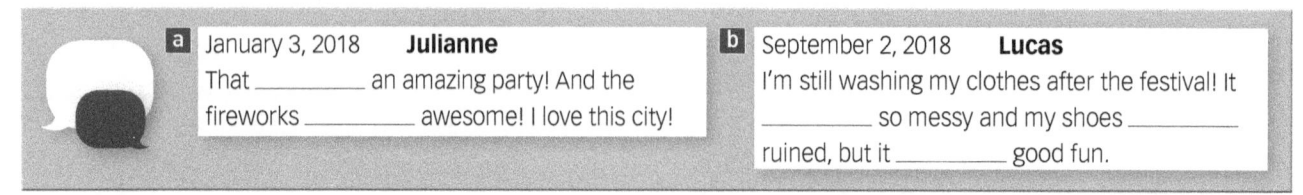

a January 3, 2018 **Julianne**
That _____ an amazing party! And the fireworks _____ awesome! I love this city!

b September 2, 2018 **Lucas**
I'm still washing my clothes after the festival! It _____ so messy and my shoes _____ ruined, but it _____ good fun.

3 Use the picture to complete the text with these prepositions.

above behind ~~between~~ in in front of next to on across from under

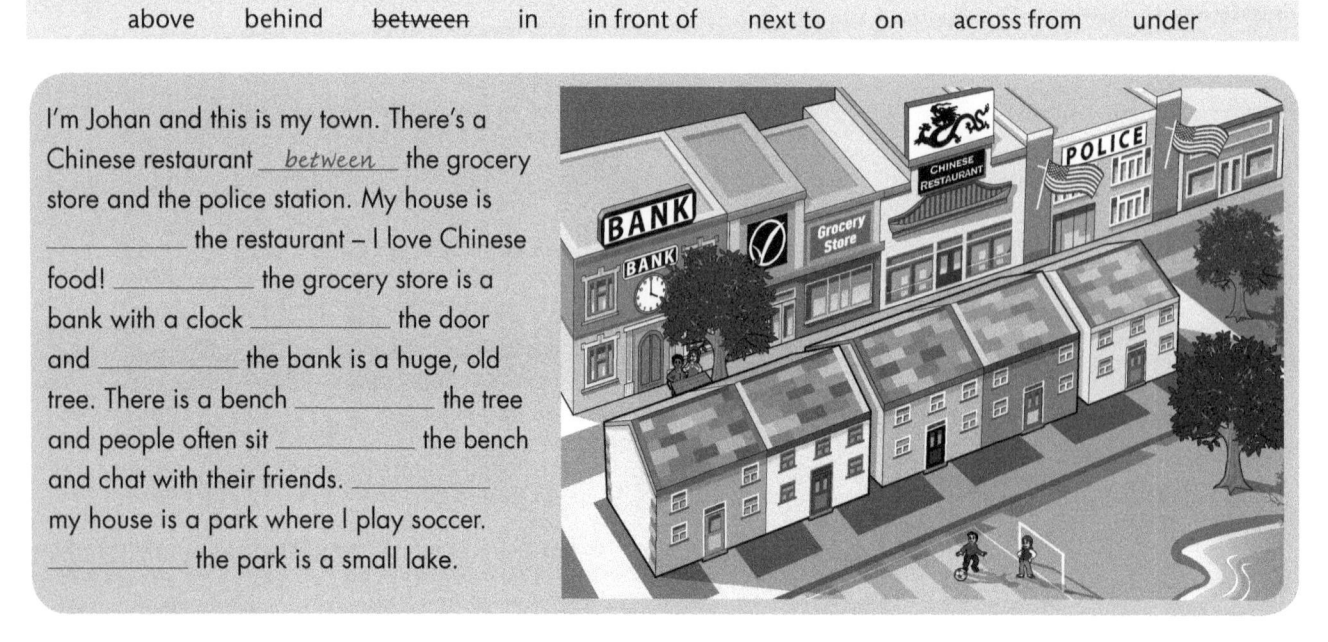

I'm Johan and this is my town. There's a Chinese restaurant _between_ the grocery store and the police station. My house is _____ the restaurant – I love Chinese food! _____ the grocery store is a bank with a clock _____ the door and _____ the bank is a huge, old tree. There is a bench _____ the tree and people often sit _____ the bench and chat with their friends. _____ my house is a park where I play soccer. _____ the park is a small lake.

4 🔵 **Make it personal** Describe your town to your partner.

7.4 Was your hometown different 10 years ago?

1 ▶ 7.6 Complete a–e with a date. Listen to check. Any surprises?

1903	1912	1972	1990	2012	2016

Famous Firsts and Lasts

a Rihanna's *Work* was a #1 international hit in _____.
b The first airplane flight with a pilot was in _____.
c The first successful communication on the Internet was in _____.
d George, the last Galápagos Giant Tortoise, died in _____.
e The Titanic's first, and last, voyage was in _____.
f The last man to walk on the moon was in _____.

2 ▶ 7.7 Look at the two pictures of André's town. Then complete the sentences. Listen to check.

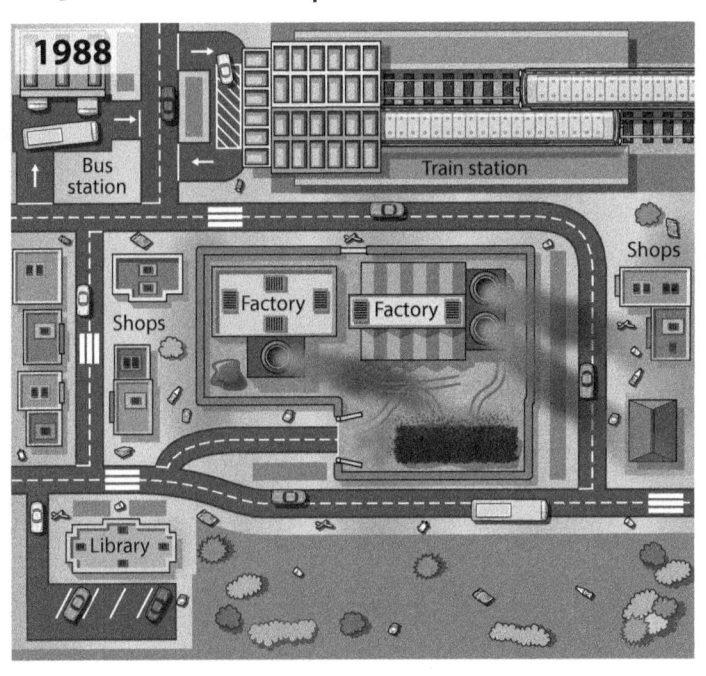

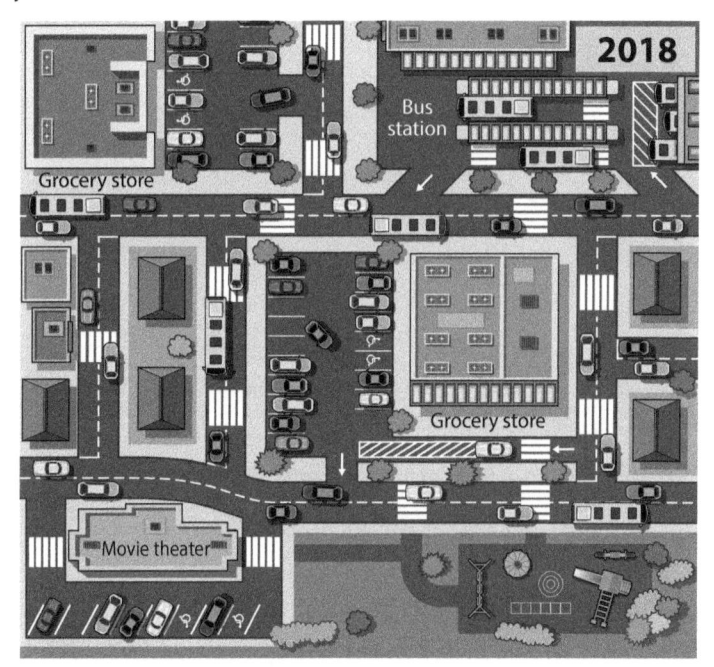

1988
There _were_ a few cars.
There _____ a train station and a bus station.
There _____ a grocery store.
There _____ a library next to the park.
There _____ two factories.
There _____ a play area for children in the park.
There _____ any big roads.
The town _____ very dirty.

Today
There _____ a lot of cars.
There _____ a train station. There _____ a big bus station.
There _____ two grocery stores.
There _____ a library, but there _____ a movie theater.
There _____ any factories.
There _____ now a big play area in the park.
There _____ a lot of new roads.
The town _____ dirty now. It is clean and beautiful.

3 🔵 **Make it personal** Are a–e True (T) or False (F) for your town?

a There were trains here fifty years ago.
b There was a lot of pollution, but it's clean now.
c There were a lot more small stores a few years ago.
d There wasn't anywhere for children to play, but now there are some play areas.
e There were some beautiful old buildings, but they aren't there now.

7.5 How about a barbecue on Sunday?

1 **Read the article and answer a–d.**
a Where is Glastonbury?
b When is the festival?
c What kind of festival is it?
d How can you buy a ticket?

GLASTONBURY FESTIVAL

Glastonbury is a small, old, historical town in the heart of southwest England. But every summer, at the end of June, around a quarter of a million people arrive there to celebrate the Glastonbury Festival, making it one of the 20 biggest cities in Britain. The world-famous music and arts festival has something for everybody, and some very big stars. To many people it is simply the best festival in the world. There was no festival in 2018, but the 2017 festival was fabulous, as usual. To get a ticket for next year register online at www.glastonburyfestivals.co.uk.

2 ▶ **7.8 Listen and match the numbers to the phrases to make statistics for Glastonbury 2016. Listen again to check.**

30	days
5	minutes to sell all the tickets
60	people in the audience
1,300	performances
Over 2,200	recycling volunteers
5,489	stages
220,000	toilets

3 ▶ **7.8 Listen again and write down three more numbers from the audio. What do they refer to?**

4 ▶ **7.9 Circle the correct word in invitations a–f. Then listen and complete with these phrases.**

a barbecue	a soccer game	a party
a restaurant	the movies	the park

a Would you like **to go / going** to _____?
b Do you **want / like** to go to _____ this weekend?
c **Do / Would** you like to come to _____ on Saturday?
d How about **go / going** to _____ after lunch?
e I'm having _____ on Friday. Can you **make / do** it?
f We're going to _____ for our 25th wedding anniversary. Can you **go / come**?

🔊 Connect

*Choose an event from **4**. Send a message to a friend to invite them to your event.*

Can you remember ...

▶ 9 rooms in a house? SB→p. 86
▶ 16 items of furniture? SB→p. 86
▶ 15 things you need for a party? SB→p. 88
▶ 9 prepositions of place? SB→p. 91
▶ how to talk about changes in a town? SB→p. 93
▶ how to invite a friend to a party? SB→p. 95

8.1 When did you start school?

1 Complete sentences a–h with the correct form of these verbs.

> agreed   died   learned   married
> started   studied   wanted   worked

a My parents got _____ in 1989. My mom wore a beautiful white dress.

b My sister _____ to drive a car last year. She isn't very good!!

c I like to help people, so I _____ to wash the car.

d Nelson Mandela _____ in 2013 in South Africa.

e We _____ to have a barbecue in the yard but it rained.

f Rihanna _____ singing when she was seven years old.

g Dominic _____ engineering at college.

h Hugh Jackman _____ as a physical education teacher before acting.

2 ▶8.1 **Read the biography and circle the correct verb forms. Listen to check.**

Robin Williams **borned** / **was born** on July 21, 1951 in Chicago. His great-grandfather was a politician in Mississippi, but his parents **weren't** / **wasn't** interested in politics. His father **worked** / **work** for Ford Motor Company and his mother **helps** / **helped** at the church.

Williams **study** / **studied** political science but didn't like it very much and **move** / **moved** to Julliard School in New York City to study theater. He **started** / **start** to work as a stand-up comedian in California and in 1978 **joined** / **join** the TV show *Mork and Mindy* as Mork.

By the 1980s, children all over the world **love** / **loved** him because his movies **was** / **were** so funny – movies like *Mrs. Doubtfire*, *Happy Feet* and *Boulevard*. However, he didn't just make comedy movies. Williams **play** / **played** roles in dramatic movies such as *Good Morning, Vietnam* and *Good Will Hunting*. He often didn't **follow** / **followed** a script but **invent** / **invented** his own dialogue and directors **was** / **were** happy to let him.

In 1998, Entertainment Weekly **list** / **listed** him as one of the 25 best actors in the world and he **receive** / **received** a Star on the Hollywood Walk of Fame on December 12, 1990.

He **loves** / **loved** sports and **was** / **were** a big fan of Rugby Union, and he often **watched** / **watch** the New Zealand All Blacks team. He also **enjoys** / **enjoyed** cycling and owned 87 bicycles.

He **married** / **marries** three times and **has** / **had** three children: Zachary, Zelda, and Cody. Cody **follow** / **followed** his father into the movie industry and is now an assistant director.

Robin Williams **die** / **died** on August 11, 2014 at home in California. He was 63 years old.

3 Reread the biography. True (T), False (F) or Not Given (NG)?

a Robin Williams' great-grandfather worked in politics.

b His first job was on a TV show.

c He was only famous for his comedy roles.

d Robin Williams enjoyed playing Rugby Union.

e He got married more than once.

f Williams' son Cody is an actor, too.

4 ▶8.2 **Listen and make sentences about Joe. Follow the model.**

Model: *study English / last weekend*
You: *Joe studied English last weekend.*
Model: *start school / in 1990*
You: *Joe started school in 1990.*

5 Write Whitney Houston's biography using the information in a–g.

a born / August 9, 1963 / Newark, New Jersey

_____

b record / her first album / 1985

_____

c receive / her first Grammy / 1986

_____

d married / Bobby Brown / July 18, 1992

_____

e star in the movie *The Bodyguard* / 1992

_____

f produce / the movie *Sparks* / September 2011

_____

g die / in a hotel / February 9, 2012

8.2 Did you go out last weekend?

1 Read about Mia and circle 18 past tense verbs. Put them in the correct spelling rules box.

> When Mia finished school, she wanted to travel. She took a gap year, studied a map of the world, and decided to go to South East Asia. Before she left her parents gave her a new camera to record all the wonderful things she saw. She flew to Indonesia in May, and when she arrived she sailed to Sumatra and got a job as a volunteer in the rainforest. She helped in a park looking after orangutans. She stayed for six months and made lots of new friends. They all cried when she said good-bye!
> She had a fantastic time in Indonesia and wants to go back there again one day.

1 - Most regular verbs	2 - Verbs ending in -e	3 - Verbs ending in consonant + y	4 - Irregular verbs
		cried	

2 Now put these verbs in the past and add them to the boxes in **1**.

> buy   come   do   go   invite   know   play   start   think   try   use

3 ▶8.3 Circle the correct preposition. Then listen to check.

Bob Marley was born **on / in** February 6, 1945 **on / in** the village of Nine Mile in Jamaica. He left school **at / in** the age **for / of** 14 to make music. **On / In** 1962, he recorded his first two singles, but the songs didn't attract a lot of attention. With his stepbrother and some friends, he created the band The Wailers **in / on** 1963. **On / In** 1966, he married Rita Anderson. The Wailers only released their first major album **at / in** April of 1973. **On / In** July, 1977, doctors discovered that Marley had cancer. He still released a new album **in / on** May 1980. He died at a hospital in Miami **in / on** May 11, 1981.

4 Complete with the correct ordinal number.
a   Bob Marley's _____ (2) name was Robert.
b   Ziggy is his _____ (1) child.
c   His _____ (11) child, Damian, was born on July _____ (21), 1978.
d   His final concert happened on September _____ (23), 1980, in Pittsburgh.
e   In 1999, *Time* magazine chose The Wailers' *Exodus* as the best album of the _____ (20) century.

5 ▶8.4 Look at the birthdates of these singers and answer the questions. Follow the model.

Model: *When was Elvis Presley born?*   You: *He was born on January 8ᵗʰ, 1935.*

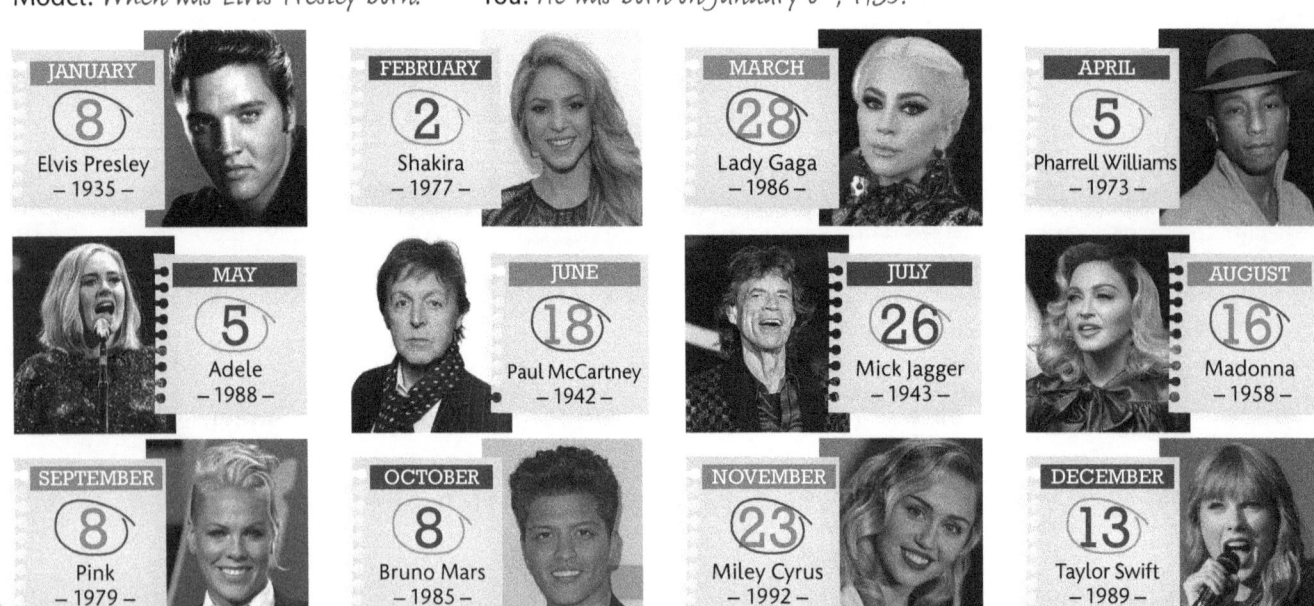

JANUARY (8) Elvis Presley – 1935 –
FEBRUARY (2) Shakira – 1977 –
MARCH (28) Lady Gaga – 1986 –
APRIL (5) Pharrell Williams – 1973 –
MAY (5) Adele – 1988 –
JUNE (18) Paul McCartney – 1942 –
JULY (26) Mick Jagger – 1943 –
AUGUST (16) Madonna – 1958 –
SEPTEMBER (8) Pink – 1979 –
OCTOBER (8) Bruno Mars – 1985 –
NOVEMBER (23) Miley Cyrus – 1992 –
DECEMBER (13) Taylor Swift – 1989 –

8.3 Where did you go on your last vacation?

1 ▶8.5 🅐 **Make it personal** Notice the pronunciation of **did you** (/dɪdʒə/). Listen and repeat. Listen again and answer.

a What *did you* do last weekend?
b What time *did you* get up on Sunday?
c What *did you* eat?
d Who *did you* see?
e Where *did you* go?
f *Did you* go to the movies?
g *Did you* stay at home?
h *Did you* have a good time?

2 Imagine a friend went to Paris on vacation. Write questions for the <u>underlined</u> parts of the sentences.

a _____?
I went with <u>my family</u>.

b _____?
We stayed <u>at the Hôtel San Régis</u>.

c _____?
<u>Yes, we did</u>. We met a nice couple from Finland.

d _____?
<u>No, we didn't</u>. We don't usually take a lot of photos.

e _____?
We bought <u>souvenirs and perfume</u>.

3 Reread the interview on SB p. 103. Correct the information about Ms. Riggs' trip.

a She went to Turkey with her husband.
She didn't go with her husband. She went alone.

b She went to Turkey on vacation.
_____

c She took a plane to Cappadocia.
_____

d The trip to Cappadocia took six hours.
_____

e They stopped at a restaurant in Istanbul.
_____

f They ate Japanese food.
_____

g She didn't like the trip.
_____

📶 **Connect**

*Use the questions in **1** to interview a friend about his / her weekend. Record your interview and send it to a classmate or your teacher.*

4 ▶8.6 Use the information below and correct these sentences. Emphasize the part you're correcting. Follow the model.

Model: *She had a train ticket to Cappadocia.*
You: *She didn't have a **train** ticket. She had a **plane** ticket.*

a plane ticket
b a ride
c Turkish food
d interesting places
e great time

5 ▶8.7 Read the blog. Use the verbs in bold in the past tense to complete the puzzle below. Listen to check.

Mike Mozey

Last weekend my girlfriend **say** (3) she wanted to go to a different place. So I **make** (2↓) a reservation for dinner at a new restaurant in town. We **go** (7) in separate cars and **meet** (2→) there.
The food was really great. We **eat** (1) good Italian pasta and **drink** (6) a bottle of soda.
At the end, when the check **come** (4), we got a big surprise: it was only one dollar!
I **know** (5) that was wrong so I called the manager. The manager **say** (3) that we were their 1,000th client, so that was a gift for us. It was perfect!

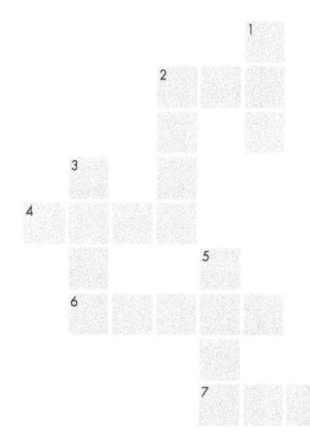

6 Answer a–d about the blog in **5**.

a Why did they go to a new restaurant?
b Did they go to the restaurant together?
c How much did they pay for dinner?
d Why did they pay that much?

8.4 When do you listen to music?

1 ▶ **8.8 Listen to this interview with singer Ginny Lomond, and check the actions she mentions.**

1	2	3
start school	record first album	move to Los Angeles
go to school	record second album	move to New York
leave school	record last album	move to Paris

2 ▶ **8.8 Listen again and answer questions a–f about the interview.**
a When did she start her career?
b Where did she study?
c Where was Ginny born?
d Who moved to New York?
e Was her first album a success?
f When did she record her second album?

3 Ask questions for the <u>underlined</u> part of the sentences.

a _____?

Time Magazine elects the 100 most influential people every year.

b _____?

Angelina Jolie divorced <u>Brad Pitt</u> in 2016.

c _____?

<u>Tom Ford</u> studied fashion design in the 1990s.

d _____?

<u>Serena Williams</u> won four Olympic gold medals in tennis.

e _____?

Steven Spielberg met <u>Kate Capshaw</u> while filming the second *Indiana Jones* movie.

f _____?

Ryan Gosling moved to <u>Los Angeles</u> in 1996.

4 ▶ **8.9 Look back at Jake's morning routine on SB p. 20 and tell it in the past. Listen to check.**

> Yesterday Jake woke up at ...

5 🎧 Make it personal   What did you do yesterday?

> I woke up early and ...

8.5 Could you help me, please?

1 ▶ 8.10 **Read the email and correct the 14 mistakes. The numbers show how many mistakes per line. Listen to check.**

○○○

From: jj_harrison@junkmail.com
To: customer_service@appliances.net
Cc:
Subject: Problems with TV

To Customer Service,

I ~~buyed~~ *bought* a new 40" flat screen TV from your   1
store on June 12 this year. And I regret this
decision every single day …

The delivery were late. Instead of three days,   1
I haved to wait one week. But then I finally   1
get my TV. To my surprise, the sound didn't   1
worked. The image was beautiful, but   1
there were only noise. So I called technical   1
support. A person come and he sayed the   2
TV needed a new part, but he didn't had it   1
there.

That was two weeks ago. I called technical
support again but they didn't knew anything   1
about the part. So another repairperson
came, look at the TV, sayed that he didn't   2
haved the necessary part, and left—without   1
fixing the TV again.

That was one week ago. Now I'm afraid of
calling technical support again and getting
another useless visit. Could you please
helped me? Could you please check the   1
reports from your repairmen and make sure
the next one brings the necessary part?

Thank you very much.

James J. Harrison

2 Reread. True (T) or False (F)?

a The buyer is happy that he bought this TV.
b The delivery took 7 days, not 3 as promised.
c The image of the TV was perfect.
d The repairmen couldn't repair the TV because they didn't have the proper part.
e Three different repairmen came to his house.

3 🔵 **Make it personal** **Use the information below to write an email like the one in 1. Add more details. Send it to your teacher or a friend.**

new cell phone
battery only lasts 15 minutes
tried recharging it
doesn't work
called support
got a new battery
same problem
called technical support again
promised a solution
no solution
a new phone

4 ▶ 8.11 **Complete requests a–i with these verbs. Listen to check and repeat each request. Be careful with the pronunciation of *could you* /kʊdʒə/ and *could I* /kʊdai/.**

borrow	have	help	hold	lend
open	pass	speak	use	

a Could you _____ the window, please?
b Could you please _____ me the salt?
c Could you _____ the door, please?
d Could you please _____ me your phone?
e Could you _____ me, please?
f Could I _____ your bathroom, please?
g Could I _____ your pen, please?
h Could I _____ the menu, please?
i Could I _____ to Mr. Green, please?

5 ▶ 8.11 **Listen again and note the replies.**

🔊 **Connect**

Use your phone to record yourself making the requests in 4. Send the recording to your teacher.

Can you remember …

➤ 10 verb phrases from Maud's biography? SB→p. 98
➤ 3 spelling rules for the simple past formation? SB→p. 99
➤ the auxiliary verb for the simple past? SB→p. 100
➤ 14 common irregular verbs in the simple past? SB→p. 100
➤ ordinal numbers 1–31? SB→p. 101
➤ 8 questions about past events? SB→p. 102
➤ 10 actions from Jay De La Fuente's daily routine? SB→p. 104
➤ 4 phone problems? SB→p. 106
➤ 7 favors and responses? SB→p. 107

1 Match the types of transportation to descriptions a–j.

☐ a bike	**a** A flying machine that is popular with the police.
☐ a bus	**b** It has four wheels and is for two to five people.
☐ a car	**c** A big flying machine that makes global tourism easy.
☐ a ferry	**d** It travels on the road and carries many people.
☐ on foot	**e** A large road vehicle that carries heavy cargo.
a a helicopter	**f** A boat that carries passengers and cars.
☐ a motorcycle	**g** A vehicle with two wheels. You power it with your legs.
☐ a plane	**h** Public transportation invented in England in the 19th century.
☐ a train	**i** It's like a bike, but it has a motor.
☐ a truck	**j** When you walk, you travel …

2 ▶ 9.1 **Which of the <u>underlined</u> letters has a different sound?**

a	t<u>oo</u>k	fl<u>ew</u>	f<u>oo</u>t
b	l<u>o</u>ved	dr<u>o</u>ve	r<u>o</u>de
c	b<u>i</u>ke	b<u>i</u>g	r<u>i</u>de
d	<u>h</u>our	<u>h</u>ouse	<u>h</u>elicopter
e	<u>ferr</u>y	t<u>r</u>ain	<u>c</u>ame

3 **Complete 1–3 with the past form of the verb.**

1 A What did you do on your vacation?
  B I ___*rented*___ (**rent**) a car and _____ (**drive**) from New York to Las Vegas.
  A Wow! How did you get to New York?
  B I _____ (**fly**) with YouAir, the food was great!

2 A Your face is red, are you OK?
  B I'm hot! I _____ (**ride**) my bike here.

3 A Sorry, I'm late. I _____ (**take**) the train and there was a problem with the line.
  B I heard about that. I _____ (**come**) by bus. The traffic was terrible!

4 ▶ 9.2 **Complete the dialogue with these words. Listen to check.**

accident	delayed	flat tire	late
traffic jam		wrong turn	

1 A Why are you so late?
  B There was a terrible _____ on the highway. We waited for two hours!
  A Oh, no. Was there an _____?
  B Yes, I think so. There was a police helicopter there.

2 A Where's Tom?
  B Oh, he called and said his car had a _____ so he took a train.
  A OK, so where is he?
  B The train was _____! He's walking from the station now.

3 A Was your flight _____ yesterday?
  B No, why?
  A Well you got here very late.
  B Ah that's because the taxi driver made a _____!

5 **Read about Isabella and her family and correct the six mistakes.**

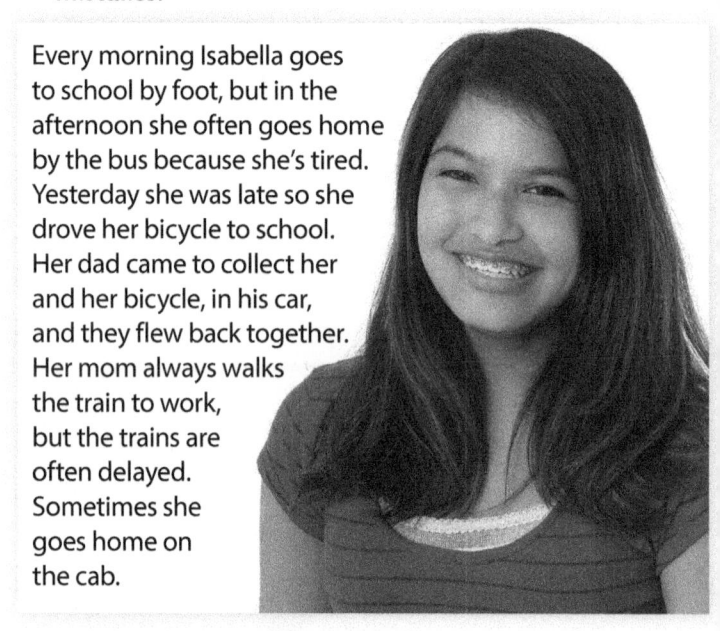

Every morning Isabella goes to school by foot, but in the afternoon she often goes home by the bus because she's tired. Yesterday she was late so she drove her bicycle to school. Her dad came to collect her and her bicycle, in his car, and they flew back together. Her mom always walks the train to work, but the trains are often delayed. Sometimes she goes home on the cab.

6 🔘 **Make it personal** **Order the words in a–f to make questions. Write short answers to them.**

a to / did / class / you / ? / get / how
  How did you get to class?   On foot.

b do / you / work / ? / to / usually / get / how
  _____

c you / do / school / ? / the / bus / to / take
  _____

d ? / ride / motorcycle / a / you / can
  _____

e you / usually / supermarket / ? / to / the / get / do / how
  _____

f your / way / ? / to / what / travel / 's / favorite
  _____

7 ▶ 9.3 **Practice the sentences. Follow the model.**

Model: *I flew / plane.*   **Model:** *She walked / foot.*
You: *I came by plane.*   **You:** *She came on foot.*

9.2 What do you do?

1 Read the magazine article and answer a–e.

Almost everybody hates their commute. The bus or the train is full of people, or there is a lot of traffic on the road. For most people, commuting is uncomfortable and boring, but at least it is safe. For the residents of Los Pinos, Colombia, things are a little different. People in the village have a choice of a two-hour walk through the mountains or a one-minute trip on a zip-line across the canyon that separates their homes from the rest of the world. There are two cables across the valley, one to get out and one to get back. They are four hundred meters long and three hundred and fifty meters high and you can go over 60 kilometers per hour! Very young children use the zip-line to get to school and their parents use it to take products to market. The government doesn't want to build a bridge because not many people live in the village. ▪

a   According to the article, what is one positive thing about the average commute?
b   How long does it take to walk through the mountains?
c   Do villagers use the same zip-line to go to and from the village?
d   Are there any age restrictions on using the zip-line?
e   Are the authorities planning to build a bridge?

2 Match words a–e from the article to the definitions.

a   to commute   ☐ a large, strong line made of metal that connects two points
b   a village   ☐ an excursion, a voyage, or a journey
c   a trip   ☐ to construct
d   a cable   ☐ a small community
e   to build   ☐ to travel regularly to the same place

3 Complete the puzzle with professions. Example: O = 👁.

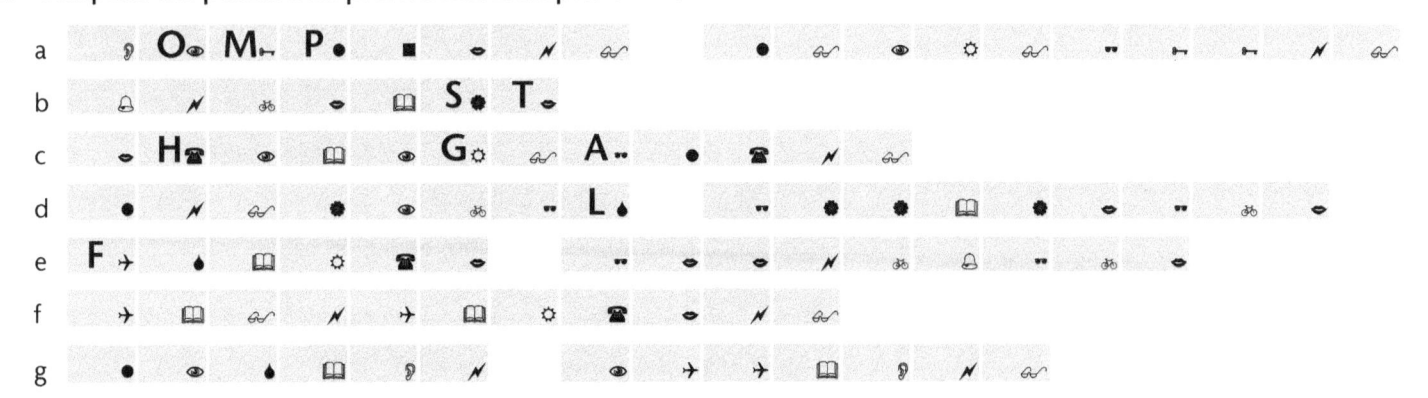

a
b
c
d
e
f
g

4 ▶ 9.4 Listen to check. Write the seven questions you hear.

5 🅐 Make it personal Check the jobs in **3** that make a lot of money and circle the dangerous jobs.

6 ▶ 9.5 Practice the sentences. Follow the model.

Model: *cook / they*   Model: *dentist / I*
You: *They are cooks.*   You: *I'm a dentist.*

9.3 Where are you going to be in 2025?

1 **Correct the mistakes in a–f.**

a What time you going to finish work tomorrow?
b Which team going to win the next World Cup?
c When are you go to go on your next vacation?
d Where are you going have lunch tomorrow?
e You are going to do your homework?
f What are you go to do next weekend?

2 ▶ **9.6 Listen to 1–6 and circle the pronunciation you hear. Match them to questions a–f in 1.**

1 I'm **going to** / **gonna** have lunch in a restaurant.
2 I'm **going to** / **gonna** stay home.
3 No. I'm not **going to** / **gonna** have time. I have to work tonight.
4 I'm **going to** / **gonna** finish early today, about 5 o'clock.
5 We're **going to** / **gonna** go on vacation at Christmas.
6 I think France is **going to** / **gonna** win the next World Cup.

> 🔊 **Connect**
>
> *Use your phone to record your answers.*
> *Send them to your teacher or a friend.*

3 👤 **Make it personal** Answer the questions in **1**.

4 **Read the article and match the predictions to the pictures.**

Once upon a time the 21st century was the future. This is how people imagined it.

In 1909 people predicted this: "in the future all important cities are going to have a roof to protect them against rain and snow."

In 1939 a newspaper made this prediction: "in the future we are going to have light-weight, solar-powered cars. We are not going to need garages because people are going to fold their cars and store them under the bed."

There are a lot of predictions about cheap and easy air travel. This is an example from the 1960s. "In the future everyone is going to have a flying car. Travel is going to be very easy and very cheap."

5 **Reread. True (T) or False (F) according to the predictions?**

a People are going to keep their cars in the house.
b Cars in the future are going to use the sun for power.
c All cities in the future are going to have a roof.
d It isn't going to snow in the future.
e Flying cars are going to be expensive.

9.4 What are you going to do next year?

1 Cross out the item that *doesn't* collocate with the verb. Which two aren't usually life changes?

a Get ~~college~~ / married / divorced
b Leave college / home / house
c Start a new job / a friend / a family
d Move house / engaged / your car
e Lose a job / a train / your keys
f Find married / a partner / a job

2 Read the article. True (T) or False (F)?

Resolutions—Make or Break

Everywhere, everybody celebrates the New Year! And we all do it in different ways, but there's one ritual that's common in many cultures: New Year's resolutions. We love them!

But how long do our resolutions usually last? A new study in the U.S. shows that after two weeks 64% of people still keep their resolutions and six months later over 40% still keep their resolutions. Not bad, huh!

So, the BIG question is ... what's the secret to success? And the answer is ... planning! Yes, plan your resolution, tell your friends about it, keep a journal and stay positive. That's your best chance of success!

You can make a resolution at any time of year, not just January 1st! Do you have any resolutions? Follow the advice in the article, make a plan and keep a journal—in English!

a Many nationalities make resolutions at New Year.
b Most people keep their resolutions for half a month.
c Only a few people keep their resolutions after June.
d Nobody has any advice to help keep a resolution.
e You should keep your resolutions secret.

3 ▶ 9.7 Match resolutions a–f with the plans. Listen to check.

a I'm going to get fit and exercise more, so
b I'm going to save money.
c I'm going to be more organized.
d I'm going to volunteer.
e I'm going to eat better.
f I'm going to try and relax more.

☐ First, I'm going to write a list. Number one ... um?
☐ I'm taking cooking classes in the evening.
☐ I'm not going to buy unnecessary clothes.
☐ I'm going on vacation next month.
☐ next week I'm joining a gym.
☐ My friend and I are helping at a homeless shelter next week.

4 Read the sentences again. What verb structures do these sentences have? Which ones are about plans with another person or organization?

5 ▶ 9.8 Practice the sentences. Follow the model.

Model: *save money next year / she*
You: *She's going to save money next year.*
Model: *find a new job tomorrow / I*
You: *I'm going to find a new job tomorrow.*

6 🎧 Make it personal Write about your plans for next year.

9.5 Would you like to be a nurse?

1 Read and match skills a–e to the reasons.

World of Work

Globalization and the Internet are changing the world fast. Analysts and experts predict that certain skills are going to become more important in the future.
In the future we are going to need:

a people who speak more than one language because …

b people who are creative because …

c people who can use social media to work because …

d people who can adapt to new situations because …

e people who can select and use data because …

☐ companies are not going to have offices and people are going to work from home.

☐ organizations are going to need people to communicate between different countries.

☐ machines are going to do all the routine jobs.

☐ the quantity of information on the Internet is going to increase.

☐ people are going to have to do more than one job in their life.

2 Check the skills you have, a–e, in **1**.

3 ▶ 9.9 Order the conversation, 1–7. Listen to check. Who's the boss, A or B?

A Fine, thank you. Listen, can I ask you something? ☐
A Oh. OK. ☐
B Sure. Go ahead. ☐
A Hi, how are you? ☐1
A Is it OK if I take the day off on Friday? ☐
B Friday? I'm really sorry, but I'm going to go to a meeting on Friday and I really need you here. ☐
B Good, thanks, you? ☐

4 ▶ 9.10 Order the words in a–f to make questions, then complete them with these words. Listen to check.

air conditioning	money	car
sit	question	photo

a I / the / ? / could / _____ / borrow / please
b I / ask / ? / you / a / can / _____
c ? / you / some / could / _____ / me / lend
d if / it / off / OK / I / is / turn / ? / the / _____
e mind / you / ? / if / I / do / _____ / here
f ? / you / your / mind / if / I / do / take / _____

5 ▶ 9.10 Listen again and repeat the questions.

6 ▶ 9.11 Listen to the complete dialogues. Check or cross a–f in **4** when they accept or don't accept.

7 ▶ 9.12 Practice the questions. Follow the model.

Model: *borrow the car / I / can*
You: *Can I borrow the car?*
Model: *open the window / I / mind*
You: *Do you mind if I open the window?*

Can you remember …

➤ 10 means of transportation and the past verbs for them? SB➔p. 112
➤ 10 jobs? SB➔p. 115
➤ 11 important life changes? SB➔p. 118
➤ 2 ways to talk about plans? SB➔p. 119
➤ 6 important jobs for the future? SB➔p. 120
➤ the difference between *borrow* and *lend*? SB➔p. 121
➤ how to ask permission with *could*? SB➔p. 121

10.1 Do you look like your mom?

1 Use the codes chart to find parts of the face, a–e. Then answer the secret question.

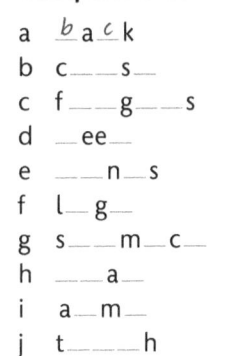

	1	2	3	4
A	a	b	c	d
B	e	f	g	h
C	i	k	l	m
D	n	o	p	r
E	s	t	u	y

E.g.: *h a i r*
B4 A1 C1 D4

a C4, D2, E3, E2, B4
b B1, E4, B1, E1
c B1, A1, D4, E1
d C3, C1, D3, E1
e D1, D2, E1, B1

A4 D2   E4 D2 E3   C3 D2 D2 C2   C3 C1 C2 B1   A1

B2 A1 C4 D2 E3 E1   D3 B1 D4 E1 D2 D1   ?

2 Add the words in **1** to groups a–e and cross out the odd word.

a kiss, see, lipstick, smile, _____
b screens, watch, talk, photos, _____
c TV, food, eat, speak, _____
d radio, listen, music, read, _____
e perfume, movies, breathe, smell, _____

3 Complete labels a–j in the picture.

a *b a c* k
b c __ s __
c f __ g __ s
d __ ee __
e __ n __ s
f l __ g
g s __ m __ c __
h __ a __
i a __ m __
j t __ h

Jay Carmen Amy Bob Joseph Cameron

4 ▶ 10.1 Complete descriptions a–e about the people in **3**, using these phrases. Listen to check.

average build	average height	fair hair	long dark hair	old
overweight	short gray hair	slim	tall	young

a Amy is about 45 and has _____. She's Jay's daughter.
b Carmen is from Colombia. She's _____ and _____. She has _____.
c Jay is married to Carmen. He's _____ and he has _____.
d Joseph is Jay's son. He's _____ and _____.
e Cameron is Joseph's partner. She's _____ and _____.

5 ▶ 10.2 Practice the descriptions. Follow the model.

Model: *Amy / fair hair*
You: *This is Amy. She has fair hair.*

Model: *Carmen / slim / long dark hair*
You: *This is Carmen. She's slim and has long dark hair.*

6 🔵 Make it personal Email a photo of friends / family to your teacher or a classmate and describe one person in the photo. Can they guess who the person is?

10.2 Are you like your dad?

1 Read the article and complete the chart with three more similarities and three differences between Nick and his dad.

Nick Johnson is 34 and a successful author. He writes suspense novels and his most recent book is The Dark Forest. Here he tells us about the influence of his father.

My father certainly inspired me to be a writer. He loves reading, and he always read to me when I was a child—all kinds of books, newspapers, poems, everything. I think that's why I love reading so much now. My father invented stories for me and my brother when we were young, and sometimes he wrote them so he didn't forget. I keep them in my office now and I still read them.

I wrote my first story when I was nine, but really I copied it from one of my father's. My teacher at school didn't know that and she gave me a good grade! Of course, I write stories now and publish them. Unfortunately, my father never published his. I think I'm going to publish them for him one day, before he dies.

Physically we are a little different. We are both tall, but I'm a little taller than he is. He has fair hair but mine is dark, like my mother's. He was very athletic and really strong when he was younger, he played a lot of sports, but I am not athletic at all.

Similarities	Differences
They both love reading.	

2 Correct two mistakes in each of a–g.

a I am more tall that my brother.

b The weather is badder then yesterday.

c My English is more good than a year before.

d My sister is intelligenter then me.

e Childrens are more happy than adults.

f Dogs are friendlyer that cats.

g My grandmother is generouser then my mom.

3 ▶ 10.3 Listen to the descriptions and label the players in the picture.

Michael   Lewis
Phil   Peter
Steve   Rory
Frank   Wayne

4 Compare the players. Use each word only once.

| happy | intelligent | overweight | ~~short~~ |
| slim | strong | tall | young |

a Rory / Phil   *Rory is shorter than Phil.*

b Lewis / Peter

c Michael / Steve

d Peter / Wayne

e Phil / Lewis

f Wayne / Phil

g Steve / Rory

h Frank / Steve

5 ▶ 10.4 Practice the comparatives. Follow the model.

Model: *Miami / hot / New York*

You: *Miami is hotter than New York.*

Model: *swimming / interesting / fishing*

You: *Swimming is more interesting than fishing.*

10.3 Who's the most generous person in your family?

1 ▶ 10.5 **Listen to the adjectives in 1–5 and check the syllable / stress pattern they follow, a–e.**

E.g.: **cri** ti cal = a

a ●●●   b ●●●●   c ●●●●   d ●●●   e ●●

☐ 1   ☐ 2   ☐ 3   ☐ 4   ☐ 5

2 **Which word in each group a–d has a different sound pattern?**

a possessive, arrogant, negative, solitary

b responsible, idealistic, perfectionist, disorganized

c calm, moody, loyal, angry

d suspicious, spontaneous, generous, romantic

3 **Read the messages from a dating website and match the people together.**

a	b	c	d	e	f
Hi, I'm female, 45. I work a lot, but I enjoy life. Want to meet a man to share all I have.	Mario, 26. Tall, dark, romantic Italian. Want to meet a lady to travel the world with.	Hi, Camilla here. I'm ambitious and a perfectionist. Want to meet a similar, successful man!	Steve, 39. Successful businessman wants to meet determined, organized woman.	Hi, I'm Lisa, 24. Want to meet Prince Charming. Buy me flowers and sing to me in Venice!	Male, 35. Fun and relaxed. Not working at the moment. Want to meet a generous lady.

4 🧑 **Make it personal** **Change the adjectives to superlatives and add them to the questions. Then answer a–g.**

a Who's _____ person you know? (**crazy**)

b What's _____ program on TV? (**bad**)

c Who's _____ person in your family? (**old**)

d Where's _____ supermarket? (**big**)

e Which is _____ soccer team in your country? (**popular**)

f Who's _____ person in your country's history? (**famous**)

g What's _____ word to pronounce in English? (**difficult**)

5 ▶ 10.6 **Complete a–e with these words. Listen to check.**

can	nightclub	park	subway station	thing

a Excuse me, I need to get to the city center. Where's the nearest _____?

b Wow, there are so many trees here! Is this the biggest _____ in the city?

c What's the most important _____ in the museum?

d So, let's go dancing tonight. What's the best _____ in the city?

e Which is your cheapest _____ of soda?

6 ▶ 10.6 **Listen again. True (T) or False (F)?**

a The subway station is next to the shopping mall.

b Green Park is next to the river.

c The most important artifact in the museum is on the third floor.

d They are in *Venom* now.

e The cheapest soda is only $2.

> 🔊 **Connect**
>
> *Use your phone to record your answers. Send them to your teacher or a friend.*

10.4 What's the best place in the world?

1 ▶ **10.7 Complete facts A–E. Listen to check.**

F UN ACTS

A Lake Superior _____ _____ biggest lake _____ _____ world.

B Aconcagua is the _____ _____ in _____ America.

C _____ _____ trees _____ _____ world _____ _____ giant Redwoods _____ California.

D Dolphins _____ more intelligent _____ monkeys.

E Tokyo _____ _____ _____ populated city _____ Asia.

2 ▶ **10.8 Practice the superlatives. Follow the model.**

Model: *Sally / good singer / the city*
You: *Sally is the best singer in the city.*

Model: *Istanbul / beautiful city / the world*
You: *Istanbul is the most beautiful city in the world.*

3 Look at the postcards. Where can you see a–h?

Madeira

ARIZONA

Indonesia

a	a big canyon	*Arizona*	d	an ugly lizard	_____	g	an extinct volcano _____
b	a beautiful island	_____	e	a high mountain	_____	h	a fantastic waterfall _____
c	a small lake	_____	f	large rocks	_____		

4 ▶ **10.9 Listen to Mary and Tess talk about vacations. Answer a–c.**

a When did Mary go on vacation?
b Did Mary go to Arizona, Madeira, or Indonesia?
c Where is Tess going to go for her vacation?

5 ▶ **10.9 Listen again. True (T) or False (F)?**

a Tess is probably not Mary's boss.
b Mary likes active vacations.
c Tess likes lizards.
d It was sunny every day on Mary's vacation.
e Tess is going on vacation next week.

10.5 Is your English better than a year ago?

1 ▶ **10.10 Do the quiz. Order facts A–E. Circle the correct word in F–J. Listen to check. How many did you get right?**

A HAVE / BLONDES / PEOPLE WITH DARK HAIR / THAN / MORE HAIR / .

B FASTER / FORMULA ONE CARS / NERVE IMPULSES / THAN / CAN TRAVEL / .

C THAN / THICKER / MEN'S HAIR / WOMEN'S HAIR / IS / .

D IS / THAN / A SOCCER FIELD / A FOOTBALL FIELD / BIGGER / .

E THAN / IS / AN AVERAGE PERSON / HEAVIER / A DOLPHIN / .

F YOUR HEARING IS **BETTER / WORSE** AFTER YOU EAT.

G WOMEN HAVE A **STRONGER / WEAKER** SENSE OF SMELL THAN MEN.

H MONDAY IS THE **SAFEST / MOST DANGEROUS** DAY OF THE WEEK.

I WE ARE **TALLER / SHORTER** IN THE MORNING.

J THE HEART BEATS **SLOWER / FASTER** WHEN YOU SLEEP.

Q U I Z

2 ▶ **10.11 Listen and answer a–c.**
a When is the fight?
b Which person is David Silver and which is Danny Belching?
c Did Danny win his last fight?

3 ▶ **10.11 Listen again and complete descriptions a–g.**
a Danny Belching is s_____ than David Silver.
b Danny Belching d_____ get t_____.
c David Silver is t_____ than Danny Belching.
d David Silver has l_____ a_____.
e David Silver h_____ a b_____ technique.
f Danny is a l_____ f_____ than David Silver.
g Danny w_____ his last t_____ fights.

4 🔊 Make it personal   Write a short paragraph comparing yourself to a friend or relative.

Can you remember ...
➤ 10 parts of the body? SB→p. 124
➤ 8 parts of the face? SB→p. 125
➤ 12 description words or phrases? SB→p. 125
➤ 9 adjectives? SB→p. 126
➤ 16 personality adjectives? SB→p. 128
➤ 9 geographical features? SB→p. 130

Audio Script

Unit 6

▶ 6.1

M = Mom   H = Hannah

M Hannah?

H Yes, Mom?

M Could you go to the store for me? The refrigerator is empty.

H Uh, I guess. Do you have a list?

M Not really, but we can write one really quickly.

H OK, so what do we need?

M Some milk and, uh, six eggs.

H OK. Oh, and we need some tea, too. I used the last bag last night.

M Hmm, do you want some fish for dinner?

H Sure.

M So get a pound of fish, too. Oh, and three onions and four potatoes to cook the fish with.

H Yummy.

M Yes. Anything else you want?

H We don't have any fruit. Can I get some apples and oranges?

M Yes, and some bananas, too. I like to eat them for breakfast.

H I know. So, is that it?

M Read it to me.

H Milk, six eggs, tea, fish, three onions, four potatoes, apples, oranges, and bananas. Is it OK if I get some chocolate as well?

M Just a small bar for you.

H OK! Then off to the grocery store I go. Call me if you remember something else.

M I will. Thanks, hon.

Unit 7

▶ 7.2

P = presenter   J = Jude

P Hello and welcome to another episode of Project Renovation, the program where we visit people on the project of a lifetime as they rebuild, restore, and renovate old houses. Today we're in Springfield, where Phillip and Jude are working on their house. Jude, what are you doing today?

J Hi. Well, today we are working on the bathroom. Uh ... In the original plans there was no bathroom, or toilet, so this is a big part of the project.

P What? No bathroom! No toilet! That's unbelievable!

J Well, there was a bathtub next to the fireplace in the living room and the ... uh ... the toilet was in the yard. Well, obviously, we want a toilet and a bathroom in the house, so Phillip is making a new bathroom above the utility room.

P I see, and are there any other big differences?

J Oh, yes, of course. In the original plans there was a kitchen and a dining room, but they were both very, very small. Oh, and there were no windows in the kitchen, so it was very dark. Uh ... now we have one big room—the kitchen and the dining room are together—and new windows, so there is a lot of light.

P That's great. So now you can cook here and ...

J Well, no, we can't cook here yet. There's no stove and no refrigerator, they are coming next week, I hope! Uh, at the moment we are using the microwave and eating a lot of pizza.

P Hmm ... healthy. So what do you like most about this house?

J Well, I know that Phillip is very excited about his new office. And I really love the yard. There's space for children to run and play, when we start a family, of course.

P Great. Well, thank you for talking to us, Jude. I'll visit again when you finish the house. Bye.

J Yes, please do! Thanks for coming. Bye!

▶ 7.4

A Wow, you look tired. What were you doing over the weekend?

B Yeah, I am tired. I was at Mari's party on Saturday until really late.

A Oh, gee! Was it a good party?

B Yeah, it was great! It was on the beach and I was there until the morning.

A Really? You were there all night? Weren't you cold?

B No, no, the night was warm, so it was ok.

A That's cool!

B Yeah, it was great. There were fireworks at midnight and a lot of pizza for the guests. Mari doesn't like cake, can you believe it?

A What? No cake? At a birthday party? I can't believe it! Well, was it a big party?

B Hmm, there were about 30 people at the beginning, but there were only five on Sunday morning! It was a great night, but I am feeling it today! And I have to work!

A Oh, well, drink a lot of coffee!

▶ 7.8

The organizers sold all the tickets in 30 minutes. The tickets were $228 each.
The festival is 5 days, but there's music on only 3 days.
There were 60 stages.
There were 1,300 recycling volunteers.
There were over 2,200 performances.
There were 5,489 toilets, and there were 300 people cleaning them.
There were over 220,000 people in the audience.

▶ 7.9

M = man   W = woman   B = boy
G = girl

a M1 Would you like to go to a soccer game?

 M2 Sure, that sounds great. When is it?

 M1 Saturday afternoon.

 M2 Saturday? Oh, no! I have to work on Saturday. Sorry.

b M Do you want to go to the movies this weekend?

 W Uh. I'm free on Saturday night. Is that good for you?

 M Yes. See you Saturday then.

c W1 Would you like to come to a party on Saturday?

 W2 I'd love to. What can I bring?

 W1 Nothing. Just yourself.

d B How about going to the park after lunch?

 G Good idea. Let's go.

e M I'm having a barbecue on Friday. Can you make it?

 W Friday? I'm sorry. I'm going to a party. Maybe next time.

f M We're going to a restaurant for our 25th wedding anniversary. Can you come?

W Oh, congratulations! Of course I can come. I'd love to!

Unit 8

▶ 8.8

A = Alyssa   G = Ginny

A Welcome to Celebrity Present and Past. I'm Alyssa Meyers. Today in our studio we're interviewing pop singer Ginny Lomond. Ginny, thank you for being here today.

G Hi, Alyssa.

A Our viewers are so curious about your life. So, when did you start your career?

G At the age of 12, actually. I was part of my school glee club.

A Really? And where did you go to school?

G I went to school here, in New York City.

A Oh, so are you originally from New York?

G No, I was born in Los Angeles, but my mother and I moved to New York when I was a baby.

A When did you record your first album?

G When I was 18, but it was a disaster!

A No, that's not possible!

G But it was! Then I recorded my second album in 2008. And I have to say, that one was a big success!

A We know it was. Well, our lines are open. If you have a question for Ginny Lomond, call now. She'll answer the questions after the break.

▶ 8.9

Yesterday Jake woke up at around 6:30 a.m., but he didn't get up immediately. He stayed in bed for three or four minutes, then he got up and made his bed. Then he exercised for 30 minutes. After that, he took a shower, shaved, got dressed, and had breakfast: coffee, juice, and cereal. Then he brushed his teeth and, finally, left home at around 8 a.m.

▶ 8.11

W = woman   M = man   B = boy
G = girl

a W1 Could you open the window, please?
  W2 Of course. Are you hot?
b M Could you please pass me the salt?
  W Here you are.
c M1 Could you hold the door, please?
  M2 OK.
d M Could you please lend me your phone?
  W I'm sorry. I don't have it with me.
e W1 Could you help me, please?
  W2 Sure. What is it?
f W Could I use your bathroom, please?
  M Yes, it's the second door on the left.
g B Could I borrow your pen, please?
  G Sure. There you go.
h W Could I have the menu, please?
  M Of course, madam. Just a minute.
i M Could I speak to Mr. Green, please?
  W Who's speaking, please?

Unit 9

▶ 9.4

W = woman   M = man

a M Excuse me. What do you do?
  W I'm a computer programmer.
b M What's your profession?
  W I'm a dentist.
c W Are you an engineer?
  M No, I'm a photographer.
d W What's your job?
  M I'm a personal assistant. I work in an office.
e M Are you a student?
  W No, I'm a flight attendant.
f M Is your job dangerous?
  W Yes, sometimes. I'm a firefighter.
g W That's a smart uniform! Are you a police officer?
  M Yes, I am.

▶ 9.7

W = woman   M = man

a W1 Did you make a resolution this year?
  W2 Yes. I'm going to get in shape and exercise more, so next week I'm

joining a gym. Or maybe in two weeks.

b M What's your New Year's resolution?
  W I'm going to save money. I'm not going to buy unnecessary clothes. I have so many shoes anyway.
c M1 Do you have a resolution this year?
  M2 Yes. I'm going to be more organized. First, I'm going to write a list. Number one ... Hm?
d W1 What's your New Year's resolution?
  W2 I'm going to volunteer. My friend and I are helping at a homeless charity next week.
e W What do you want to change this year?
  M Well, I'm going to eat better. I'm taking cooking classes in the evening.
f W What are you going to change this year?
  M I'm going to try and relax more. I'm going to go on vacation next month.

▶ 9.11

W = woman   M = man   B = boy
G = girl

a B Dad, could I borrow the car tonight?
  M Uh ... where are you going?
  B Oh, only to Joe's house. We need to ... hmm ... work on our school project.
  M Sure, go ahead. But drive slowly!
b M1 Can I ask you a question?
  M2 Yeah. Go ahead.
  M1 Do you make a lot of money?
  M2 I'm sorry, but I don't like to talk about money.
c W1 Could you lend me some money for the drink machine?
  W2 No problem. Here you are.
d W Is it OK if I turn off the air conditioning?
  M Oh, are you cold?
  W Yes! Really cold!
  M Oh, sorry. Go ahead.
e B Do you mind if I sit here?
  G I'm sorry, but my friend is sitting here.
f W1 Do you mind if I take your photo?
  W2 Not at all. Cheese!

Audio Script

▶ 10.1

This is Amy. She's about 45 and has fair hair. She's Jay's daughter. And this person is Carmen. She is from Colombia. She is slim and young and she has long dark hair. Next to her you can see Jay. He is married to Carmen. Jay is old and he has short gray hair. On the other side of the picture you can see Joseph and Cameron. Joseph is Jay's son. He is average height and average build. Cameron is Joseph's partner. She is tall and overweight.

▶ 10.3

This is a picture of my soccer team. So, the player at the front, the slim one, that's Michael. He's slim and he's very fast! And the player next to him is Lewis. We call him the Mad Scientist because he looks like Albert Einstein. But he's clever, he's more intelligent than the other players. Uh... Who else? Oh, yes! This is Wayne, he's more overweight than the other players, but he's still a good player! And this one's Frank. He's happier than all the others. Frank's always happy, even when we lose.

And this is Phil, he's only 17. He's younger than the rest of the team. Then, at the back you can also see Peter. He's so tall, over two meters! He's taller than everyone else in the team. And there's Steve, too. He's stronger than the other players and he's not very friendly. And this one is little Rory. He's shorter than everyone, but he's a very good player!

▶ 10.5

a perfectionist, spontaneous, disorganized
b angry, moody, loyal
c possessive, romantic, suspicious
d idealistic
e arrogant, negative, positive

▶ 10.6

W = woman   M = man   G = girl
B = boy

a W Excuse me. I need to get to the city center. Where's the nearest subway station?

M It's a couple of blocks from here. Just keep going straight. It's in the shopping mall.
b G Wow, there are so many trees here. Is this the biggest park in the city?
W No, the biggest one is Green Park. It's next to the river.
c B What's the most important thing in the museum?
W We have some Egyptian artifacts on the second floor. They are very rare.
d M So, let's go dancing tonight. What's the best nightclub in the city?
W Sorry? What did you say?
M The best nightclub.
W Oh. That's *Venom*. It's behind the movie theater.
M Ok, let's go!
e G Which is your cheapest can of soda?
M It's this one.
G OK. I'll take one of those.
M That's two dollars, please.

▶ 10.9

T = Tess   M = Mary

T Hi, Mary, where were you last week? You weren't at work.
M Oh, Tess, didn't I tell you? I was on vacation.
T Awesome. How was it?
M It was beautiful! I went swimming in the ocean and did some sunbathing on the beach and I went walking in the mountains. There were lots of lizards sitting on the rocks in the sun, they were so cute! I enjoyed it a lot.
T Lizards! Ugh! I hate them. But the ocean sounds nice. Was it hot?
M Oh, the weather was perfect, it only rained once. How about you? Are you going on vacation this year?
T Yes, I am. I'm going to Indonesia next month. I'm really excited!
M I can imagine. Everyone says Indonesia is amazing.

▶ 10.11

M1 = man 1   M2 = man 2

M1 Do you like wrestling?
M2 Yeah, it's great! Are you going to watch the fight next weekend? David Silver against Danny Belching.
M1 Of course! Who do you think is going to win?
M2 That's a difficult question. I think

maybe Danny Belching. He is stronger and he has a lot of energy, he doesn't get tired.
M1 That's true, but David Silver is taller and his arms are longer. I think his technique is better, too. I think he's going to win.
M2 It's true that he is taller, but Danny is a little faster. And remember, Danny won his last two fights, but David lost his. I think it's going to be Danny's night.
M1 Hmm, maybe you're right. Let's wait and see.

Answer Key

Unit 6

6.1

1 a chocolate b fish c lettuce d spaghetti
e oranges f tomatoes g vinegar h potatoes
i chicken j sugar
Sentence: We went to the grocery store and
bought lots of things.

2 Some milk, six eggs, some tea, some fish, three
onions, four potatoes, apples, oranges, bananas,
chocolate.

3 a the last bag
b fish / dinner
c fish / onions / potatoes
d bananas / breakfast
e chocolate

4 Personal answers.

5

Countable	Uncountable
carrot	
onion	tea / coffee
egg	milk
banana	bread
grape	butter
orange	cheese
apple	oil
kiwi	rice

6.2

1 a a can b a cup c a piece d a slice e a bowl
f a glass g a bottle

2 some, any, a, a, any, some, some, any, an, any

3 a coffee with milk, bread and butter
b sometimes c vegetables d orange juice
e chocolate f every day

4 Personal answers.

6.3

1 a little, a little, a few, a few, a little, a little

2 a healthy diet b fast food c (a little) fruit
d a lot of

3 (Second column sequence) b, d, c, e, a

4 a a little b a little c a few d a little e a few

5 Personal answers.

6.4

1 a F b F c F d T e T

2 1 Do you have a healthy diet?
2 how much fruit do you eat every day?
3 how many bananas do you eat every week?
4 Do you like all vegetables?
5 How many vegetables do you usually eat every
week?
6 How much meat do you eat?
7 How much fast food do you eat?
8 How many cups of tea or coffee do you drink
every day?
9 Do you eat anything unhealthy?
10 how many slices of chocolate cake do you eat
every week?

3 meat, onion, tomatoes, tomato, oil, salt

4 How much, a little, a few, How many, how much,
a few, How many, a lot, How much, a little

6.5

1 **Down:** 1 grapes 3 steak 4 spinach
Across: 2 pepper 3 salmon 5 pie 6 onions
7 strawberries

2 **Courses:** starters, main courses, desserts
How it's cooked: pureed, grilled, barbecued,
sautéed, steamed, baked
Fruits: lemon, melon, pears
Vegetables: lettuce, carrots, onions

3 Would you, don't, Would you, like, would you,
wouldn't, liked

4 Can I have the menu, Would you like to order a
starter, I'll have the chicken salad, Anything to
drink, I would like a diet soda, Could you bring
me a clean plate

Unit 7

7.1

1
Odd word	Room
b fireplace	bathroom
c armchair	kitchen
d oven	office
e bathtub	bedroom
f bed	living room
g fan	garage
h shower	dining room
i TV	laundry room

2 a bedroom b living room c kitchen d basement
e laundry room f office g garage h bathroom
i dining room

4 Personal answers.

5 a T b F c F

6 a was no b was c wasn't d were no / weren't
any

7 a bathroom b utility room c dining room
d stove e microwave f office

7.2

1 b balloons c cake / candles d snacks
e lemonade / cola f coffee / tea g plates /
napkins / glasses h fireworks i music

2 Personal answers.

3 b How was **it**? c Where **was** it? d What **was** the
weather like? e **Was** there a lot of food? f **Were**
there fireworks? g **Was** there a cake? h How
many people **were** there at the party?

5 a On Saturday. b Great. c On the beach.
d Warm. e Yes, there was pizza. f Yes, there
were. g No, there wasn't. h About 30.

6 Personal answers.

7 h, c, a, g, e, b, d, i, f

7.3

1 a New Year's Eve in Rio
b Mardi Gras
c Tomatina

2 **Julianne** was, were
Lucas was, were, was

3 across from, Next to, above, in front of, under, on,
Behind, In

4 Personal answers.

7.4

1 1 a 2016 b 1903 c 1990 d 2012 e 1912 f 1972

2 1988
was, wasn't, was, were, wasn't, weren't, was
Today
are, isn't, is, are, isn't, is, aren't, is, are, isn't

3 Personal answers.

7.5

1 a In the southwest of England.
b In the summer, at the end of June.
c A music and arts festival.
d You have to register online at
www.glastonburyfestivals.co.uk.

2 5 days
60 stages
1,300 recycling volunteers
Over 2,200 performances
5,489 toilets
220,000 people in the audience

3 The tickets were $228 each.
There are only 3 days of music.
300 people cleaning the toilets.

4 a *to go* / soccer game
b *want* / the movies
c *Would* / a party
d *going* / the park
e a barbecue / *make*
f a restaurant / *come*

Unit 8

8.1

1 a married b learned c agreed d died e wanted
f started g studied h worked

2 was born, weren't, worked, helped, studied,
moved, started, joined, loved, were, played,
follow, invented, were, listed, received, loved,
was, watched, enjoyed, married, had, followed,
died

3 a T b F c F d N e T f F

5 a Whitney Houston was born on August 9, 1963
in Newark, New Jersey.
b She recorded her first album in 1985.
c She received her first Grammy in 1986.
d She (got) married (to) Bobby Brown in July 18,
1992.
e She starred in the movie *The Bodyguard* in 1992.
f She produced the movie *Sparks* in September
2011.
g She died in a hotel in February 9, 2012.

8.2

1 1 finished / wanted / sailed / helped / stayed
2 decided / arrived
3 studied / cried
4 took / left / gave / saw / flew / got / made /
said / had

2 1 played / started
2 invited / used
3 tried
4 bought / came / did / went / knew / thought

3 on, in, at, of, In, in, In, in, In, in, on

4 a second b first c eleventh / twenty-first
d twenty-third e twentieth

8.3

1 Personal answers.

2 a Who did you go with?
b Where did you stay?
c Did you meet anyone?
d Did you take a lot of photos?
e What did you buy?

3 b She didn't go to Turkey on vacation. She went
on business.
c She didn't take a plane. She got a ride.
d The trip didn't take six hours. It took thirteen
hours.
e They didn't stop at a restaurant in Istanbul.
They stopped at a restaurant in Ankara.
f They didn't eat Japanese food. They ate Turkish
food.

g She liked the trip.

5 1 ate 2 made / met 3 said 4 came 5 knew
6 drank 7 went

6 a Because his girlfriend wanted to go to a
different place.
b No, they went in separate cars.
c Only $1.
d Because they were the 1000th client.

8.4

1 1 go to school 2 record first album, record
second album 3 move to New York

2 a At the age of 12. b In New York City. c In Los
Angeles. d Ginny and her mother moved to New
York. e No. f In 2008.

3 a Which magazine elects the 100 most influential
people every year?
b Who did Angelina Jolie divorce in 2016?
c Who studied fashion design in the 1990s?
d Who won four Olympic gold medals in tennis?
e Who did Steven Spielberg meet while filming the
second Indiana Jones movie?
f Where did Ryan Gosling move to in 1996?

4 Yesterday, Jake woke up at around 6:30 a.m., but
he didn't get up immediately. He stayed in bed
for three or four minutes, then he got up and
made his bed. Then he exercised for 30 minutes.
After that, he took a shower, shaved, got dressed
and had breakfast—coffee, juice and cereal. Then
he brushed his teeth and, finally, left home at
around 8 a.m.

5 Personal answers.

8.5

1 *The correct form of the verbs are in bold.*
To Customer Service,
The delivery **was** late.
Instead of 3 days, I **had** to wait ...
But then I finally **got** my TV.
... the sound didn't **work**.
... but there **was** only noise.
A person **came** and he **said** the TV ...
... but he didn't **have** it there.
... but they didn't **know** anything ...
... another repairperson came, **looked** at the
TV, **said** that he didn't **have** the necessary
part ...
Could you please **help** me?

2 a F b T c T d T e F

3 Personal answers.

4 a open b pass c hold d lend e help f use
g borrow h have i speak

Unit 9

9.1

1 b a car c a plane d a bus e a truck f a ferry
g a bike h a train i a motorcycle j on foot

2 a flew b loved c big d hour e ferry

3 1 drove / flew 2 rode 3 took / came

4 1 traffic jam / accident 2 flat tire / late
3 delayed / wrong turn

5 by foot – **on** foot, by the bus – **by** bus, drove –
rode her bicycle, flew – **drove** back, walks – **takes**
the train, on the cab – **by** cab

6 b How do you usually get to work?
c Do you take the bus to school?
d Can you ride a motorcycle?
e How do you usually get to the supermarket?
f What's your favorite way to travel?

9.2

1 a It is safe.
b Two hours.

c No, there are 2 cables.
d No. Very young children can use it.
e No, because not many people live there.

2 (Second column sequence) d, c, e, b, a

3 a computer programmer b dentist
c photographer d personal assistant
e flight attendant f firefighter g police officer

4 a What do you do?
b What's your profession?
c Are you an engineer?
d What's your job?
e Are you a student?
f Is your job dangerous?
g Are you a police officer?

5 Personal answers. Suggested answers:
Computer programmers and dentists make a lot
of money. Dangerous jobs are a firefighter and a
police officer.

9.3

1 a What time **are** you going to finish work
tomorrow?
b Which team **is** going to win the next World Cup?
c When are you **going** to go on your next vacation?
d Where are you going **to** have lunch tomorrow?
e **Are** you going to do your homework?
f What are you **going** to do next weekend?

2 1 going to 2 gonna 3 gonna 4 going to
5 going to 6 gonna
a 4 b 6 c 5 d 1 e 3 f 2

3 Personal answers.

4 Picture 1: lightweight, solar-powered cars
Picture 2: a city roof to protect against rain and
snow
Picture 3: people are going to fold their cars and
store them under the bed

5 a T b T c F d F e F

9.4

1 b house c a friend d engaged e a train
f married
Losing your keys and moving your bag aren't life
changes.

2 a T b T c T d F e F

3 (Second column sequence) c, e, b, f, a, d

4 Next week I'm joining a gym.
My friend and I are helping at a homeless shelter
next week.
I'm taking cooking classes in the evening.
I'm going on vacation soon.
These sentences all have Present Continuous.

6 Personal answers.

9.5

1 c, a, b, e, d

2 Personal answers.

3 (Dialogue order) 3, 7, 4, 1, 5, 6, 2

4 a Could I borrow the **car**, please?
b Can I ask you a **question**?
c Could you lend me some **money**?
d Is it OK if I turn off the **air conditioning**?
e Do you mind if I **sit** here?
f Do you mind if I take your **photo**?

6 a ✓ b ✗ c ✓ d ✓ e ✗ f ✓

Unit 10

10.1

1 a mouth b eyes c ears d lips e nose
Secret question: Do you look like a famous person?

2 a lips / see b eyes / talk c mouth / TV
d ears / read e nose / movies

3 b chest c fingers d feet e hands f legs
g stomach h head i arms j teeth

4 a fair hair
b slim / young / long dark hair
c old / short gray hair
d average height / average build
e tall / overweight

10.2

1 **Similarities:** write stories, tall
Differences: Nick publishes his stories. Nick has
dark hair. Nick's father was athletic.

2 a I am **taller than** my brother.
b The weather is **worse than** yesterday.
c My English is **better** than a year **ago**.
d My sister is **more intelligent than** me.
e **Children** are **happier** than adults.
f Dogs are **friendlier than** cats.
g My grandmother is **more generous than** my
mom.

3 **Front, right to left:** Michael, Lewis, Rory, Phil,
Wayne, Frank.
Standing right to left: Peter, Steve.

4 b Lewis is more intelligent than Peter.
c Michael is slimmer than Steve.
d Peter is taller than Wayne.
e Phil is younger than Lewis.
f Wayne is more overweight than Phil.
g Steve is stronger than Rory.
h Frank is happier than Steve.

10.3

1 1 b 2 e 3 d 4 c 5 a

2 a solitary b idealistic c calm d spontaneous

3 a-f, b-e, c-d

4 a the craziest b the worst c the oldest
d the biggest e the most popular
f the most famous g the most difficult

5 a subway station b park c thing d nightclub
e can

6 a F b T c F d F e T

10.4

1 a is / the / in / the
b highest / mountain / South
c The / tallest / in / the / are / the / in
d are / than
e is / the / most / in

3 b Madeira / Indonesia c Indonesia d Madeira
e Madeira / Indonesia f Arizona g Indonesia
h Arizona

4 a Last week. b Madeira. c Indonesia.

5 a T b T c F d F e F

10.5

1 A Blondes have more hair than people with dark
hair.
B Nerve impulses can travel faster than Formula
One cars.
C Men's hair is thicker than women's hair.
D A soccer field is bigger than a football field.
E A dolphin is heavier than an average person.
F Your hearing is **worse** after you eat.
G Women have a **stronger** sense of smell than
men.
H Monday is the **most dangerous** day of the week.
I We are **taller** in the morning.
J The heart beats **slower** when you sleep.

2 a Next weekend.
b Danny Belching is stronger and he has a lot
of energy, he doesn't get tired. David Silver is
taller and his arms are longer.
c Yes, he did.

3 a stronger b doesn't / tired c taller
d longer arms e has / better f little faster
g won / two

4 Personal answers.

Phrase Bank

This Phrase Bank is organized by topics.

Invitations

Unit 7
Are you free on Friday?
Do you want to come to a barbecue?
I'm sorry. I already have plans.
How about going to a movie tonight?
Sure. That sounds good. / Sounds great.
I'm having a party on Saturday. Can you come?
Of course I can.
Sorry, I can't. But thanks for the invitation.
Maybe next time.
It's my birthday this week. Do you think you can come?
Sounds great! What can I bring? / What time?

Houses

Unit 7
In my opinion, a bed is absolutely essential.
This is the living room and that's the bathroom.

My town

Unit 7
There was(n't) a lot of traffic downtown.
There were / weren't a lot of malls / people.
Twenty years ago there was a park near my house.

Parties

Unit 7
What kind of party was it?
It was Jane's birthday party, at her house / home.
Was there a lot of food?
Yes, there was. / No, there wasn't.
Were Jane's parents there?
Yes, they were. / No, they weren't.

Past expressions

Unit 7
I was at a great party last month / yesterday evening.
It was awesome!
Were you (at) home last night?
Yes, I was, all evening.
Where were you (at 7 o'clock) yesterday morning?

Dates

Unit 8
My great grandmother was born on October 14th, 1861, and died on April 3rd, 1961.
Miley Cyrus was born in 1992, on November 23rd.

Favors

Unit 8
Could I ask you a favor? / Could you help me, please?
Could you do me a favor?
That depends. What do you want?
Could you open the door for me, please?
Sure. There you go.
Could you please do the dishes for me?
I'm (really) sorry, but I can't.
Come on, I can do it tomorrow.
OK. I'll do it now.
Don't worry, I'll get it.

Asking and giving permission

Unit 9
Can I ask you something?
Could I take the day off?
Can I take the car?
Could you lend me ... ?
Do you mind if I turn off the air conditioning?
That's fine.
Sure. Go ahead.
Of course. No problem.
Help yourself.
Not at all.
No, I'm busy.
Maybe next time.
No, I'm sorry, you can't.
I'm sorry, but ...
I'm sorry, but it's too cold.

Phones

Unit 8
Can I borrow your charger?
Can I use my phone? I left mine at home.
Can you tell me the Wi-Fi password, please?
I can't get a signal.
I can't talk right now can I call you later?

Reactions

Unit 8
That's fantastic!
That's incredible!
Oh no!
Wow!
You're kidding!
That's amazing!

Phrase Bank

Unit 10

Really? I didn't know that.
That sounds great. Problem solved!
That's terrible! Poor thing!

Vacations

Unit 8

Did you have a good time enjoy your vacation?
Yes, I did. It was great. / No, I didn't. It was …
How did you get there?
I went by car.
What did you do?
I went to the beach.
Who did you go with?
I went with my family.
What did you do last vacation?
What did you eat?
Where did you stay?

Food

Unit 6

My grandmother counts calories.
For breakfast I can only have a bottle of water.
I can't eat any meat. I'm a vegetarian.
I don't like oranges.
There was a special offer on bananas.
There's some milk in the refrigerator.
What do you have when you get up?
Yes, I can. But only a little.

In a restaurant

Unit 6

Would you like to see the menu?
Are you ready to order? / Can I take your order?
What would you like for your starter? / to start?
I'll have the soup, please.
Would you like to order the main course now?
I'd like the chicken, please.
(Can I get you) anything else?
No, that's all, thanks.
What would you like to drink?
Can I have a soda, please?
Can you bring us the check, please?
OK. Just a moment, please.
What do you have when you get up?
Yes, I can. But only a little.

Intentions

Unit 9

What are you going to do (when you finish school)?
I'm going to go to grad school.
I'm going to make a few changes.

Fixed future plans

Unit 9

After lunch he's meeting his teacher.
Tonight, he and his mother are having dinner.

Jobs

Unit 9

What do you do?
You can / can't make / earn a lot of money.
You help / don't help a lot of people.
You work alone / with other people.
I'm unemployed.
It's interesting / dangerous work.
You work / don't work long hours.
It's a job of the past / future.
It's a job I'd like / woulnd't like to do.

Transportation

Unit 9

How did you arrive here?
I came on foot.
How do you usually get to school / work?
I go by car. / I drive.
He rode his motorbike.

Describing people

Unit 10

Are you like your dad?
Do you look like your mom?
What is he / she like?
He's fun and spontaneous.
She has long dark hair.
She's short and slim and has brown eyes.
They're both energetic and very strong.
This person is tall with long, dark hair.
What color is her hair?
What does she look like?
What's he like?
Your sisters look identical!

Making comparisons

Unit 10

I'm more athletic than him, but he's taller.
I prefer Italian food, but it's more expensive.
Home is the nicest place in the world.
My writing is worse than my speaking.
Our apartment is bigger than Sheila's new house.
My dad is friendlier than I am. I'm a little shyer.

Making choices

Unit 10

Where do you want to go?
I can't decide where to go.
What do you recommend?
I'm not sure, but ...
Why don't we go to the beach?
OK, let's go to the beach.

Other useful expressions

Unit 9

Great to see you!
I'm so pleased you came!
I never use elevators.
It isn't going to be easy.
That sounds boring / fun.
What happened?

Word List

This is a reference list. To check pronunciation of any individual words, you can use a talking dictionary.

Unit 6

Food and drink
apple
banana
beans
bread
butter
cake
candy
carrot
cheese
chicken
chocolate
coconut water
coffee
cream
egg
fish
fries
fruit
grapes
ice
ice cream
juice
kiwi
lemonade
lettuce
mango
meat
melon
milk
nuts
oil
onion
orange (juice)
pasta
pear
pepper
pizza
potato
rice
salad
salt
soup
spaghetti
spinach
sports drink
steak
strawberry
sugar
tea
tofu
tomato
vegetables
vinegar
water
yogurt

Unit 7

Parts of the house
basement
bathroom
bedroom
dining room
garage
kitchen
laundry room
living room
office

Furniture
armchair
bathtub
bed
chair
closet
fan
fireplace
microwave
oven
refrigerator
shelves
shower
sink
sofa
stairs
storage space
stove
table
toilet
TV
window

Party items
balloons
birthday cards
cake
candles
coffee
glasses
invitations
juice
napkins
plates
presents
snacks
soft drinks
tea
water

Adjectives to describe places and events
amazing
awesome
beautiful
cold
fabulous
fantastic
magical
special
terrific
wonderful

Unit 8

Ordinal numbers
1st first
2nd second
3rd third
4th fourth
5th fifth
6th sixth
7th seventh
8th eighth
9th ninth
10th tenth
11th eleventh
12th twelfth
13th thirteenth
14th fourteenth
15th fifteenth
16th sixteenth
17th seventeenth
18th eighteenth
19th nineteenth
20th twentieth

Unit 9

Transportation
bike
bus
car
ferry
helicopter
motorbike
on foot
plane
train
truck

Professions
civil engineer
computer programmer
cook
dentist
designer
financial advisor
firefighter
flight attendant
hairdresser
market research analyst
nurse
optician
personal assistant
photographer
police officer
software developer
student

Life changes
find a girl/boyfriend
get engaged
get divorced
get married
leave college
leave home
lose a job
move
start a (new) job
start a family
retire (from a job)

Unit 10

The body and the face
arm
back
chest
ears
eyebrows
eyes
fingers
foot / feet
hair
hand
head
leg
lips
mouth
nose
stomach
teeth
toes

Description words and phrases
average build
average height
overweight
short
slim
tall

Adjectives
active
ambitious
angry
arrogant
athletic
bad
calm
courageous
critical
depressed
determined
disorganized
energetic
extraordinary
friendly
generous
happy
hard
heroic
idealistic
loyal
moody
nice
ordinary
passive
perfectionist
possessive
relaxed
responsible
romantic
sad
solitary
spontaneous
strong
suspicious

Geographical features
canyon
cave
forest
island
lake
mountain
river
rock
underground river
volcano
waterfall

Richmond

58 St Aldates
Oxford
OX1 1ST
United Kingdom

ISBN: 978-84-668-3248-9

Fifth reprint: 2024
CP: 105588

© Richmond / Santillana Global S.L. 2019

Publishing Director: Deborah Tricker
Publisher: Luke Baxter
Media Publisher: Luke Baxter
Managing Editor: Laura Miranda
Content Developers: Paul Seligson, Deborah Goldblatt, Neil Wood
Editors: Sarah Curtis, Hilary McGlynn
Proofreaders: Lily Khambata, Diyan Leake, Rachael Williamson
Design Manager: Lorna Heaslip
Cover Design: Lorna Heaslip
Design & Layout: Rob Briggs (ROARR Design), Jon Fletcher Design
Photo Researcher: Magdalena Mayo
Audio Production: John Marshall Media Inc.

We would like to thank all those who have given their kind permission to reproduce material for this book:

SB Illustrators: Alexandra Barbarozza, Alexandre Matos, Beach-o-matic, Bernardo Franca, Bill Brown, Guillaume Gennet, Diego Loza, Gus Morais, Alvaro Nuñez, Klayton Luz, Leonardo Teixeira, Martins CG Studio, Rico

WB Illustrators: Alexandre Matos, Andrew Pagram, Vicente Mendonça

SB Photos:
V. Atmán; 123RF/Juan Bauitista Cofreces, Antonio Balaguer Soler, Tatjana Baibakova, oleksiy, Gerold Grotelueschen, ALFREDO COSENTINO, Julian Peters, Cathy Yeulet; ALAMYAKP Photos, Peter Forsberg/People, WENN Ltd, Pictorial Press Ltd, Simon Grosset, Ilene MacDonald, Collection Christophel, Stefan Sollfors, Inner Vision Pro, dennizn, Granger Historical Archive, Don Douglas, Michael Wheatley, Everett Collection Inc, Wm. Baker/GhostWorx, dcphoto, Martin Thomas Photography, carlos cardetas, AF Archive; GETTY IMAGES SALES SPAIN/Fuse, Enjoynz, FOX, E+, Anna Frajitova, Stockbyte, Amarita, AJ_Watt, Londoneye, tBoyan, Tomazl, Xavier Arnau, TriggerPhoto, CJ Rivera, Nikada, Maskot, Zxvisual, Lisafx, Caziopeia, Onston, Drbimages, Vostok, Klaus Vedfelt, wakila, Phive2015, Alvarez, AntonioGuillem, Andresr, Byrdyak, DimaChe, CSA Images, Eyewave, Gerenme, Kaantes, Jabiru, Klasu Tiedge, Stockcam, Ipopba, CaronB, Jeff Kravitz, Dragonimages, Bill Baptist, Win McNamee, Nazar_ab, Pingebat, Serts, Leeser87, JoKMedia, Pekic, Jaromila, Mr.nutnuchit Phutsawagung/EyeEm, NurPhoto, Bas Vermolen, Boston Globe, Erik Isakson, Image Source, Robynmac, Scanrail, Klaus Tiedge, Totororo, WPA Pool, Wsfurlan, PaoloGaetano, Adie Bush, Alan Graf, Ansonmiao, Ricky Vigil, bowdenimages, Chalabala, Cindy Ord, Designalldone, FatCamera, Heshphoto, LJM Photo, Luis Cataneda, Martin-dm, Mixdabass, Nancy Ney, Rafael Fabres, Polka Dot, Ridofranz, StockFood, Janoka82, Tuan Tran, Westend61, icarmen13, karandaev, Adam Gault, Ajr_images, Buyenlarge, Eric McCandless, Dreamnikon, Drewhadley, EnolaBrain, Eri Morita, FSTOPLIGHT, Grandriver, Hillwoman2, Maica, Gkrphoto, Flavijus, Kali9, Flashpop, Harold Stiver/EyeEm, Georgeclerk, Dmitry_7, JackF, Filadendron, Bettmann, Eva-Katalin, Don Farrall, Yvdavyd, Fudio, Futureimage, TangMan Photography, Hero Images, Ildo Frazao, Jay's Photo, Jesse Grant, Karinsasaki, Karwai Tang, Lovelypeace, Arnab Guha Photography, Rose_Carson, Ryan MacVay, Sam Edwards, Shapecharge, Simoningate, Svariophoto, The_burtons, Igor Kisselev - www.close-up.biz, 10'000 Hours, Photo by Ivan Dmitri/Michael Ochs Archives, BamBamImages, Tom Werner, spooh, Pixelfit, Recep-bg, Tom Merton, Gpointstudio, BraunS, RichLegg, Juice Images, Karin Dreyer, Karl Tapales, Kevin Winter, YinYang, Thinkstock, Ligia Botero, Michael Tran, Mike Cameron, Momentimages, Morsa Images, Oneinchpunch, Brian Cullen/EyeEm, PeopleImages, Raymond Hall, Rustemgurler, South_agency, Stocksnapper, Tim Robberts, Travis Payne, Theo Wargo, Spinkle, Ayzek, AlasdairJames, Andersen Ross, Ariel Skelley, Carsten Koall, Dan Bannister, Thatpichai, Gabriel Bouys, Inti St Clair, Istanbulimage, Jamie Garbutt, Johner Images, Joseph Okpako, Jupiterimages, Ryan McVay, Merinka, Mikkelwilliam, Mitchell Funk, Mlsfotografia, Pacific Press, Paul Bradbury, Peathegee Inc, Peter Cade, Samir Hussein, Serhil Brovko, Stephen Marks, Steve Granitz, Ullstein Bild, _human/iStock, Anadolu Agency, OJO images, Marcaux, Caracterdesign, David De Lossy, Digital Vision, Dzphotogallery, FS Productions, Image_By_Kenny, Kryssia Campos, LauriPatterson, Martin Barraud, Shannon Finney, SinghaphanAllB, Zero Creatives, franckreporter, Axel Bernstorff, Aonip, Fabrice LEROUGE, JGI/Jamie Grill, Lutsina Tatiana, MakiEni's Photo, Mario Gutierrez, Michael Dunning, Philippe Regard, Philippe TURPIN, Piotr Pawelczyk,

Adam Lunde/EyeEm, Aurelien Maunier, Crady Von Pawlak, Education Images, Kansas City Star, MangoStar_Studio, Asia Images Group, Mike Prior, Alexander Tamargo, Abel Halasz/EyeEm, MiguelMalo, Lawcain, Yulia_Davidovich, C Squared Studios, ColorBlind Images, ElenaNichizhenova, Jonathan Paciullo, Malcolm P Chapman, Maya Karkalicheva, PeterHermesFurian, Vi Ngoc Minh Khue, AleksandarGeorgiev, Richard E. Aaron, Buena Vista Images, Enrique Diaz/7cero, Jason Merritt/TERM, Jonas Hafner/EyeEm, Julie Moquet/EyeEm, Katra Toplak/EyeEm, Larry Busacca/PW18, Oksana Vejus/EyeEm, PamelaJoeMcFarlane, Razvan Chisu/EyeEm, Tim Clayton-Corbis, Burcu Atalay Tankut, Dan Thornberg/EyeEm, Dave and Les Jacobs, Elizabeth Fernandez, Lars Baron, Quynh Anh Nguyen, Teresa Recena/EyeEm, The Washington Post, Axelle/Bauer-Griffin, Classen Rafael/EyeEm, Color Day Production, Fabiano Santos/EyeEm, Jose Luis Pelaez Inc, Monkeybusinessimages, Nils Hendrik Mueller, Santiago Bluguermann, Aaron Fortunato/EyeEm, Andriy Mykhalchevskyy, Sara Herrlander/EyeEm, Science Photo Library, Peter Macdiarmid, Athletea Widjaja/EyeEm, Cynthia Lafrance/EyeEm, Hinterhaus Productions, James Haliburton/EyeEm, Gallo Images-Stuart Fox, chokkicx/Digital Vision, Benedetta Barbanti/EyeEm, Caiaimage/Agnieszka Olek, Szabo Ervin-Edward/EyeEm, Jules Frazier Photography, Thomas Roetting/LOOK-foto, Paul Mansfield Photography, De Agostini Picture Library, Jon Feingersh Photography Inc, John Fenigersh Photography Inc, JB Lacroix, LIU JIN, Michael Rheault - madfire@gmail.com, Compassionate Eye Foundation/Gary Burchell, Poba, ANDREYGUDKOV; ISTOCKPHOTO/Getty Images Sales Spain, Susan Chiang, Juanmonino, Chmiel; NASA; SHUTTERSTOCK/Arts Illustrated Studios, Moviestore Collection, ESB Professional, ParrySuwanitch, Happy Together, Ken McKay, AlexLMX; Louisville Convention & Visitor Bureau; Tumbleweed Tiny House Company; Kaitlyn Schlicht; Kelly Bruno; Dotta; Helen Chelton López de Haro; Jorge Cueto; United Nations; ARCHIVO SANTILLANA

WB Photos:
J. Jaime; 123RF/Fabrizio Troiani, brulove, Tatiana Popova; ALAMY/Steve Skjold, Michey, Skyscan Photolibrary, Image Source Plus, Erwin Zueger, Dmitry Melnikov, AF Archive, Elena Elisseeva, Zoonar GmbH, F1online digitale Bildagentur GmbH; GETTY IMAGES SALES SPAIN/RB, Liam Norris, SolStock, JoKMedia, Paul Bradbury, By Vesi_127, Floortje, Kupicoo, Steve Granitz, Hackisan, Hero Images, Nattrass, Thomas Francois, Antonello, Drbimages, Electravk, NetaDegany, DigiStu, D-Keine, Photoservice, Gofotograf, Subjug, David Lees, MarianVejcik, Rob Kroenert, Gradyreese, Karaandaev, Kojihirano, G-stockstudio, NicoElNino, Thinkstock, Zak Kendal, Altayb, Donvictorio, Georgeclerk, Guenterguni, Jeff Greenberg, John Rowley, JohnnyGreig, Kevin Mazur, David Livingston, OksanaKiian, Philipphoto, Roger Kisby, Sam Edwards, Taylor Hill, Xavierarnau, 10'000 Hours, Morsa Images, Kevin Mazur/Billboard Awards 2014, Chris Ryan, Westend61, Image Source, IakovKalinin, Phil Fisk, Diana Miller, Ismailciydem, Kali9, Liesel Bockl, MachineHeadz, Deepblue4you, Mike Kemp, Noel Vasquez, PeopleImages, Dcdr, David Buchan, Sezeryadigar, South_agency, Tim Robberts, Caroline Sale, Chris Clinton, Fiona Goodall, Dave J Hogan, James Devaney, Jamie Garbutt, Jeffrey Mayer, Johner Images, Jupiterimages, Michael Kovac, Oliver Furrer, Istetiana, China Photos, Terry O'Neill, Yasser Chalid, Anthony Harvey, Cecilie_Arcurs, Hulton Archive, Ida Mae Astute, Axelle/Bauer-Griffin, LauriPatterson, Marc Romanelli, Martin Hospach, Newstockimages, JGI/Jamie Grill, Photos.com Plus, Stefanie Grewel, Victor Ovies Arenas, Andrew Merry, Jay L. Clendenin, Jeffrey Richards, Gareth Cattermole, Gonzalo Marroquin, Jonathan Paciullo, Oktay Ortakcioglu, RightFieldStudios, Robyn Breen Shinn, istock/Thinkstock, Stanton J Stephens, DEA / G. NIMATALLAH, Dave and Les Jacobs, Rajibul Hasan/EyeEm, Teresa Recena/EyeEm, Ian Gavan, Imv, BJI/Blue Jean Images, Caiaimage/Tom Merton, Gints Ivuskans/EyeEm, Jose Luis Pelaez Inc, Monkeybusinessimages, Tim Clayton - Corbis, Caiaimage/Sam Edwards, Dan Thornberg / EyeEm, Mendowong Photography, Science Photo Library, Tatiana Dyuvbanova/EyeEm, Jules Frazier Photography, Universal History Archive, Dennis Fischer Photography, Simpson33, Julia Finney; ISTOCKPHOTO/Getty Images Sales Spain; SHUTTERSTOCK/Kseniia Perminova, threerocksimages, Sergey Peterman, Ilya Sviridenko, PhotoHouse, eurobanks, AJR_photo, hxdbzxy, kurhan; ARCHIVO SANTILLANA

The Publisher has made every effort to trace the owner of copyright material; however, the Publisher will correct any involuntary omission at the earliest opportunity.

Printed in Brazil by Forma Certa
Lote: 796377
Cód.: 290532489